D1293761

# THE
# PSYCHOTIC
# PERSONALITY

# THE
# PSYCHOTIC
# PERSONALITY

By
## Leon J. Saul, M.D.

Emeritus Professor of Psychiatry,
Medical School of the University of Pennsylvania
Honorary Staff, Institute of the Pennsylvania Hospital
Dean, The Philadelphia Academy of Psychoanalysis

and

## Silas L. Warner, M.D.

Clinical Associate Professor of Psychiatry,
Medical School of the University of Pennsylvania
Attending Staff, Institute of the Pennsylvania Hospital
Consulting Psychiatrist, Haverford and Swarthmore Colleges
Executive Committee,
The Philadelphia Academy of Psychoanalysis

VNR VAN NOSTRAND REINHOLD COMPANY
NEW YORK   CINCINNATI   TORONTO   LONDON   MELBOURNE

Library of Congress Catalog Card Number 81-15928
ISBN 0-442-27764-4

Manufactured in the United States of America

Published by Van Nostrand Reinhold Company Inc.
135 West 50th Street, New York, N.Y. 10020

Van Nostrand Reinhold Limited
1410 Birchmount Road
Scarborough, Ontario M1P 2E7, Canada

Van Nostrand Reinhold Australia Pty. Ltd.
17 Queen Street
Mitcham, Victoria 3132, Australia

Van Nostrand Reinhold Company Limited
Molly Millars Lane
Wokingham, Berkshire, England

15 14 13 12 11 10 9 8 7 6 5 4 3 2 1

**Library of Congress Cataloging in Publication Data**

Saul, Leon Joseph, 1901-
  The psychotic personality.

  Includes index.
  1. Psychoses. I. Warner, Silas L. II. Title.
[DNLM: 1. Psychotic disorders. 2. Personality
disorders. WM 200 S256p]
RC512.S28    616.85'82    81-15928
ISBN 0-442-27764-4      AACR2

*To those who are dedicated to easing human suffering and preventing the human race from destroying itself*

## OTHER BOOKS BY LEON J. SAUL

*The Library of Psychodynamics:*

The Childhood Emotional Pattern: The Key to Personality, Its Disorders and Therapy

The Childhood Emotional Pattern and Corey Jones

The Childhood Emotional Pattern in Marriage

The Childhood Emotional Pattern and Maturity

The Childhood Emotional Pattern and Psychodynamic Therapy

The Childhood Emotional Pattern and Human Hostility

Dependence in Man (with H. Parens)

## OTHER BOOKS BY SILAS L. WARNER

Preschool Child's Learning Process (with W. Rosenberg)

Your Child Learns Naturally (with E. Rosenberg)

# PROLOGUE

Here is how one of our best and most conscientious current authors struggles to understand one of his own characters—a girl who seems to fit the category "psychotic personality" because she is superficially pseudonormal in her daily relations but nearly psychotic in her views and behavior:

*I pondered the question [of her behavior] . . . reviewing her motivation as I understood it. It wasn't sex, because her behavior with Nazrullah, Zulifiqar and Stiglitz had an almost sexless quality; she was neither driven by desire nor faithful to anyone who fulfilled it. I wondered if she might be suffering from some kind of schizophrenia, but I could find no evidence that she was; no one was persecuting her; she persecuted herself. At one point I had thought she might be a victim of nostalgia for a past age, but she would have been the same in Renaissance Florence or Victorian England; history was replete with people like her, and although she despised this age, no other would have satisfied her better. It was true that like many sentimentalists she indulged in an infantile primitivism; if bread was baked over camel dung it was automatically better than bread baked in a General Electric range, but many people were afflicted with this heresy and they didn't wind up in a caravan at Balkh. There remained the possibility that she suffered from pure jaundice of the spirit, a vision which perverted reality and made it unpalatable; but with Ellen this was not the case. She saw reality rather clearly, I thought. It was her reaction to it that was faulty. And then I heard the dry, emotionless voice of Nexler reading from the music professor's report:* I saw her as a girl of good intention who was determined to disaffiliate herself from our society. *This didn't explain* why *she acted as she did, but it certainly described* what *her actions were.*

James Michener, *Caravans*
New York: Random House, Inc. 1963

*. . . though the man's even temper and direct bearing would seem to intimate a mind peculiarly subject to the law of reason, none the less, in his soul's recesses, he would seem to riot in complete exemption from that law, having apparently little to do with reason further than to employ it as an ambidexter implement for affecting the irrational. That is to say: towards the accomplishment of an aim which in wantonness of malignity would seem to partake of the insane, he will direct a cool judgment sagacious and sound.*

*These men are true madmen, and of the most dangerous sort—it is secretive and self-contained: so that when most active it is, to the average mind, not distinguished from sanity, and for the reason that whatever its aims may be (and the aim is never disclosed) the method and the outward proceeding is always perfectly rational—can it be this phenomenon, disowned or not acknowledged, that in some criminal cases puzzles the courts?*

Herman Melville, *Billy Budd*

*Between his heart and mind—both unrelieved*
*Wrought in his brain and bosom separate strife.*
*Some said that he was mad; others believed*
*That memories of an antenatal life*
*Made this, where now he dwelt, a penal hell . . .*

Shelley, *Prince Athanase*

# PREFACE

This book presents some of our clinical observations, deductions and tentative conclusions as to the diagnosis and psychodynamics of the "psychotic personality." This subject is no small circumscribed problem, but an entire area of psychopathology. Some cases even suggest an organic etiology in some part—but organic or hereditary elements are beyond our scope or concern here. Our purpose is limited to the application of the psychodynamic approach to the problems of definition and cause. Science is a collective, cooperative, and self-correcting procedure, and classification of phenomena is one of its basic tools. We are well satisfied if this effort adds something to the clarification of an important area of human psychological suffering in individuals and in society.

The interested analyst and psychodynamicist have ample opportunities for observing people other than the few they see in their offices over a year. Such opportunities for observation are greater if they are consultants to certain institutions and agencies. Without citing statistics, it is obvious that, as Freud pointed out, in many if not most people, the ego (the orderly operation of the conscious mind) is under constant pressure from the forces of instinct, conscience, and the outside world. The more one observes this, the more natural it seems that many people are living under the threat of neurosis or psychosis. We can all identify with these struggles, and they provide the material for fiction and drama. Many people, not just a rare few, are under such severe stress from an early age that they barely control powerful tendencies toward psychosis. They are just now being recognized and studied, and upon them this book is focused.

Our procedure has been to write out vignettes of all the 60 patients and other individuals we have seen in therapy or in consultation who were more than simply neurotic but not clearly psychotic. We then studied our vignettes for what impressed us as the most striking of the deeper, more permanent characteristics, trying these out as criteria for diagnosing the psychotic personality. They seem to work for us in defining those pathodynamics but must of course be critically tested by others to see if they help narrow down this particular syndrome to something sufficiently definable to be recognizable and useful as a diagnosis.

### CRITERIA FOR THE PSYCHOTIC
### PERSONALITY DISORDER (PPD)

This condition is characterized by the depth, level, or age of the fixation or regression, in which the frustration or trauma and the consequent fight-flight reaction to it cause:

1. an *intensity* of *hostility* which creates difficulties of some kind or at least is prominent and usually is in part handled by *projection;*
2. serious *withdrawal* from human relations (i.e., repressed or deficient object interest and relations);
3. heightened *narcissism* in the form of emotional absorption with self and self-interests (possibly like Freud's amoeba with pseudopods withdrawn from object interest into itself);
4. warping of *the sense of reality,* somewhat repressed;
5. the psychotic elements *diffuse* throughout the personality or ego; they are not apparent as specific psychotic symptoms but are repressed behind a mask of reality.

We assume that the reader of these vignettes describing what we call "psychotic personalities" will have in mind for a control series an adequate background of relatively normal or neurotic individuals with which to contrast these cases and criteria.

Not all psychotic personalities are tyrants, but many a tyrant—petty or major—is a psychotic personality. The frustration caused by feelings of inferiority stemming from the depth of the fixation or regression to an early age and stage of development generates more than average feelings of inferiority, reactively heightened narcissism, and therefore frustration and the fight-flight reaction, with consequent hostility and withdrawal. Often the hostility is too freely vented because of the lack of identification with the victims, which is part of the failure and deficiency of object relations and interest, the withdrawal of human sympathy, the remoteness from people. The hidden distortion of the sense of reality is often revealed if the tyrant meets reverses; he then complains that he did nothing wrong but is simply misunderstood and mistreated by others. When the tyrant is in a family, one or more of the children will be ruined for life. Many of these psychotic personalities who are ubiquitous in society come to the attention of lawyers and the courts, where they are mostly as poorly understood as they are in the world of business, in universities, and elsewhere.

# ACKNOWLEDGMENTS

Susan (Mrs. Vernon) Bender, my ever-reliable, unsurpassable secretary, has most directly made this book possible with her always practical suggestions, her prompt and accurate typing and retyping, and her saving of my energies in a thousand ways. June Strickland, librarian of the Institute of the Pennsylvania Hospital has been indispensable in her willing and rapid providing of books, articles, and references. Mr. Eugene Falken and his fine, friendly, and efficient staff—Ella Harwood, secretary, Alberta Gordon, editor—have been a pleasure to work with on the endless details involved in publishing this book, and I am most appreciative of their attitude and substantial help. Indirectly but no less importantly, the understanding and devotion of my wife, Rose, and of my children and grandchildren—especially Mark and Anne, who are old enough to understand—have given me the emotional replenishment to write this book, as well as to practice and carry other responsibilities.

LEON J. SAUL

Thanks to my wife, Elizabeth Severinghaus Warner, and to my children, with my sincere gratitude for their patience and understanding during the long hours taken in writing this book; and my thanks to my secretary, Constance Bertholet.

SILAS L. WARNER

# CONTENTS

Prologue / vii
Preface / ix
Acknowledgments / xii

SECTION I: THEORETICAL CONSIDERATIONS / 1

1. Instincts and Reality / 3
2. Hypothesis: Theoretical Formulation / 19
3. Nature of the Concept / 29
4. The Psychotic Personality: Varieties / 38
5. Some Points About Narcissism / 51
6. Review of the Literature and Differential Diagnosis / ˏ80

SECTION II: SOME EXAMPLES OF THE CLINICAL OBSERVATIONAL DATA / 119

7. In the Transference / 121
8. Psychotic Personality or Neurotic Character? / 132
9. Four Types of Passive-Regressive Withdrawal / 136
10. Five Types of Paranoid-Hostile Behavior / 150
11. Reactive, with Psychosis and Suicide: John Orbison / 166
12. Compulsive Type: Ella Lowry / ·173
13. Suicidally Depressed Type: Wynne / 179
14. Emotional Isolation: Mackley / 184
15. Marital Problem: Mahlon Bowe / 188
16. Lois Dunston / 197

SECTION III: PSYCHOSOCIAL MEDICINE / 209

17. Psychosocial Medicine / 211
18. Cults / 221
19. Destructive Type: Hitler / 262

20.  Constructive Type: Mary Baker Eddy  /  275
21.  Psychodynamics and Society  /  293
22.  The Perennial Revolution  /  300

Index  /  303

# SECTION I
# THEORETICAL
# CONSIDERATIONS

# 1
# INSTINCTS AND REALITY

*For my part I am of the opinion with mad Johnson that all mankind are a little mad.*

John Adams

*We often hear of prisoners at large. The majority of mankind are madmen at large. They differ in their degrees of insanity. . . .*

Benjamin Rush
(Both quotations from *The Spurs of Fame: Dialogues of John Adams and Benjamin Rush*)

*Whether we have a crisis or not depends on who wins the race between belief and disbelief. . . .We [gnomes] stand for disbelief. We are basically cynical about the ability of men to manage their affairs rationally for very long.*

Adam Smith, *Paper Money*

## CIVILIZATION

Civilization is a term used broadly and in many ways. (1) It seems to imply a social organization, i.e., a gathering of people who are related to each other, whether closely or at a distance, having in common their existence as part of the organization of the group, the group being relatively permanent. An obvious example is a nation. (2) Another characteristic of civilization is the treatment of one another in a "civil" manner. (3) Most civilizations are also characterized by some degree of surplus of life's necessities, so that there is time available beyond the constant struggle to obtain the indispensable essentials of food, clothing, and shelter. (4) This makes possible some amount of culture, which arises from sublimation of the animal instincts into the products of thought and art, i.e., mostly artistic and scientific creation. Science is at bottom a cooperative, systematic way of learning the facts about nature and ourselves as part of it. It is a method of learning about reality, both physical and psychological.

Which instincts are sublimated? Here we tread on shaky ground, because there is still disagreement on the meaning of *instinct*. Psychoanalysts have long believed that their field lacks a sound theory of instincts. Yet if we keep to the obvious, instincts mean simply the most basic and constant motivations of a living organism as a unit. We can reduce the question to: What main motivations and reactions do we see in humans throughout their lives, from birth onward, during their entire life cycle? The experienced analyst finds in his clinical work ample opportunity to study this question.

The following list includes obvious, powerful, and permanent drives in the life of every human being, drives which motivate the organism as a unit and not, for example, a part reflex like breathing. This list is of course only a first approximation, but it is based entirely on clinical analytic observations. The more simple and comprehensive a theory is, the better. However, at this stage of psychodynamics as a science, it is not possible to list exclusively pure, fundamental, permanent, irreducible, unanalyzable urges. Freud (1930) tried to achieve this goal but had to sacrifice a close relevance to clinical usefulness and come down to his Eros-Thanatos, love and death, instincts which correspond to anabolism and catabolism in biochemistry. However correct, these concepts are so broad and the gap to biology is so wide that they are of little practical use in dealing with the true basis of science, namely, observable and verifiable facts (as Planck's thermodynamics, Einsteins's theory of relativity, and Darwin's theory of evolution do). A list of instincts includes the basic emotional forces as they are observable in the human mind, where they are rarely seen in pure form but appear mostly in interplay with other emotional forces and reactions (Saul, 1979, Part II). Further experience will lead to a better instinct theory. For the present we will sacrifice depth, breadth, and elegance of theory for closeness to observable facts. It is a consoling thought that the atom as known to modern physicists is far different from the unit of matter envisioned by Democritus.

## INSTINCTS

1. Certainly the newborn infant is completely *dependent* upon its mother (or substitute) for its very survival. Moreover, every analyst and every careful observer sees signs of this dependence, whether frank and overt or partially hidden, throughout every person's life. The need for this dependence with which all humans are born, which existed before birth, in the womb, is certainly a major lifelong emotional force and can properly be called an instinct.

2. Every human child from birth (and probably every other mammal) requires caring and demonstration of affection—in a word, *love.* (a) This *need for love* which continues for life is also an instinct. Feeling itself loved is the child's (and the adult's) assurance of being cared for and thus of survival. (b) Not so necessary for survival as the need *for* love—perhaps more a part of the mature instinct for race preservation than for personal survival—is the drive to *give love.* Nevertheless, whether one desires to get or give it, love is omnipresent and surely must be listed with the instincts.

3. The instinct for *self-preservation* is obvious throughout the animal kingdom and, like the other instincts, is seen in various manifestations and connections (consider the paradoxical mass rush into the sea of lemmings when threatened with overpopulation). One of the manifestations of the instinct for self-preservation is *self-love,* narcissism, or vanity. This manifestation is usually less obvious and often subtle but is nonetheless universal, so powerful and permanent in fact as to justify placing it with the instincts. One result of this is *envy.*

4. Another deep, lifelong urge is the *sexual.* Normally this instinct encompasses: (a) the desires for closeness to an individual of the opposite sex, and (b) the physiological drive for coitus and orgasm. This powerful reproductive drive is seen in a vast variety of manifestations.

5. Also readily observable is the *fight-flight reaction,* basic to understanding every human. This reaction is seen clinically as a response to any danger, frustration, or irritation by impulses to remove the threat through destroying it or fleeing from it. Unfortunately, the *hostile* part of this reaction is often mistakenly referred to as "aggression," although this latter term can mean energetic action for constructive

purposes. In civilized societies, it is not possible to *act out the hostility* freely or even express unrestrainedly the feeling of anger associated with it. If this were done, the society would cease to be civilized, would destroy instead of protecting its members, and would eventually cease to exist.

The *flight* part of the reaction to escape danger by removing oneself from it cannot be freely acted out either, as the earth becomes more congested with our species and little space remains to which one can flee. Yet flight from both external and internal frustrations and dangers can be achieved in some part—at great cost to maturity and the sense of reality—through a psychological return to patterns of thinking, feeling, and behavior which worked in the past, i.e., by *regression* to patterns of childhood (neurosis) or infancy (psychosis), with or without the aid of alcohol or other drugs. This tendency to regression mixes or even fuses with the longings for childish dependence and makes some tendency to flight by regression universal, and thus should be ranked as an instinct.

6. Rarely if ever does an animal live alone in nature. Animals gather in herds, flocks, schools, just as humans gather into tribes, families, and societies. Our strongest feelings, negative and positive, are toward other persons. The universality of this attraction of animals into groups confirms the instinct of *social cooperation.* It is rarely seen in pure form because, like all instincts, it is conditioned by the early experiences of childhood, especially in humans, during the tender, most formative years from birth to about age six or seven (0 to 6). Because of this conditioning it can be facilitated and encouraged, inhibited or warped, and even made antisocial.

7. It may seem strange to conceive of a *drive to know,* but the facts seem to support such a drive. We see it in human *curiosity,* certainly in sexual curiosity but also (however sublimated) in scientific curiosity and gossip, as well as in the curiosity involved in a sense of suspense, in wanting to know "how it will all come out," as exhibited in drama and fiction, gambling, and psychoanalysis.

More mental than the physical urges we have listed above as instincts, but still essential for survival, is this *cognitive drive,* for in truth, one must know something about oneself and others in one's society even to survive, let alone to live satisfactorily—knowledge is indeed power. The infant and young child soon *learn* what behavior will bring them love, approval, and the care they require to survive, and they are *conditioned* to these patterns of appropriate behavior in relationships with other humans. Curiosity and the wish to know (i.e., the cognitive drive) are thus intimately interrelated with the instinct to social cooperation and to a tendency toward conditioning by experience in learning how to win love.

8. This mixture of instincts and the results of conditioning and learning by experience shapes a part of the personality which dictates much of its control and direction of the physical instincts, and thus of a person's basic behavior and his ability to adapt to and live within his society. Freud called this conditioned, learned part of man's personality the *superego.* The emotional propensities of curiosity, conditioning, and learning lead to superego formation and to the motivations the superego contributes to the thinking, feeling, and behavior of every personality. These become so intrinsic and are so constant and enduring as to be termed an instinct. Essentially, it is the need for living with others, the drive to social cooperation, which necessitates the training of every newborn child, especially during its 0 to 6, and the formation of its superego.

9. *Sense of Reality:* The interactions of the instinctual forces which must be controlled by humans (by the ego) and not freely *acted out* if people are to live in societies cause every person to feel powerfully impelled but at the same time unable to act except as permitted by his training and experience (i.e., by his superego). This conflict between instincts and superego puts every human mind under the pressure of emotional forces. Unable to achieve relief through immediate action as an animal might in nature, humans seek expression and gratification of their instincts in fantasies. Venting of instincts through fantasy interferes with the perception of reality. Delusions and even hallucinations occur when the fantasies not only fill the mind but overwhelm the sense of reality. Except in earliest childhood, when the infant's needs are met by its parents, a human being cannot adapt and survive unless he or she sufficiently recognizes reality. The *sense of reality* is an essential for survival and may thus be called an instinct, although we are not accustomed to conceiving of it as a drive or an urge like the others.* The sense of reality is contributed to by the

---

*The entire history of humanity is, in a major aspect, the story of the progress of the rational knowledge of reality over superstition and mysticism, as these latter are generated by the fantasies formed by the more or less repressed instincts.

cognitive drive, the drive toward social cooperation, and a healthy superego—by learning reality from emotionally healthy parents. Interestingly, Freud initially attributed the sense of reality to the superego.

The scientific process consists essentially of drawing general truths from observable facts and then testing these theories with further facts. Psychodynamics can be as scientific as any other study. Every field has its own special difficulties. The difficulty in studying the human mental and emotional life lies in its abstractness and its inaccessibility. However, just as in the physical sciences, there are special methods and tools for detecting and interpreting the unconscious emotional forces. One tool is communication through speech, by free association at random and to the visual elements of dreams. There is no lack of data; rather, excessive amounts exist. Generally, only those persons who seek relief from suffering are sufficiently motivated to reveal themselves fully. This communication during psychotherapy may go on for long periods before the individual is well understood by the analyst; the raw data to establish reasonably confident conclusions would comprise whole volumes—enormous amounts of ore for very little pure metal. Yet this must all be studied by others to be certain that the interpretations drawn correspond to reality. Because it is not practicable to publish many volumes of associations to prove even a small point, psychoanalysts have always taken shortcuts, describing conclusions which they trust other analysts will confirm from their own clinical observations.

We believe the observations regarding the instincts listed above to be so obvious and universal as to be readily confirmed by others from their own data.

## INSTINCTS AND FANTASIES

The emotional pressures in every human being of all these interacting fundamental feelings create the fantasies with which most or all human minds teem. If these fantasies are sufficiently strong, they affect the person's sense of reality. Although the interactions of these emotional forces (the psychodynamics) are not identical in any two human beings, certain similarities are frequently perceptible either (a) in the psychodynamics or (b) in their effects on the sense of reality.

For example, it is not uncommon to observe persons whose hostilities and guilts so distort their reality sense as to make them feel that certain individuals or groups are against them, responsible for their lack of success or their unhappiness, or even threatening and persecuting them. These particular similarities we label "paranoid," or paranoia, and consider this to be a recognizable symptom and diagnostic category in psychiatry. Other persons are withdrawn and gloomy, and full of forebodings of suffering and catastrophe for themselves and others; to this distortion of the reality sense we give the diagnosis "depression." If the distortions of the sense of reality are gross enough we call such individuals "psychotic" and group all such severe distortions as psychoses. At the extremes, the pressure of the emotional forces deranges the orderly operations of the mind, the memory, reason, and the grasp of reality (the whole ego) to cause disorientation as to time and place and also illusions, delusions, and hallucinations.

The working of the reality sense, like that of the other emotional forces, is observable across a whole spectrum of kind and severity. A broad band of disturbances of the ego, milder than the psychoses, is made up of the neuroses. For example, the hostility and guilt may affect the reality sense so as to create only a sense of anxiety, of some unidentifiable harm that may ensue if one goes out in crowds, is alone on a broad thoroughfare, or goes above a certain height. If such irrational fears are enough in evidence they provide another diagnosis: the "phobias" which are included under the general rubric "psychoneuroses."

From the most severe psychoses to the mildest, most nearly normal psychoneuroses stretches an intricate spectrum. The spectrum of light extends from shorter to longer wavelengths, from short lengths (the gamma rays), even below x-rays, to the largest radio waves; the other variable for light is frequency. However, the variations in shades of feeling and intensity within human emotional forces are far more complex and subtle. Moreover, this psychodynamic spectrum involves all sorts of distortions of the ego's perceptive, integrative, and executive functions, besides its grasp of reality. It extends from psychoses to neuroses to criminality, and covers the endless variety of disturbances in ego functions which we properly call "borderline" (including "psychotic personalities") to distinguish them from the more readily definable psychoses and neuroses. Thus lying between psychoses, neuroses, and criminality, borderline personalities are properly manifestations of psychopathology. Simply discerning the similarities in this varied, multifarious *intermediary group*, if we succeed in defining them, does not end our problem: we can assign many of them to the area of psychiatry, but once we recognize the psychiatric problems of these persons, we cannot fail to see the sociological, political, military, and even religious manifestations of the individual's thinking, feeling, and behaving. The analyst is accustomed to understanding a patient and his deepest dynamics as seen (1) in his dreams, which are indeed the royal road to the unconscious; (2) in the transference (a sample of his human relations as seen toward the analyst); and (3) in the patient's patterns of behavior in his life. Usually the analyst focuses mostly upon the patient's intimate personal life, which is what comes through most specifically in his free associations. If we discern the roots of his sociological, political, and religious ideas and feelings, we notice how irrational and unrealistic so many of these views usually are: hence the common admonition not to discuss politics or religion.

Just as similarity in *effect* is what leads to such diagnoses as paranoia, depression, or phobia, so other similarities can lead to mutual attempts at therapy—such as Alcoholics Anonymous—or to similarity in political feelings, thinking, and behavior which can result in groups of liberals, conservatives, or extremists of the left or the right. We readily see paranoia in politics: some blame all the ills of society on the wicked rich people of Wall Street and on the oil companies, while others blame all ills on the unrealistic radicals and revolutionaries. If the analyst can discern the roots of such convictions, usually passionately and compulsively held, he finds them to spring from emotional forces instead of from reason, and often to be a form of paranoia in political guise. Many alcoholics can cooperate therapeutically in AA, and many paranoids can cooperate in groups of the extreme right or left, with a common feeling of persecution by those people whom they unite in fearing and hating, and whom they can attack with the rationalization of self-defense. Some groups are generally recognized as pathological and called the "lunatic fringe." The better a person fits into a group—however neurotic or psychotic—the less apt he is to see his own emotional problems.

The less developed a person's sense of reality and the more powerful the force of his feelings, the greater is his confusion in perceiving whether these sensations come from within or without, i.e., the stronger is the tendency to project these inner feelings and fantasies upon the outside world from which they now seem to originate.

The instincts, including the aftereffects of training, experience, and learning (the superego), are to some extent frustrated by (1) their conflicts between themselves and (2) the external world. The frustration (internal or with the external world) adds the fight-flight reaction to all these motivations. All these emotional pressures fill the human mind with fantasies of satisfaction, and it may be that no human can live without some illusions. Nevertheless, everyone must live with the realities of himself and of his world, and it is not too much to say that at this stage of our evolution anything that compromises, warps, distorts, confuses, or makes astigmatic the human sense of reality eventually opposes human well-being, health, and survival. The fantasies that fill the mind provide the material for mankind's greatest art and contribute to science which is humanity's great cooperative procedure for understanding the external and internal realities with which we must live. Yet when the fantasies take forms that obscure, distort, or lead away from reality, then they become dangers to individual lives and to society, i.e., as in superstitions of all sorts and even in religious forms such as cults.

Fantasies can cause all forms of mental and emotional disorder, as well as asocial and antisocial behavior, which shape our social, political, economic, and religious scenes. The future happiness and very survival of human life on this planet seem to lie (a) in the knowledge of psychological and physical reality through science, and (b) in the proper rearing of children with love, understanding, and respect for their personalities, especially from conception to age six or seven (0 to 6). Whatever furthers the human understanding of the realities of nature and of mankind is helpful; whatever opposes man's grasp of reality endangers his happiness and very existence.

## A SUMMARY LIST OF INSTINCTS

Human beings cannot live together in societies unless they control or modify their animal instincts. What are these instincts? Freud, searching for the deepest, had to go rather far from clinical observations with the opposing tendencies of love and death. We must agree that these are unmistakable. However, if we shun the controversy over what an instinct is (accepting it simply as a basic motivation of the organism as a unit) and if we keep close to what is observable by every analyst daily (accepting the interconnections of these instincts in individual psychodynamics and the fact that we do not see them in pure form), then we observe the basic, universal, lifelong motivations which we discussed above. They are:

1. Dependence
2. Growth, maturity, independence
3. Love
    a)  Needs *for* love
    b)  Urges to *give* love
4. Self-preservation:  self-love, vanity, narcissism
5. Sexual drives
    a)  Closeness to person of opposite sex
    b)  Coitus and orgasm
6. Fight-flight reaction
    a)  Attack
    b)  Regression connected with dependence
7. Social cooperation:  conditioning to social living and superego
8. Curiosity and the cognitive drive
9. Reality sense

The *interplay* of these instincts (psychodynamics) keeps every human under emotional pressures, most of which he cannot vent in immediate *action* as an animal in the wild can; instead, man seeks expression and gratification in *fantasy*. The pressure of fantasies interferes with the perception of *reality* and is the source of all sorts of *psychopathology* and of *superstition* and *mysticism*. The child survives in the care of responsible loving parents; the adult human can adapt and survive only with a relatively unimpaired instinct for *reality*.

This instinct theory, despite its limitations and inadequacies, is clinically verifiable and clinically useful.*

## A TENTATIVE VIEW OF HUMAN LIFE

What then do we see when we look at the people in our streets, our towns, our cities, our nation, the world? We see great numbers of beings who give all the signs of being animals, unmistakably built like other mammals and particularly the great apes, only more upright and almost hairless, yet of almost identical physiology, biochemistry, and methods of survival: taking in food by mouth; excreting the waste as urine and feces; reproducing by sex, coitus, impregnation, gestation, and birth; caring and educating their young. All these individuals have intensely strong reactions to one another, especially to certain intimate ones: they are like atoms with negative and positive charges—attracting, repelling, destroying. In this vague analogy, the particles represent the basic motivations and reactions of each individual. Thus each person's powerful feelings are directed toward others close to him. He usually also feels intensely toward certain larger groups with which he identifies—*his* (or her) family, city, church,

---

*A comprehensive definition of "instinct" was not formulated even by Charles Darwin after his lifetime of study, but there is no reason not to follow so great a scientist in listing what is observable. The following is from *The Origin* by Irving Stone (New York, Doubleday, 1980):

Charles' chapter on instincts was one of the most exciting and puzzling in the book to write. . . .The incredible mathematical judgment in the wax cell construction of hive bees. The power of communication among ants; their ability while in deadly strife with nests of similar species to recognize their own comrades. The wisdom of snails in searching out better pasture, returning for weaker members, and guiding them to food along the deposited layer of slime; and of the oyster, which shut its shell when taken out of water, enabling it to live longer. Of the beaver accumulating pieces of wood, even in dry places where no dam making was possible. The instinct of the ferret to bite the back part of the head of the rat at the medulla oblongata, where death was most easily achieved. How digger wasps dropped their prey and inspected their burrows before bringing in food for their young. How young sheep dogs, without instruction naturally ran round the flock and kept it together. The astonishing migration of young birds across wide seas; and of young salmon from fresh into salt water, and the return to their birthplace to spawn. The lava-colored marine iguanas of the Galapagos who went into the sea only long enough to feed on submerged algae and quickly returned to the shore rocks out of harm's way of the sharks.

nation—often identifying so strongly as to fight for them and die for them. How can an individual know and understand a whole city, church, or nation which is beyond his experience? He cannot, but the intense feelings born of all his instincts shape fantasies in his mind, and he accepts these fantasies as reality which he attributes to such fragments of information, rumor, or propaganda as may come his way.

The individual, homo sapiens, seethes with the interactions of his instincts, his basic biological urges and reactions, the forces of training, learning, and experience, and his reactions to the dangers and demands of the outside world in which he must live.

These feelings, thoughts, and behavior reveal to us psychoses; psychotic personalities; neuroses; perversions; addictions; asocial, antisocial, criminal, and every variety of behavior within and outside the law—the entire social and political scene, including the sublimated expressions in religion, music, art, and literature. Thus it is that the interactions of the instincts—intrapsychically within each person and interpersonally between individuals and groups—produce all we see and know of mankind; the dynamics of the individual personal and social psychopathology of humanity's earthly lot; the individual's suffering and the suffering imposed on intimates by his or her psychoses, neuroses, and sadism; the social ills of wars, tyrannies, revolutions, and exploitation; everyday cruelty, widespread divorce, battered wives and children, exploited husbands; increased crime so that the peace-loving citizen is endangered in his own community; and, finally, the threat of possible extinction through overpopulation, pollution, inflation, and atomic warfare (Mudd, 1964).

Where does the hope for bettering humanity's lot (mostly abominable) lie? The problem is made especially difficult because, in examining human motivation and behavior, there is so much resistance to recognizing whatever touches the observer's own feelings, and generally because the sense of reality is so greatly shaped and distorted by the other instincts. This makes it even more difficult to see the realities of the psychological sciences than the realities of physical science in which most observations are made through our senses, amplified by instruments, and not through our emotions, yet psychodynamics, young as it is, has clearly demonstrated that human motivational and emotional forces and reactions can indeed be studied scientifically. This is the first and most promising pathway of hope for bettering mankind's misery, namely, ascertaining the psychological realities and methods of amelioration through cooperative scientific study and working out ways of diminishing the suffering.

A few fundamentals are already known although they require much further study: it seems that relatively few individuals mature properly or sufficiently for satisfactory marital, parental, or social living. The path from conception and the newborn infant to the mature adult is one of long, complicated development—to develop adequately and learn to live with other persons in human society require love, sympathetic understanding, and respect for other personalities (not overcontrol, domination, interference, neglect, or hostility). Only if these requirements are met will the child mature properly and adequately, just as the tree will not grow straight, strong, and healthy without proper soil, moisture, sunlight, and the presence of other trees around it. It is also known that the foundation of the child's personality is laid down from conception to age about six or seven (0 to 6), by which time its emotional health or psychopathology as an adult for the rest of its life is mostly determined.

It seems obvious that the kind of world we have, with all its violence and man-made suffering, is a reflection of the kinds of personalities which compose it: Christ and his followers in contrast with Hitler and his followers; democracies and their confusions, and dictatorships with their tyrannies and antihuman cruelties. It is most unlikely, therefore, that any particular kind of social organization alone will bring a better life, whatever the theories of conservatives, liberals, socialists, communists, fascists, Yippies, protestors, and adherents of other -isms. As long as the *individuals* who compose a group are hostile, envious, self-centered, and cruel (i.e., still basically immature, emotionally *disturbed children* under their facade of adulthood), no kind of *organization alone* can work. The failure of each instinct to mature adequately leaves inner feelings of childishness, immaturity, and inferiority in the adult, these frustrations keep the fight-flight reaction aroused, with consequent rage and hate on the one hand, and impulses to escape by regression on the other. This results in all the myriad forms of psychopathology we see in personality and therefore in social ills.

Only the relatively mature are good, constructive spouses, parents, friends, and citizens, and children mature and are socialized adequately only if reared with love, sympathetic understanding, and respect. If we had a body politic of mature, realistic, friendly, loving individuals, it would be little problem to make a workable organization that would give humankind all the benefits of social living without all the disorders, dangers, and frustrations which we find increasingly to be the rule rather than the exception.

## PSYCHODYNAMICS AND SOCIAL SCIENCE

A major difficulty in sociological and political theory has been the failure of those fields of study to be based on a correct concept of human nature. No well-established concept existed until Freud developed psychoanalysis, which gave birth to the new science of psychodynamics. Some social and political theorists based their conclusions on the assumption that humans are universally self-centered, selfish, power-hungry and hostile (for example, Machiavelli and Pareto; Marx thought only capitalists were thus evil, while proletarians were magically reasonable and of good will e.g., in Edwin Markham's "Man With the Hoe," where we read of "the league of sober folk, the workers of earth, bringing long peace to farmland, alp and sea.")

Others, like Locke, Bentham and Jefferson, believed man was so far good as to be able to form a state which could guarantee life, liberty and the ownership of property. None of the famous social and political thinkers from Plato on fully recognized the extent to which each person has in him both the depths of evil and the heights of nobility and good—both devil and saint—infantile and mature. The fact is that the human constituents of a population are not all the same; "human nature" is a complex mixture of unsocialized, partly socialized and adequately socialized animal impulses. Yet parts of the personality (parts of the animal and parts of the moral) are the same in all people in the sense that all faces are identical in their *features* of ears, eyes, nose and mouth, while differing enormously in details.

In this way there is a human nature common to every human, including (depending on which forces are strongest) saints and sinners, pacifists and war lovers, law-abiding citizens and lifelong criminals, etc. It is impossible to understand social or political science without the recognition of the heterogeneity of human personality and the fact that these differences are not caused solely by the prevailing ideology of the particular age or by the socioeconomic position or occupation of the individual, important as these are. The essential facts of human nature for the social and political scientist are that (1) while the prevailing ideology is one important determinant of an adult human's views and feelings and (2) another powerful determinant is his socioeconomic position and occupation, (3) there are also personal inner differences in attitudes and motivations arising from inner, unconscious sources in the individual personalities.

The determinant the dynamic psychiatrist sees daily in every patient is the effect on his personality development toward emotional maturity of the emotional soil, atmosphere and experiences during the most formative days, weeks, months and years of his life, from conception to age about six or seven (0 to 6). Here lie the causes of healthy emotional maturity or of pathological warping, the making of the mature adult of good will, the good spouse, parent, friend and peaceloving, responsible, productive citizen—or else the childishly fixated neurotic, psychotic or pervert, or the criminal, the sadist or war lover. All that is required for social peace and personal satisfaction in living is the rearing of their young by humans with love, understanding and respect for their personalities—*primum non nocere:* the first task (in childrearing) is to do no harm.

Generally humans do not rear their young with as good feelings toward them as do other animals. It is common for humans to cause their children severe trauma, and everyone is familiar with the terms, if not actual instances, of "battered babies," "battered wives," and wives who subtly drive their husbands and children to neurosis, psychosis or even death.

It is inordinately difficult to get our children properly reared, when "proper" means only with good feelings between child and family members and not any sort of indoctrination, supplying the warmth of love and understanding which permits the child to grow in its own way, as the tree or plant does. *Keeping good feelings is the essential.* But it is difficult because most adults are so warped themselves that the problem comes down to: how to get infantile, emotionally-disordered parents to raise emotionally healthy, mature children, even if all that is required is to love them and leave them alone? We can clearly see the opposite: if children are traumatized during their most formative years (0 to 6), their personalities become so warped

1818

and pathological as adults, so infantile, frightened and hostile, that no ideological propaganda or political measures will make them into mature spouses, parents and productive citizens of good will or give us security from hostility, violence, crime and war.

Difficult as it is, the only task in childrearing is to keep good feelings between the growing child and those close to and responsible for him while winning him over to the necessary degree of socialization.

## REFERENCES

Freud, S. (1930): Civilization and its discontents, *S.E.* 21.
Mudd, S. ed. (1964): *The Population Crisis and the Use of World Resources.* Bloomington: Indiana University Press.
Saul, L.J. (1979): *The Childhood Emotional Pattern and Maturity.* New York: Van Nostrand Reinhold.
____(1980): *The Childhood Emotional Pattern and Human Hostility.* New York, Van Nostrand Reinhold.
SEE ALSO:
Alexander, F. (1942): *Our Age of Unreason.* Philadelphia: J.B. Lippincott.
____(1960): *The Western Mind in Transition.* New York: Random House.

# 2
# HYPOTHESIS:
# THEORETICAL FORMULATION

Does there exist, even approximately, a time period or a certain broad level of development of the human personality between, say, the ages of two and three, when its characteristics of feeling, thinking, and behaving—although healthy for a child of that particular period—would be considered psychotic in an adult? That is, if an adult, through fixation, regression, drugs, or other reasons showed characteristics of thinking, feeling, and behavior like that of a healthy one-, two-, or three-year-old child, would the adult be considered psychotic? We know that however healthy and happy a child might be, its grasp of reality, its feelings in relating to others, and its control of its own feelings will not be the same when it is adult. Are any of those qualities we consider completely healthy and normal in the child necessarily psychotic when evidenced in the adult? If an adult should regress far enough into childhood, will he show psychotic manifestations? Would this hold true even if the level of childhood to which he regressed was a healthy, normal one?

Understanding of the psychotic personality might answer some of these questions. It is not uncommon to see an individual who is in some part fixated at such an early level, or partially regressed to such a level, temporarily or permanently.

We need to determine whether these partial fixations or regressions of some elements of the patient's dynamics are the source of the psychotic manifestations. There seems to be one particular type of psychotic personality in which most of the personality is responsible, productive, and independent (RPI), operating maturely and realistically, but in which certain elements such as a specific pattern toward mother, father, or sibling are fixated at an old infantile level. This differs from the psychotic personality in which *almost the whole personality* is withdrawn to passive, receptive, dependent attitudes and motivations (PRD) and has not developed adequately emotionally beyond the infantile level of attachment to the parent.

Average level of
adult functioning

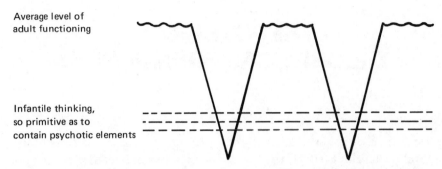

Infantile thinking,
so primitive as to
contain psychotic elements

Figure 1. Psychotic elements minimal. Here the average of the major dynamics and the functioning of the ego are well above infantile feelings and thinking on a psychotic level, and only a few parts (the downward spikes) dip below this level.

If our formulation (see Figs. 1 through 3) is correct, would it not also be applicable to all other emotional disorders of every kind and variety? The cases in this book indicate that nowhere does fixation or regression occur unless there was trauma which formed such a pattern. Conversely, no healthy, happy, well-adjusted infant or small child ceases developing without trauma. We see Mahlon Bowe (p. 188), a strong, successful man whose whole love life subtly manifests his pathodynamics, or Irma (p. 136), who never developed enough to achieve a life of her own. Had they been raised with only free, easy, loving feelings and with respect for their personalities, would they have no appreciable psychopathology? Was not the level to which they were fixated or had regressed determined by some early long-range trauma and their reactions to it?

Average adult
level

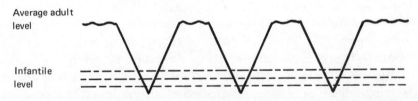

Infantile
level

Figure 2. Here the average of the major dynamics and of the ego is down close to the level of infantile thinking. The psychotic features are readily identifiable, but the condition is not frankly full-blown psychosis. The downward spikes represent psychotic characteristics.

Figure 3. Here almost all of the dynamics including the ego are into or below the infantile levels and the condition is psychosis.

The following hypothesis was first formulated by Freud: if the fixation or regression is to a near-preverbal level or younger, then the manifestations are generally psychotic in nature, producing either frank psychosis or psychotic personality; if the regression is not to so early an age, level of development, and verbal stage, then unless the trauma was very severe, the manifestations are only neurotic.

The essence of the psychotic personality and the formula for all the forms it takes can be represented schematically on a graph. The first element comprises the major dynamics of the psychotic condition as these appear in each person in specific and individualized form. Within these dynamics one or another characteristic may be especially regressive, such as a *specific,* extremely infantile pattern toward a certain individual of childhood which would warp the sense of reality in adult relations with substitutes for this figure sufficiently to introduce psychotic elements (Fig. 1). The other element is the *entire average level* or depth of specific dynamics—the extent to which the whole personality is fixated at an early infantile emotional and motivational level (Fig. 2). This is represented schematically in Figures 1 through 3.

The correctness of the representations shown in Figures 1 through 3 depends on several factors. First, can an individual's dynamics be observed to have certain elements that are appreciably more infantile than others? This can be answered in the affirmative with confidence, simply by a survey of one's patients at a given time.

More fundamental is the question of whether there exists, however roughly, a level that represents infantile, preverbal psychotic elements. If such a level exists, then this concept can easily include the pathodynamics, all the traumata contributing to the disorder, and also those factors which the age level alone causes. The feeling, thinking, and behavior of a specific individual can thus be readily represented in the concepts of the ego and regression with which every analyst is thoroughly familiar.

This concept, although developed as a hypothesis for the psychotic personality, by no means need be limited to this condition; it is applicable in understanding the complete range of neurotic, psychotic, and criminal conditions and all forms of emotional disorder.

\*   \*   \*   \*

A friend of mine who is usually reliable in matters of animal ethology once told me of two little foxes who met in the woods. One was male, the other female. In the natural course of events, they had sexual intercourse and then they went their separate ways; but they never forgot each other, always thereafter recognizing and responding warmly to each other.

Whether such facts are established I do not know, but even if this is only a quaint tale it contains a fundamental psychodynamic truth: namely, that there is a tendency to integration, not only in the ego (Saul, 1979, p. 469) but in the total personality. This may well be another "built-in conflict" (Saul, 1977, p. 275) between the tendency to *integrate* and the tendency to *split off.*

The warm recognition of each other by the little foxes after the one casual sexual episode would be intelligible if their sex drive were integrated with the mating instinct and warm (loving?) feelings toward each other. Whatever the psychology of the little foxes, in the human animal we see, in happy marriages, the sexual relations in the setting of mating, reproduction, and the rearing of young in family living, i.e., the integration of the sex drive and activity with mating and homemaking—desire integrated with love. However we also see, very frequently, the splitting off of the sex drive from the mating instincts; the man or woman is sexually active extramaritally and may even divorce in order to be free and promiscuous sexually without settling down into mating, reproducing, and rearing young—the desire and the love going separate ways.

This same sort of splitting off is seen in many forms throughout psychopathology. It is clear in the monosymptomatic neurotic conditions in which an otherwise emotionally healthy person works, plays, and loves easily and smoothly, but has an irrational fear of water or of heights and may be unable to go above the second floor of a building. In such cases it seems that all the frustrations, angers, and regressions unite and split off from the rest of the personality into this one irrational symptom.

Sometimes the conscience splits off: a loving, intelligent young mother uncharacteristically let her anger at her beloved young son vent itself in a verbal scolding of him, after which she was overwhelmed with guilt and self-reproach. She awoke that night from a nightmare in which many people were accusing her of some misbehavior for which they were trying to send her to prison.

In the psychotic personality, the forces of integration hold sufficiently that no clear-cut psychotic episode splits off from the rest of the personality. Instead, the psychotic elements are held in and diluted by all the rest of the personality. It is a little like a powerful electromagnetic field keeping agitating molecules, ions, and electrons from flying off.

Perhaps in the psychotic personality the actual behavior, the final common path, often comes out as relatively normal, although the intensities warp certain feelings and perceptions. In such cases, the diagnostic label indicates chiefly *distortion of the ego in its perception and in its integrative* rather than its executive functions. One way of judging whether a diagnosis of psychotic personality is correct is to consider the end result. If the characteristics that seem amiss became much worse, would the end result be simple neurotic disorder or would the end result be psychotic manifestations?

A psychotic personality does not preclude neurosis. The difference in diagnosis is difficult because it lies in the ego and not in the general dynamics. The psychodynamics are identical in the classic symptom neuroses and the neurotic character—the difference being that certain of the dynamics which cause symptoms in the neuroses are *acted out* in the neurotic character; but in the psychotic personality the dynamics are of such intensity that *certain of the ego functions are distorted, and these distortions are to some extent repressed.*

This fits into our basic concept of all emotional disorders manifesting a failure to mature adequately. In general, every person is still very much the child he once was, and the question becomes: In what mixture of age levels and of emotional traumata does the child live on in the adult? Many a "successful" man or woman is seen, on close scrutiny, to be a combination of a two-, three-, four-, or five-year-old child and perhaps also an adolescent. Insofar as this is true, the earlier the fixations, the greater is the chance that perception and integration will be as remote from reality as the mind of a young child. Generally, the younger the mind and the more under emotional stress it is, the more unrealistic and poorly integrated and less able it is to cope with the exigencies of adult life, i.e., the closer it is to psychosis, psychotic traits, or psychotic personality.

The severity of the psychopathology in the psychotic personality, as in the neurotic personality, is determined by at least two factors or variables: (1) how early in the child's life the emotional patterns were formed which are not outgrown and (2) the degree of abnormality (psychopathology) of these patterns, i.e., how severely disordered (by traumata) are the feelings toward self and others. Before the age of about three, and particularly before mastery of speech, the child's capacity for comprehension of its feelings and control of them is severely limited. The ability to deal with emotional problems is a function not only of (1) age but also of (2) the nature and (3) the intensities of the emotional pressures themselves, which are generated within the child, especially by those closest to him and responsible for him; as well as of (4) the kind and amount of support he receives in handling the emotional pressures. These strongly affect the development in kind and intensity of: (1) the child's dependence upon others, (2) its needs and ability to get love from others and to give it, (3) its sense of self-worth and of competitiveness, (4) its ideals and standards, (5) its conscience, (6) its fight-flight reaction, (7) its sexuality, and (8) its grasp of reality (Saul, 1979).

In general, every person shows the strains of his emotional forces, especially of his emotional pathology, upon his ego. From these emotional stresses and strains can come, as we know, the expression of a whole gamut of psychopathological symptoms: psychosomatic disturbances; classic neuroses; anxiety; depressions; perversions; and every form, extent, and degree of acting out (including the neurotic personality and the psychotic personality) from self-injuring masochism to all forms of hostility—criminality, torture, murder, and sadism. If the motivations express patterns of too early a period in life or if they are too intense, too pathological, or all of these, then the distortion of the ego (how a person thinks, feels, and behaves), which is the essence of emotional disorder, may take as one of its forms spotty, diffuse psychotic variations in the person's accustomed thinking, feeling, and behavior (i.e., some form and degree of psychotic personality). No wonder this condition is so common and takes so many different forms. Also, the earlier the age and stage of the regressive motivations, the more prominent becomes the self-centeredness and, therefore, usually the *narcissism* and the *distortion of reality*. Every human shows every kind of residual childhood reaction (Saul, 1979) such as excessive or disordered dependence, love needs, inferiority feelings, egotism, competitiveness, superego motivations, and all manifestations of the fight-flight response. When we diagnose headache or depression or paranoia, we only indicate the *most prominent* of a number of childhood patterns of reaction which everyone has in some degree.

In diagnosing psychotic personality, *sense of reality, narcissism,* and *hostility* must be considered, and also the withdrawal from emotional relations with other persons—object interest. Whether this is a neurotic or psychotic personality comes down to a matter of *degree,* especially concerning the above points. Are the distortions of the sense of reality, the extent of the narcissism (in whatever form, especially self-centeredness and prestige needs), and the intensity of the hostility sufficient to warrant the label "psychotic personality disorder" (PPD)?

If emotional forces (e.g., needs for love, rivalry, frustration, rage, revenge, escape, withdrawal, and so on) are so powerful that they threaten *loss of control* and *of sense of reality,* but are in a state of *diffusion throughout the personality* in all its thinking, feeling, behavior, and human relations, this very diffusion will act as a psychological defense against their power. If they ever coalesced, they might form a precipitate which, being unified or integrated, would break through like a beam of coherent light as organized psychosis.

If this is correct, then an essential of the psychotic personality is that in it we witness the ego's *defenses by diffusion* against a psychotic breakdown. It would be correct to say that the diffusion serves to defuse the explosive power which is present in the psychodynamics but not organized.

Is fear of being overwhelmed by overt psychosis (i.e., breakdown of the orderly operation of the mind) the main anxiety in all psychotic personalities? Is it also the main anxiety in *all* personalities except the most fortunate, most harmonious ones who are able to relax under the pressure of volcanic emotional forces? Many psychotic personalities go through life, if their diffusion and controls are good enough, with few if any other individuals perceiving the degree of pathology behind the mask of reason or sensing what could be triggered to explode into psychosis, suicide, or murder. (Very many murderers are described by friends and acquaintances as most gentle, pleasant, and considerate, the "last person in the world" they would have expected to do such a thing.)

In general, the prognosis for the psychodynamic treatment of the neurotic character is usually good, especially if there is considerable suffering; but it remains to be learned whether the prognosis for the psychotic personality is good or not. From our experience, it is generally not good, although we have had some excellent results even in paranoid jealousy, masochistic self-defeat, and hostility plus withdrawal. However, the therapy is apt to be very long (1) because the individual's ego and superego controls, reason, and sense of reality have to remain in command during therapy, and while under severe pressure from his biological (id) impulses for a longer period of time; (2) because of the possibility of periods in which therapy might temporarily intensify this pressure of the powerful, barely repressed emotional forces; (3) because the patient's reaction to unpredictable and uncontrollable incidents and situations in his life may produce more violent emotional reactions (see the case of Ursula, p. 152); (4) because the emotional withdrawal tends to make a weak and very hostile transference; and (5) because the earlier and deeper the regression, the longer is the developmental road back to maturity and reality.

In the earlier days of psychoanalysis, if the patient did not progress well, someone would suggest (with tongue slightly in cheek) that it was because the patient was really a latent schizophrenic. In these days of predominantly personality disorders, if the patient does not do well we must beware of falling back on the easy out of saying that this is not a neurotic but a psychotic personality. That diagnosis may well be correct, as cases in this book illustrate, but it would be a failure in conscientious responsibility to jump to this diagnosis as an excuse for failure while we are still studying the psychotic personality and ways to increase the effectiveness of therapy for it. After our years of study, we do accept psychotic personalities for therapy if there is enough healthy ego to work with and sufficient therapeutic urge in the patients, but we recognize that the therapy will be long and exhausting for patient and analyst, although it can bring a new, much more gratifying life to the patient and in some cases prevent deterioration into a psychosis.

A perceptive analyst, in discussing a man who had seen four analysts, said: "How long do you think it will take his new analyst to recognize that he is a psychotic personality?" In the hope of helping others to recognize and diagnose this state, we repeat the features that have impressed us during the study of our patients:

1. fixation of a considerable portion of the personality (but not all of it, which would be psychosis) at a level of

2. serious *withdrawal* (flight reaction) from human relations (deficiency of identifications and of object interest and relations),

3. heightened *narcissism* as psychological absorption with only self and personal interests (possibly like Freud's amoeba, with pseudopods withdrawn into self),

4. *hostility* (fight reaction) more or less chronic and intense enough to make difficulties of some kind, or at least to be evident and usually in part projected,

5. more or less repressed warping of the sense of *reality*,

6. *diffuseness* of the psychotic elements without definite psychotic symptoms.

Our competence and analysis of the psychotic personality is entirely psychodynamic but one neurophysiological reference warrants mention: Hughlings Jackson's (1958) concept of functional levels of the central nervous system has long proven real and useful. Paul MacLean (1973) extended this through the cortex in its embryological and evolutionary aspects as:

1. a brain stem transmitting bodily reflexes;

2. on top of which evolved the R-Complex, the reptilian brain, coordinating sex, self-preservation, and other behavior as seen, for example, in snakes and crocodiles;

3. on top of which developed the mammalian brain like that of the apes;

4. finally, the cerebral cortex, overshadowing all below it and uniquely characteristic of homo sapiens, making possible the human mind and all science, including the science of its operation—psycho-

dynamics. Only a beginning has been made as yet in revealing the neurophysiological connections of the mind with the brain, but the question sometimes arises in studying certain psychotic personalities: Does the fixation or regression observed psychologically reflect a dominance over the cortex of lower levels of the central nervous system, such as functions of the mammalian or even the reptilian brains?

## REFERENCES

Jackson, John Hughlings (1958): *Selected Writings of John Hughlings Jackson,* Vol. 2, ed. by James Taylor. New York: Basic Books.

MacLean, Paul (1973): *The Triune Concept of the Brain and Behavior.* Toronto: University of Toronto Press.

Saul, L.J. (1977): *The Childhood Emotional Pattern: The Key to Personality, Its Disorders and Therapy.* New York: Van Nostrand Reinhold.

____(1979): *The Childhood Emotional Pattern and Maturity.* New York: Van Nostrand Reinhold.

# 3
# NATURE OF THE CONCEPT

The neurotic personality or neurotic character is well recognized clinically. It was described most clearly by F. Alexander (1961) as a logical insight derived from Freud's *The Ego and the Id* (1923). It is a condition in which a person's pathodynamics, rather than causing physical or psychological symptoms as seen in hysteria or compulsion neuroses, are acted out in behavior although the person's ego (perception, integration, and executive functions) is relatively intact. In some persons, however, the ego is swamped by these dynamics and there is such gross distortion of the sense of reality (Freud, 1924) that they can no longer be termed neurotic, but are called "psychotic personalities" or psychotic characters, analogous to the neurotic personality—in which there is not a well-organized neurosis but acting out of pathological patterns that may only be recognizable over many years, for example, repeated successes and self-ruinations in business or in marriages and divorces. So in the psychotic personality disorder (PPD), *there is no circumscribed, organized psychosis, but a diffuse distortion of the ego functions.*

The diagnostic category of psychotic personality seems to be a step toward filling that gap in psychoanalytic theory which lies in the presently ill-defined area between neurosis, psychosis, and criminality.

Distilled to its essentials, the concept can be stated briefly as follows: the basic psychodynamics of a personality can contain strong and extensive psychotic elements; these elements can manifest themselves in different ways in different individuals, for example,

(1) in overt psychotic episodes,

(2) in coloring a person's whole outlook on life while never breaking through as frank psychosis, and

(3) by unconsciously employing the reality sense and rationality in the service of irrational, psychotic goals which may or may not be

achieved or even detectable for many years. There are many outcomes and combinations of the above.

By psychotic we mean failures of maturing, with weaknesses and distortions in the forces of repression from ego and superego, especially with impairment and warping of the sense of reality. Within the psychotic personality the reason and the sense of reality may be relatively intact, but used for irrational goals, and the psychotic elements are so diffused through the ego and superego that they are not readily identifiable.

Before Freud, classification was simple: the crazies, the insane, were locked up inside. Those on the outside were sane. With Freud, the center of focus shifted to neurosis. It became evident that the great mass of disorders occurred on the outside, that almost everyone is, to some extent, neurotic. Those on the outside *nearly all* had some emotional disorder, and it is only the extremes of disorder that are on the inside. Psychosis may be qualitatively different from neurosis; some psychoses may be organic rather than emotionally caused, but still there is a continuum from the less emotionally disordered to the extremes.*

There seems to be a band in this spectrum that contains those individuals who are not merely neurotic and not overtly psychotic, but in whom there is *sufficient psychosis to show through in some form* in the personality. It is these individuals we are studying; our working label for them is *psychotic personality disorder* (PPD). The assonance of the term "psychotic character" makes it more euphonious, but it has a tinge of implication of the moral character, or specifically, the superego. Perhaps the essence can be expressed in this way: *these individuals appear rational but are pursuing irrational goals, and we ask whether these goals are those of emotional patterns of early childhood.*

If the concept of psychotic personality proves true, then it is likely that our view of humanity must alter. Instead of a rather limited, relatively constant number of extreme psychotics and a preponderant mass of neurotics and neurotic personalities, we may see that a certain appreciable percentage of the population consists not merely of neuro-

---

*This book is devoted only to the psychodynamics of the psychotic personality and does not include any structural, organic, physical, or chemical factors that may occur in any cases. Organically caused disorders are beyond our purview.

tic personalities but of psychotic personalities. It is these which are now being discovered by analysts and about whom so much is being written. Freud's original remark that "everyone is a little bit neurotic" may yet be amended to "and everyone is a little bit psychotic, at least at times."

This alone brings a new perspective on *the sense of reality,* which seems to be enormously more sensitive, unstable, and subject to warping than is generally supposed or taken for granted. We have noticed that few persons can live without rationalization. Amazingly, rationalization was not included in Anna Freud's classic study (1937). The sense of reality is at the mercy of the emotions and readily distorted by the emotions. This is evident in almost every discussion of politics or religion.

Discerning psychotic elements in the childhood emotional pattern presents observational difficulties. These difficulties for the analyst arise first from having to recognize them by reconstruction from what the adult tells and, secondly, because they probably enter in most cases before the age of three, i.e., before the individual has sufficient conscious memory to recollect and verbalize them. Many small children act "a little bit crazy," but the family usually defends against recognizing this and blots it out as a passing phase of no significance unless it becomes too severe and persistent to be denied. However, to detect it retrospectively by present analytic methods of personal history taking and interpretation of unconscious material (Saul, 1977, 1980a) is usually extremely difficult. Therefore, this part of the theory of the dynamics of the psychotic personality remains to be worked out, probably by longitudinal studies and collaboration with interested, research-oriented child analysts and other direct observers of children.

In trying to discern the nature and cause of psychotic tendencies within the individual's childhood emotional pattern, the psychoanalyst looks for (1) some weakness or defect in the development of the reality testing capacity of the ego, which is at best very delicate, and (2) the presence of a relatively healthy ego with normal reality testing, but subjected to such powerful emotional forces from within that normal reality testing is distorted.

One feature seen frequently in the psychotic personality is extreme selfishness and self-centeredness. This is no doubt a form of infantilism and might be considered narcissism, but that may be too broad a term for it. It is seen clearly in the case of Mackley (p. 184). The thinking is only of "what *I* want": "*I* am not happy, therefore *I* will change my life style, divorce my wife, leave my children; all that matters are my own desires." Such thinking exists entirely on the pleasure-pain level with a conspicuous absence of sympathetic understanding and responsibility for others, of object interest, of identification with others, of love for others. There is a lack of capacity for close relations with another person. This typical psychotic personality can relate loosely to people, but not closely to single individuals. Therefore, he or she may have many acquaintances but no close friends, and may not be able to tolerate the intimacy of marriage. Yet typically, the psychotic personality thinks the reason lies in others and not in himself. This failure in close human relations seems to be partly libidinal, an absence of such relations during early childhood, and also partly hostile, so that sooner or later an attempt at closeness (usually with parents or siblings, acquaintances or co-workers, or through an extramarital affair) ends with the emergence of naked hostility and often hatred. The common formula is: *failure of closeness* in relationships, often denied, plus deeply *repressed hostility*.

Life is human relations and not only the self-indulgence of one's own desires, especially the infantile ones, regardless of the well being and happiness of other persons.

It can be said of many psychotic personalities and perhaps of many of us that, as we will illustrate in our case studies:

Each one kills the thing he loves.
Some do it with a bitter look,
Some with a flattering word.
The coward does it with a kiss,
The brave man with a sword.
Some kill their love when they are young,
And some when they are old;
Some strangle with the hands of lust,
Some use the hands of gold.
Some do the deed with many tears,
And some without a sigh.*

Why does the poet write so insistently and passionately that each man kills the thing he loves? Is he only playing with words or with

---

*With apologies to Oscar Wilde, in "The Ballad of Reading Gaol."

an idea? Or has he struck a poignant truth? One need not look far to find the latter.

Our first love object is normally our mother, or some equally close person: father, grandparent, aunt or uncle, sister or brother. This first great love also involves *a need to be loved and cared for.* It starts at birth but does not reach awareness until that part of the mind capable of awareness is sufficiently developed, approximately from age one to three, and then it expands and deepens until about age six or seven. If the child receives love, care, and respect, its own love continues to grow and expand and deepen. However, the love object—mother, other family member, or substitute—does not always give unalloyed love, respect, and understanding to the infant. Indeed, it is often the opposite: impatience, irritation, overcontrol, domination, physical violence, outright cruelty, and every form of human hostility (the three Ds: deprivation, domination, depreciation). The small child is weak and helpless, and cannot strike back. Often it continues to love, because for its own existence it needs its mother, upon whom it depends for both emotional needs and physical survival. If the mother, however, continues to treat the child badly, whether by neglect or active abuse, then inevitably and automatically the child will hate her and feel impulses either to flee from her or to attack and destroy her. Thus many small children come to hate the thing they love.

The universal popularity of this poem attests to the accuracy of the poet's perception. When a child is mistreated so as to stimulate its pain, fear and hate, especially under the age of three, it is far too young to have the use of language and thus be able to understand, handle, digest, and manage such a mixture of intense, conflicting feelings. The part of its mind that has the capacity for awareness is confused and warped in its development by something beyond its powers to control and understand. The child's accuracy of awareness, i.e., its sense of reality, is injured permanently, leaving scars or weak spots, vulnerabilities, and points of fixation for later regression. The poet's thread of ambivalence toward the love object runs through each case presented in this book, indicating how unconsciously each man kills the thing he loves, and how the pattern was set in childhood by parental mistreatment. If this experience was too intense before the age of three, the disturbance in the sense of reality may be severe enough to result in a psychotic personality or perhaps an incorrigible criminal.

It seems quite usual to say "incorrigible criminal," but scientifically this expression is moralistic and legal rather than psychodynamic, i.e., based on understanding the human personality.

We have said that the psychotic personality lies in the area between neurosis, psychosis, and criminality. Our clinical vignettes of patients support this statement. It also raises an important question. Hitler's behavior helped start a war which resulted in the death of 50 million people, including the fully goal-conscious mass murders of the Poles and of the Holocaust. Thus there is no question about the criminal element in his dynamics, meaning the open, conscious, planned acting out upon others of his hostilities. These seem to have been generated in his childhood emotional pattern chiefly toward his father (see Chapter 19). Hitler did not, however, become a "common criminal," or simply a murderer (many of whom are personally charming people whose acquaintances are amazed that such gentle, considerate persons could do such things). Thus the question becomes: If a person represses his hostilities but they cause symptoms, he fits the diagnostic category called psychosomatic condition or neurosis; if his hostilities break down the orderly socialized functioning of his ego, he is psychotic; but if the hostility is acted out in criminal fashion against others in antisocial behavior, then is not *criminality* just as much a *psychiatric diagnostic category* as neurosis and psychosis? And if so, should it not be included in our psychiatric diagnostic manuals? We believe so.

We have not recognized and used this obvious fundamental before, so far as the authors are aware, because we are accustomed to thinking of criminality as a province of the law, not a problem of psychiatry. However if we view it as a psychiatric diagnostic category, the effects upon the law might be much needed and healthy. We are all acquainted with the spectacle of psychiatrists appearing in court to testify as "experts" in criminal cases, the testimony of one diametrically contradicting that of the other. We also have heard passionate pleas for and against capital punishment. If criminality is a pathological psychiatric condition, then the issue is not primarily a moral one of severity of punishment, and the whole idea of treating antisocial behavior by punishment becomes of secondary importance and must be seen in a different light. The central point becomes diagnosis and prognosis, with treatment based upon these. For example, the following specific questions would be asked. Is this a condition of criminality? Is it a rational reaction to danger? Is this a deep-seated personality disorder? What is the prognosis, the chance that this individual will not trouble society again? Is it treatable—by punishment? by psychotherapy? by anything else? (Saul, 1980b, Chapter 12).

The function of the psychiatrist in court is to be an expert psychiatrist and not part of the adversary system. Everything the expert psychiatrist or analyst knows can be expressed in everyday language, intelligible to a jury. He can judge the diagnosis and prognosis of psychosomatic conditions, neurosis, and psychosis, and can with experience learn to estimate the prognosis for the diagnostic category "criminality" with or without the most promising kind of treatment. It would not be easy because no two persons are alike in their personalities or their psychopathology, be it neurotic, psychotic, or criminal. Nevertheless, we must see the fundamental psychological realities clearly, and base our attitudes and approaches on these realities.

Each personality is shaped by the inner drives, feelings, and responses he is born with interacting with the external world, especially that of other human beings, and also interacting with certain innate characteristics of his own. This is somewhat analogous to the relation between paranoia (in which there is fear of outside forces, usually other people) and hypochondria (in which the fear is of damage from within, usually some kind of disease). Apart from such psychopathology, our emotional patterns react to, and are shaped by, perfectly healthy characteristics—bodily ones such as size, strength, and coordination, and psychological ones such as intelligence and scientific and artistic capacity.

The most obvious characteristics that enter into the shaping of our personalities are those of our *body*. Build and strength enter directly or indirectly. For example, a young man who is strong and healthy and achieves a height of six and a half feet is apt to be tempted by the immediate financial rewards of professional basketball. Even more obvious is the reaction and adjustment of a girl to being either beautiful or "plain," even though in the long run it is usually personality that is basic. Less blatant than physical looks, strength, and coordination are *talents*. The hereditary factor in these can be strong although hard to establish and recognize. For example, a man who has been happily married for many years (and has five children grown to young adulthood) has absolute pitch for music, and this talent has been evident since birth. Because of it, he studied piano, the only one of four siblings to do so. Although trained in classical music, the socioeconomic situation after his marriage led him into popular music, where the money was. He never "made it big." The competition with tens of thousands of pianists was enormous, and he was glad to have steady employment in a nightclub. Only one of his five children had his talent. He was neither sad that his other four children lacked this musical gift nor pleased that the one did—rather, he feared it. From his own experience, he knew that this son would enjoy music in his youth, but feared that he would be attracted to a musical career in which the income was uncertain, unless one were a near-genius, and in which the hours were almost prohibitive for a family man who wanted children and a home.

The talent for making enormous amounts of money seems to arise from special forms of psychodynamics. It is, however, a special talent. "If you are smart why aren't you rich?" A mind as brilliant and profound as Einstein, H.A. Lorenz, Bohr, or Fermi can work on many subjects but not be good for money-making. Even traits developed from dynamics shaped in early childhood may cause problems for the rest of the personality. For example, a man was intrigued by mechanical problems and had a gift as an inventor and as a salesman. His vanity (his form of narcissism) favored both the inventing and the selling, because his own overestimation of his invention infected potential buyers. However, this same sense of his own superiority blinded him to what a poor businessman he was until he brought the business to the verge of bankruptcy. Only then did he recognize that failure could indeed happen to him. So narcissism can help or hinder as well as be healthy or pathological (Freud, 1914). Because of its role in the psychotic personality, we shall devote Chapter 5 to a discussion of some points about it.

## REFERENCES

Alexander, F. (1961): *The Scope of Psychoanalysis.* New York: Basic Books.
Freud, A. (1937): *The Ego and the Mechanisms of Defense.* London: Hogarth Press.

Freud, S. (1914):  On narcissism, an introduction, *S.E.* 14, p. 73.

_____ (1924):  The loss of reality in neuroses and psychoses, *S.E.* 19, p. 183.

_____ (1932):  The ego and the id, *S.E.* 19.

Saul, L.J. (1977):  *The Childhood Emotional Pattern: The Key to Personality, Its Disorders and Therapy.* New York:  Van Nostrand Reinhold.

_____ (1980a):  *The Childhood Emotional Pattern and Psychodynamic Therapy.* New York:  Van Nostrand Reinhold.

_____ (1980b):  *The Childhood Emotional Pattern and Human Hostility.* New York:  Van Nostrand Reinhold.

# 4
# THE PSYCHOTIC PERSONALITY: VARIETIES

To sharpen his picture of the "neurotic character," Franz Alexander placed it in relation to neurosis, psychosis, criminality, addiction, and perversion (1962, pp. 56-73). Glover (1955) recognized the existence of the psychotic personality, but neither he nor the other earlier authors that mention it succeeded in defining it and its dynamics with precision or in pointing the way to such delineation. This is in some part because the psychotic personality takes so many different forms, appears as we say, in such protean manifestations, and results in part from a combination of elements found in the dynamics of the neurotic character, psychosis, and criminality. Alexander's classic description is good today and, only slightly amended, will serve as a synopsis. The following conditions are arranged in order of decreasing capacity of the ego for repression:

1. In *neurotic symptoms,* unconscious impulses are displaced and manifested in the person's feelings by substitute gratifications.

2. In the *neurotic character,* the unconscious impulses are acted out to yield disguised but real gratification.

3. In *psychosis,* defenses fail, with breakdown of the ego, yielding undisguised but inner gratification, usually of very regressive impulses.

4. In *criminality,* defenses fail, but with ego intact, permitting undisguised, direct, acting out gratification. (Addictions and perversions are omitted. Of course, the above are rarely, if ever, seen in pure form.)

5. In the *psychotic personality,* we see
(a) neurotic dynamics acted out, as in the neurotic character;
(b) failure of defense with ego organization intact and some uninhibited acting out gratification, as in criminality;

(c) usually extreme narcissism and egocentricity—one's own wishes and desires being paramount over identification, empathy, and sympathy with others or with most others so that these feelings are often minimal;

(d) minimal or *repressed insight* into illness;

(e) the acted-out id impulses justified to the ego by distortion of reality (as in psychosis). This distortion is not extreme, is mostly rationalization, and is not beyond possible reality; this defense mechanism, rather than being relatively circumscribed as in a clear-cut psychosis, is more *diffused* throughout the ego and therefore more difficult to perceive and to describe. Indeed, the analyst may sense intuitively that one of his patients is a psychotic personality without being able to support this feeling for a considerable period by solid observational facts.

The essentials of the psychodynamics seem to be as follows: as all analysts know every child is born with certain potentials which interact with his emotional and physical environment to form an emotional pattern of reaction, the nucleus of which is usually well established by the age of about six. In general, the younger the child, the greater are the effects of the environmental influences. Insofar as these effects of omission and commission are traumatic, the child's emotional pattern of reacting to others is warped. Also, insofar as this warping distorts the ego, and superego, and sense of reality, it produces the potentials for psychosis. If the distortion is severe enough, the groundwork for a lifelong psychosis is laid. In general, the earlier in life the traumatic influences are exerted, the more apt they are to cause psychotic distortions. In other words, the distortions in the childhood emotional pattern (Saul, 1977) result in these psychotic elements in the child's psychodynamics which form a psychotic personality or the potential for psychosis itself when the child grows up and the rest of his psyche matures (see Chapter 1).

Terminologically, we shall use "psychotic personality disorder" (PPD) until good psychodynamic reasons are developed for preferring a different descriptive term (we have already noted that psychotic "character" is less desirable because of the tinge of moral character and of emphasis on the superego). Historically, there was a trend toward using the word "character," following Freud's *Character Types Met with in Psychoanalytic Work* (1916). However, after

Freud's *The Ego and the Id* (1923), it was felt that he had expanded psychoanalysis to a study of the total personality and this term appeared more widely (as in Anna Freud's *The Ego and the Mechanisms of Defense* (1937) and Alexander's *The Psychoanalysis of the Total Personality* (1930), both written in reaction to *The Ego and the Id.* Historically and in psychoanalytic usage, these terms appear mostly without sharp definition or distinction. Therefore, we shall use the broader term "psychotic personality" (or PPD).

Cases exemplifying psychotic personality in this book fall into the following types: (1) diffuse, (2) regressive withdrawal, (3) hostile, (4) schizoid, (5) paranoid, (6) depressive, (7) criminoid, and (8) criminal. These are little more than rough descriptive categories, although the symptoms do imply some dynamics.

What the basic psychodynamics or even diagnostic characteristics of the psychotic personality are, however, is not easy to discern. There seem to be two essential dynamics found in different proportions in all cases deserving this diagnosis:

1. The first of these is, at the extreme, the direction of entirely unimpaired reason, rationality, and sense of reality to *unconscious, irrational, infantile goals.* (An example is a man who married at age 66, then blamed and later tried to divorce his much younger wife for having ruined his entire life.)

2. The second is the *diffusion* of the psychotic dynamics throughout the personality in such fashion that thinking, feeling, and behavior are seriously influenced but without the formation of any frank, definitely psychotic symptoms such as would justify a diagnosis of "psychosis." It is as though the psychotic elements remained diffused and never coalesced into overt psychotic symptoms. Probably the most important characteristic of these is the warping of the sense of *reality* combined with some degree of impairment, loss, or warping of *controls.* This type is often hard to differentiate from very mild, transient psychotic episodes, sometimes lasting only a few hours or a few days.

Because psychoses take many forms while having certain basic features in common, such as a disordered sense of reality, it can be expected that psychotic personalities will also take many forms. Our *problems include:*

1. Is there a psychological condition which can be recognized as "psychotic personality," as distinct from "mild psychosis"?
2. If so, what are its features?
3. How do these features differ from "psychosis"?
4. Can its varieties be clearly defined and illustrated?
5. Can these varieties be classified?

\* \* \* \*

A charming, kindly, highly intelligent man of 60 came to talk with the analyst about his daughter. She had a good marriage and four children. The man was anxious about his daughter, first about her physical health and then about her marriage. Was it really a happy one? He had heard fragments of talk that suggested his daughter's husband might be having an affair. In fact, maybe his daughter was having an affair also. After three visits, with the analyst questioning the gentleman in detail about the evidence and the actual behavior of the family, it appeared that his case for worrying had evaporated. The analyst told him that there seemed to be no adequate, realistic reason for his anxiety about his daughter. From other sources the analyst had gotten information about the family and learned that they had long recognized his extremely unrealistic overconcern. With this reassurance and suggestion that he have more confidence in his daughter and son-in-law, he seemed genuinely relieved.

However, as he was leaving the office he said, "Oh, I should have told you about my other daughter—she is the one who *really* has the problem. When can I talk to you about *her?*" He returned to discuss his three daughters and his son. His wife had died some years before. With his permission, the analyst contacted the psychiatrist they had both seen before the wife's death, and the psychiatrist indicated that his behavior had been going on for 20 years. The patient originally had been worried about his wife, who had come for help in dealing with him. His dynamics were those of the overprotective mother. They went so far, however, that he actually believed his worries were justified and, like the paranoid or hypochrondriac, built up most of them from a small kernel of truth. Here, then, were neurotic dynamics acted out, with ego intact but so distorted in its sense of reality that apparently rational thinking and behavior were used for irrational acts of interference, dependence, and hostility to his children and their families.

The *paranoid* type of psychotic personality is readily illustrated by the frequently seen, unreasonably critical type of wife. A woman of 35 was appealing because of her blonde beauty and charm of personality, combined with a contrasting "little-girl" element that seemed to express a plea for love. Her handsome, adoring husband worshipped her, but she was usually so angrily complaining about him that when she was reasonably pleasant he was grateful. There were two daughters and a son. She had been a good mother until the children began to emerge from childhood at the age of eight or ten. Then she became critical of them also: "Why did you do this?" or "Why did you not do that?"

Her complaints about her husband were endless and expressed two main themes—that he was controlling and that he gave her no time, interest, or help. This was almost pure projection, as was unmistakable from interviews with the husband and from the wife's own account. She was the one who completely dominated the household. She gave the orders and made the demands. Her husband emptied the garbage exactly her way and on her schedule, did the dishes, hung up the laundry, and everything else. She controlled the sleeping arrangements, the lovemaking, the restricted social life. Her conversation was mostly critical and hostile. If she mentioned football, an enthusiasm of her husband's, it was in terms of the players swarming out onto the field like vermin out of the woodwork. She came to me to complain about her husband, but she complained about the butcher and the baker too—their products, the neglect, the abominable service—never seeing that her arrogant, regal, hostile treatment of them provoked their attitudes. Nor could she see that her husband was a saint to put up with her, let alone love her and patiently remain devoted and faithful. She saw his reactions to her endless demands, criticisms, and hostilities only as indicative of all *his* problems and of what an awful person he was. If he put out the garbage at the appointed hour for a year and then forgot or delayed a single time, she launched an unending tirade at him. If he was driven to losing his temper she might attack him physically, sometimes dangerously, with whatever was handy.

She did not come to see a psychoanalyst to get help for herself, but to get her husband to come and to change. For if this "monster" who so ill-treated her did not change she would throw him out and get a divorce. There was a shocking absence of any sense of what he, poor man, must be feeling.

Her mother had been depriving and dominating during the patient's very early years. After the patient was five or six, the mother treated her better. .Her analyst had only hints of this but had the opportunity of checking it with her older brother. The patient had transferred her image of her mother to her husband, to her friends, to acquaintances, to her whole world. This was evident in her comments on plays, books, and people, and in her conversations as well. Her outlook was through paranoid glasses. She was mildly paranoid in a diffuse way. She was not psychotic; she was well organized and effective in the home and in any job she undertook. You could introduce her into any group with confidence in her being accepted. It was all but impossible to give her any insight into her own hostilities and provocative dynamics. Impervious and thoroughly defended against insight into illness, she was barely defended against her own unconscious demands and hostilities, which expressed the pattern of reaction to her mother. She justified these demands by a generalized distortion of reality. Just as the depressed person sees the world through dark glasses, this patient saw it in a way that was keenly perceptive and realistic so far as it went, but selected and toned such behavior of others to make her feelings of frustration and anger seem natural, indeed inevitable.

This patient was physically and psychologically in fine shape. She relished her food, was indefatigable, fell soundly asleep on hitting the pillow, had no complaints at all except that she had to put up with such a husband and such a world. Her paranoid outlook kept her comfortable because all the problems were in others and not in herself. Yet her ego, *undamaged* in structure, was so deeply *colored* by her id impulses as to make her thinking, sense of reality, and behavior psychotic rather than neurotic in quality. The relation to criminality is evident in her extreme lack of identification and empathy with her husband and in the physical attacks, some made with knife or poker and mortally dangerous, that she made upon him. He sensed a danger that sometime her hostility might break through her defenses completely during one of these rages and he would not be safe if his back were turned at such a time.

With both patient and husband in therapy, the deterioration of the marriage halted and some very slow improvement began. They were seen on and off, as indicated, for ten years while this improvement continued; five years later, the wife phoned to tell me her husband had died. She outlived him for another five years.

\* \* \* \*

The difficulties in determining whether a patient should be termed a "psychotic personality" can be seen in Bartley's case. He was six feet tall, beautifully proportioned and possessed of superior coordination. Bartley was handsome—one could say he had a perfect physique with regard to build, looks, health, and athletic ability. His intellect was also superior and his personality most attractive. He was universally popular; girls wanted to sleep with him, live with him, marry him—anything and everything. At age 16, he had a beautiful 15-year-old girl all his own and enjoyed full sexual relations with her. His pleasure was alloyed, however, by feeling that he was too dependent on her.

Then Bartley got a sports car and became absorbed in tinkering with it. The girl interfered with this and he now thought she was too dependent upon him. He still tinkered and polished the car; the relationship with the girl ended.

At age 20 Barlety felt little interest in girls. His greatest pleasure was his sports car, especially when he was driving it. However, if there was any car behind him he felt tense and anxious, and that spoiled his pleasure. His parents could willingly afford any schooling he wished. He had youth, health, perfect body and intellect, and attractiveness, but Bartley could not be interested in or enjoy these gifts; he gradually came to the conclusion that life for him was not worthwhile and the only answer was suicide.

He met with firm resistance the idea that he have a physical exam, that his blood sugar might be too high or too low, or that some other condition might exist or be found. He also refused a short trial of lithium. The central feature of his psychology seemed to be this regressive trend—in ordinary language, this infantile quitting attitude.

He seemed to say, "If everything is not just as I want it (even though in reality he had everything) then I'll quit, I just will not play." This is the attitude of a small, very spoiled child. The striking absence of manhood, of fighting spirit, of the will and the desire to live are all apparent. How different this is from the famous line:

And though this world, with devils filled, should threaten to undo us; We will not fear, for God hath willed His truth to triump through us. (Martin Luther)

Bartley had a normal conscious wish for independence, but tried to express it only in ways certain to keep him dependent, namely, by fighting every step that might assure his physical and psychological health and true independence.

What shall we call this? Is this just a severe neurosis? Is it a psychosis—if so, what kind? Schizophrenic withdrawal? The depressive, suicidal elements seem much more a result rather than the basic condition. At age 20 and possessed of every advantage, he could not enjoy living and was frustrated to the point of suicide. If this is psychosis, is it not diffused throughout this whole personality rather than a specific combination of symptoms—and therefore best labeled *psychotic personality?* This leads to the following considerations: a powerful feeling (from the id) such as anger may be blocked in a particular person by the conscience (or the superego) so that it cannot be vented in unmitigated cruelty and violence, but yet it may be so strong that it distorts the ego functions, the reason, the memory, and the sense of reality. If these faculties are sufficiently distorted, we call the condition *psychosis* and the person *psychotic.* As an example of a psychotic episode: a superior man, Rufus, believed that he had devised a formula of great potential good for mankind but that a gang was plotting to steal it from him. In fear of "them" he began to travel, fleeing from city to city. Apart from this delusion (which it was), his ego was intact with good memory, judgment, sense of reality; but whatever the topic of conversation, in about 15 minutes he would bring up his delusion and manifest a distressing combination of fear and rage. This psychosis was paranoia, and although so severe that for a time he had to be hospitalized, it was a transient, circumscribed disorder. It ended and he returned to his life and his profession. This was not a paranoid personality, but a transient paranoid psychosis.

In other cases the psychosis is not thus sharply delineated. For one young man it was subtle, diffuse, permeating his whole thinking. Even the most extreme paranoid delusions and delusional systems are generally built up by distortions and exaggerations of a kernel of truth. Ryan was a sophomore in college, a loved child who was still overly dominated by both parents, yet nevertheless was permitted and encouraged to defy them. Stereotypes and thinking in stereotypes usually mean seeing groups and categories of people as part of one's own childhood emotional pattern. Ryan typically projected his childhood pattern onto the social scene: the "establishment" was too controlling, "young people" today want more freedom, they do not want domination, they show spirit in defying and rebelling, and so on. He could not see that our country, while not perfect of course, had achieved a greater *degree* of democracy than any other in history; that police were necessary; that military preparedness was essential for survival in the world as it existed; that the university he attended was sincerely trying to do its job well. There was indeed a kernel of truth in every abuse he listed, but it was all seen through the eyes of his being controlled, as in reality he had been by his parents in early childhood; only now he saw this control as coming from *all* authorities, from the establishment. This had been his early conditioning, and this conditioning had spread (in psychoanalytic terms, "transferred") to others, to all who could be seen as having power. And his emotional reaction, as in childhood, was fear and rage. The fear and the rage kept this view going; they distorted his sense of reality, his reason, his judgment, not so grossly as to call it frank paranoia but yet so pervasively—so saturating his views on food, dress, bathing, music, sex, politics, economics, in short on everything— that Ryan could correctly be called a *paranoid personality*.

Another man saw revolutionaries everywhere. In other words, paranoid distortions can be projected on anything and are clearly evident in political extremism of both right and left, or any orientation. In the Joseph McCarthy period, it was from the right that this paranoid distortion came, and even our greatest patriots such as General George Marshall and President Dwight Eisenhower were publicly accused of being subversive Communists. At present, among students the distortion is mostly in the other direction. Many of these extremists cannot be diagnosed as definitely paranoid, but their whole outlook, including the political—whatever the kernel of truth—is so suffused with this distortion of reality that their total personality is colored by it. If such coloring is dark and pessimistic and severe enough to twist reality, then it is a psychotic personality of the depressive type. If the person acts out his feelings on the basis of this hostile, fear-ridden, distorted view of reality then his is a psychotic personality off paranoid *acting out* type; this may take various forms—personal, political, and criminal. The political form of acting out can be seen, for example, in those extremists who try to rationalize their violence which achieves no real purpose and exists only for its own sake, that is, the satisfaction of acting out internal feelings of hate and hostility. Acting out can, of course, occur in all variations and combinations of these forms. In general, extremists of all sorts seem to be mostly emotionally disordered people. To comprehend the problems of society it is important to clearly recognize this, but of course it is only the beginning of the problem. What are the limits of the healthy human personality? At what point does pathology begin?

The paranoid type of psychotic personality is exemplified by Geraldine, who was an incessant complainer and criticizer, always in a directly hostile way. She was a hostile personality or, to use a more usual psychiatric term, a paranoid personality, to such a degree of intensity and with such disregard of reality as to be unmistakably borderline psychotic rather than neurotic. Two brief incidents illustrate this.

She lived in a small town in Indiana where she had beaten the spirit out of her husband and antagonized all their friends, totally extinguishing their social life. A cousin who had been a good friend during Geraldine's early childhood, when she had been brutally mistreated by her own mother, felt sorry for the woman and invited her to visit for a week in San Francisco. This cousin's husband was wealthy and generously sent her a large check to cover her travel and sightseeing expenses in Chicago, en route to San Francisco. Her reaction upon receiving the check, instead of gratitude, was rage: "He sent this check to me here because he knows I have no bank in Chicago!"

She did go to San Francisco, however, and there she shopped. At one store the salesgirl tore off her portion of the sales slip in a manner to which this woman was not accustomed, and her reaction was again rage: "She only did that to charge me more without my knowing it!" Even when her cousin showed her the exact price, unchanged, on her portion of the sales slip, Geraldine could not be placated or appeased.

On another occasion, a distant male relative who knew of her difficulties stopped off to say hello. Knowing that her occasional visits to Chicago were the only hints of relief in her life, if not of pleasure because she seemed incapable of pleasure, he offered to drive her to Chicago for the day. Her reaction again was rage: "He only invited me because that's what *he* wanted to do himself."

In the psychotic personality of the *criminoid* type (Saul, 1980), injury is done to others, which may be flagrant but is within the law. A garden variety example of such behavior within the family is Lester, a husband who, after 12 years of devotion, decides that he is no longer interested in his wife or children and asks for a divorce to marry a young girl, with no feeling at all for his family or their suffering by his actions. The main dynamics of this case were as follows: the usual dependence upon the wife, which the husband sought to compensate for by acting as the "big" man ("macho") with the young girl; a desire to escape from family responsibilities to "play" with a young girl; spoiling and domination by his mother in his childhood, which apparently generated a lifelong undercover rebellion against her and against all that she emphasized as proper, including responsibility for wife and children. So this husband was in full rebellion. Home meant submission, and he declared his freedom and independence. He indulged in undisguised selfishness and in hostile rejection of wife and children and of his mother—showing no sign of identification, empathy, or sympathy despite their obvious anguish and the children's reactions to all this by their failures in school, growing sullenness, and misbehavior. This husband justified his hostility and egocentric indulgence as mature independence, which he had won for himself at long last. He saw loyalty, love, and responsibility simply as arguments that his wife and friends were using to control him, just as his mother had. His ego organization remained intact as he ruthlessly went ahead with his determination to satisfy himself regardless of others. The pattern soon repeated itself toward his new young wife, and he divorced her almost immediately after their child was born.

A patient of neurotic rather than psychotic personality, possessed of an attractive family, got himself into the same position as the one described above—an affair with a young girl. However, his ego was less colored and his reality sense less distorted; his love and empathetic identification remained. Feeling the pain he was causing his family and seeing the damage to his children, he was guilty and miserable. He also saw his inability to forego the gratification of the other woman. He had enough insight to recognize this as a problem and to seek treatment.

Another example of the psychotic personality who acts out politically is the boy who was locked in a domination-submission conflict with his father from his earliest years, and came to see himself as submissive and infantile. This was intolerable, it hurt his narcissism, his adult masculine pride, and his need to identify with his father as a strong adult male, and it enraged him. At other times he saw himself as sadistically dominating others, utterly crushing all opposition, and his whole inner drive was devoted to achieving this. It colored his entire outlook. His ego organization was intact and he had a certain political genius in perception and action, but he justified his hostile drives for domination, destruction, and sadism—devoid of sympathy and empathy—by coloring and molding his view of his country and its "enemies" to fit these impulses. The fearsome fact is that many millions accept such distortions to justify their unrestrained indulgence of every id impulse. Rationalization, not reason, rules the world.

We reemphasize the point that rarely is any outcome of emotional disorder seen in pure form; there are so many motivations that the differences are mostly quantitative, and all combinations and gradations are seen in any given individual. The public's usual view is naive in the extreme: for example, in 1981 a young man shot the President of the United States, causing an injury from which he recovered. Public reaction was, "What's his motive?" There were of course many, at all psychological levels. However, the motive which the public liked was that the would-be assassin did it to impress a girl he had never met. This was probably not a motive but a rationalization. Many real motives probably lay in his unconscious childhood patterns of hostility, unknown to himself.

To summarize the psychotic personality: (1) the dynamics of the neuroses (2) acted out as in the neurotic character, (3) with extreme narcissism, selfishness, egocentricity, hostility, and failure of empathetic, sympathetic identification, and (4) with these id impulses rationalized by distortion of reality as in psychosis, less in circumscribed ways as specific delusions but more by diffusion throughout the ego, (5) with minimal or repressed or no insight into illness, and (6) as in criminality, with failure of defenses against id impulses, although the rest of the ego organization is intact. Since almost everything in the psychic life is quantitative, all combinations and gradations are seen. Examples have been given of four types of psychotic personality: simple, paranoid, criminoid, and political.

Every child is born with certain potentials which interact with the physical and emotional environment to shape in him* a specific individual childhood emotional pattern which is usually well established by the age of about six. If this pattern so distorts the ego and superego, especially the sense of reality, as to cause psychotic elements or coloring, a psychotic personality develops, or at least, the potential for psychosis.

## REFERENCES

Alexander, F. (1962): *The Scope of Psychoanalysis.* New York: Basic Books.
_____ (1930): *The Psychoanalysis of The Total Personality.* New York: Nervous and Mental Disease Publishing Co.
Freud, A. (1937): *The Ego and the Mechanisms of Defense,* 1-3. London: Hogarth Press.
Freud, S. (1916): Character types met with in psychoanalytic work, *S.E.* 14.
_____ (1923): The ego and the id, *S.E.* 19.
Glover, E. (1955): *The Technique of Psycho-analysis.* New York: International Universities Press.
Saul, L.J. (1977): *The Childhood Emotional Pattern: The Key to Personality, Its Disorders and Therapy.* New York: Van Nostrand Reinhold.
_____ (1980): *The Childhood Emotional Pattern and Human Hostility.* New York: Van Nostrand Reinhold.

---

*Throughout, we use "he," "him," "his" generically to include both male and female sexes.

# 5
# SOME POINTS ABOUT NARCISSISM

*The first love in a man's heart is love of self. Heaven put that love first in order that man would want to live, whatever his sorrows. Now, when self-love is wounded, no other love can survive, because when self-love is too much wounded, the self is willing to die, and that is against Heaven.*

Pearl Buck, *Pavilion of Women*

As we have seen, "psychotic personality" refers to those patients who manifest psychotic elements, not as frank, overt psychosis, but in some way, shape, manner, or form which is diffuse and often subtle and difficult to define.

The psychoanalytic literature burgeons with papers about this and related topics: narcissistic personality, borderline personality, self-psychology, the analysis of the self, etc. The narcissistic element is so often prominent in the psychotic personality that a few remarks are required here.

Freud's paper on narcissism is in part an application of the libido theory to this topic. With his love of mythology and flair for the dramatic, the tale of Narcissus abandoning Echo and falling in love with his own image reflected in a pool provided Freud with the dynamics he wanted; he apparently took the term from P. Näcke and Havelock Ellis. Freud (1914) introduced his concept by stating that:

. . .isolated features of the narcissistic attitude are found in many people who are characterized by other aberrations. . .narcissism would be the libidinal complement to the egoism of the instinct of self-preservation. . .schizophrenics suffer from megalomania and have withdrawn interest from people and things.

Like many psychoanalytic concepts, this one of narcissistic self-love has been used even by analysts in a broad fashion with a variety of emphases: being in love with oneself, sexual interest in oneself, preoccupation with oneself, etc. Perhaps Heinz Kohut's simple definition covers it most broadly—"cathexis of the self" (1971).

Narcissism is indeed a broad concept with a minimum of three basic components:

1. the biological element, from the id, of the instinct of self-preservation (as stated in Freud's quotation above) more or less eroticized;
2. the residues in the superego of the original attention and adoration of the mother and other family members, especially from conception to the age of six or seven, and the residues of the Oedipus complex,
3. the interaction with the outer world, where to achieve any security in human society, every person must acquire some amount of admiration and love and also his own self-respect.

Withdrawal of interest from people and pursuits seems to be a feature of the psychotic personality. Psychodynamically, is the characteristic narcissism in this condition perhaps a natural result of emotional isolation, a withdrawal of interest or libido?

"Narcissism" has thus come to include vanity and pride; self-interest; egoism, egocentricity, selfishness; needs for prestige, status, admiration and recognition; conceit, exhibitionism, self-praise; ostentation, self-importance. The narcissism takes different forms in different people. Perhaps the everyday, nontechnical term "vanity" encompasses most of these feelings. In this chapter we will present briefly the dynamics of narcissism as observed in the course of psychodynamic treatment, in a random series of patients.

Freud's "primary narcissism" appears to be at bottom the instinct of self-preservation, identical with Darwin's survival of individuals and species best adapted to their environment. (Darwin's psychological insights into mental and emotional characteristics and attitudes are constantly impressive.) This kind of self-preservative love of self, or cathexis of self, is a perfectly normal instinct, like such other instincts as sex, mating, and the dependence of mammalian young on their mothers. Such universal healthy narcissism follows a course of development and vicissitudes just like all other instincts. It is not the same in infancy or childhood as it is in adulthood. In childhood, it is largely the desire for the love and approval of the parents which is the helpless little child's only guarantee of survival, and it is the natural result of the child's main task, namely, its own growth and development. The small child has little more at its service than the fight-flight reaction of self-defense, escaping a danger or destroying it (a capacity of R-4, the reptilian brain). It is not yet served by a well-developed ego and by social organization, such as the "higher" mammals have (flocks of geese or herds of deer). In humans the narcissism becomes inextricably involved with the interplay of many instincts,* emotions, and reactions, and with part or all of the psychodynamics of the total personality.

This connection of narcissism with primitive self-preservation is seen in animals who fight for a higher position of dominance. The higher the dominance, the greater is the access to resources, e.g., food and mates (Saul, 1980, p. 9). There seems to be a prestige element in those riding horses that strongly insist on leading the string. There is no question of the need for prestige—vanity—as a deep motivation in many other mammals besides humans. The dominance hierarchy may well be one of the deepest biological links of narcissism with the instinct of self-preservation; higher dominance brings the rewards of greater access to resources and privileges. This is probably reinforced psychologically in humans by the long period of childhood during which nearly all access to resources is possessed by the dominant individuals in the family—the parents. The child, weak if not helpless for so many years, grows up with the frustration of seeing his parents monopolize the privileges of authority, power, mating and sex, and whatever financial control can provide. This must be a serious wound to the child's biologically rooted vanity and prestige needs, and must cause strong reactive narcissism. Incidentally, something very similar to the dominance hierarchy in animals is seen within human communities as the psychosocial phenomenon of snobbism and power structure which is usually

---

*Although general agreement on a scientific definition of "instinct" is still lacking, we find the term useful for fundamental motivations and reactions of the organism as a single unit.

based on social position and maintained by wealth and positions of power, as witness "The Four Hundred," "Boston Brahmins," "Southern Belles," or the English vis-á-vis high caste Hindus, each sure of their superiority over the other. "Macho" is a form of expressing male superiority to women; many young boys (and girls) start smoking cigarettes to show their peers how superior and grown-up they are, until the real addiction—physical or psychological—develops.

From clinical observation, it seems that any strong emotional force (e.g., narcissism, as well as hostility) can be "projected," or perceived as coming from another person rather than from oneself.

Harry, with his thick blonde hair, small but fierce-looking mustache, and blue eyes, looked like a modern Viking. He was a man of superior insight and maturity, but so constantly critical of his wife that, despite all the reasons he gave, one inevitably wondered if there were not an element of paranoid projection at play. In one analytic hour, Harry spoke of his distaste as a child for anything feminine, of the rage he felt at his mother and sister if they intimated that he might be a good cook and could darn his own socks, of anger at the faintest innuendo that he might have feminine traits or talents. What he finally remarked clearly was that he hated the very idea of anything in himself that could possibly be considered feminine. Harry had long since read of the bisexuality of both men and women, but it was for him only an intellectual idea. After many hours of analytic work he realized his hostility to his mother and sister in his childhood, and now his repetition of it to his wife. With his usual honesty and courage, he gradually perceived that this hostility was generated (1) by a constant sense of frustration for not receiving from them sufficient love, care, help, and attention; (2) as a defense against admitting that he needed and wanted this tender, loving care at all; and (3) as a defense against identifying with his mother, and therefore admitting any feminine characteristics. He resented the fact that she was expected only to do housework, while his father, and later himself, were expected to go out into the big, bad world and earn money. He defended against a partially negative Oedipus complex. The chief reason for this defense was masculine narcissism, denying any hint of feminine traits. Of course when, in the analysis, he maturely rose above his narcissism and could freely acknowledge all these feelings that offended his masculine pride and vanity, his own self-regard and also the analyst's private opinion of him rose. Everybody has every-thing in his unconscious. Respect is aimed directly at the individual's ego and superego, in recognition of his standards and of his courage and honesty in facing feelings and traits even if they offend and pain his pride.

Harry's hostilities during early childhood (0 to 6) were sharply de-marcated. His respect, closeness, and affection went mostly to his father and older brother, while the complaints and resentments were directed mainly toward his mother and sisters. He felt as a child that his mother was responsible for the home and children, and therefore if anything went wrong it was her fault.

Harry sensed a chronic frustration within himself, a feeling that his mother did not sufficiently satisfy his dependent love needs, that he never got all he should have gotten from her. This feeling carried over in his feelings toward his wife. It seems that no adult can really satis-fy the needs of childhood that live on within him. Now Harry chal-lenged this belief. He was fully determined to have a try at getting from his wife the satisfactions he wanted as a child but felt he never got from his mother. He was no longer a child and his wife was not his mother. The sense of frustrated passive-dependent love needs was part of his childhood pattern in his own mind—which made fail-ure inevitable. When he acknowledged this, he resigned himself to accepting reality and gained much relief and peace.

Harry spontaneously related a memory of early childhood: his mother was passing a tray of candies around the table after dinner. His siblings were all scrambling for them, fighting each other for the best and the most. Suddenly the thought came to him: "No! I am no longer going to fight like these children for my share. I would rather do without." This seems quite mature for a child, but Harry says that the idea sank in and he never again fought like a child for his share, preferring doing without to demeaning himself by such selfish, childish struggles, but also believing he could get them in other ways.

It seems that this step increased his identification with his father and older brother, thereby increasing his poise and dignity, but of course at the sacrifice of a portion of what his dependent, receptive love needs craved. Now, in middle age, it seemed that Harry was going through life with this repressed and frustrated craving emerging toward his wife in the form of often vague feelings that she did not give him enough of what he wanted and needed in order to be satisfied with his life. It was not easy for him to admit that his dissatisfaction and frustration might lie not all in his wife, but in his own childhood dynamics. He was able to rise above this narcissistic resistance, however, and fearlessly face any truth about himself in spite of it.

Then Harry told a current dream which dealt yet another blow to his self-regard. It was of a large insect that had bitten his hand and was so firmly attached to it that he could not shake or pry it off. To this dream he associated some guests, old friends of his, who were coming to visit for a week. Then a small dream fragment of his wife returning from vacation to take care of these guests led into the entire area of his resentment against any demands being made on him. Once, on a day some other long-awaited old friends of his had arrived to visit, Harry found a reason to absent himself, leaving the entire welcome to his wife.

He admitted that he had made a great point to his wife and children of the virtues of commitment and responsibility, but now he found himself resenting his own responsibilities and efforts in the home. Again, he rose above his narcissism and faced whatever traits or dynamics emerged. He could see his hostility to his own feminine tendencies, which he had hitherto never acknowledged, and could see the hostility he felt toward his wife as the living representative of femininity. Lacking sympathetic acceptance of what he considered his own femininity, he had been unable to give sympathetic acceptance to his wife's femininity. As is generally true of everyone, what the individual defends against in himself he resents in others. In this case, Harry could not tolerate the femininity in himself or, therefore, in his wife.

Even deeper in his dynamics, however, was the difficulty in relating intimately with individuals, especially women. Handsome and attractive, he had sown his wild oats successfully, but rarely got close to any woman emotionally or continued a relationship for more than a few weeks. When he noticed some inhibition in his wife's sexual responsiveness, this became a burning issue for him because unconsciously it served as a rationalization for withdrawal from closeness to her. He suffered from feeling this lack of closeness, just as he had with his mother, but attributed it entirely to problems in his wife and not in himself. In retrospect, perhaps, he should never have married but continued as in earlier years to have sexual affairs without the problems of getting close emotionally. Harry did not want a divorce—he clung to what attachment he had with his wife, but its difficulty and pain led him to gradually disengage himself so that he was married but not very close to her. This was his childhood pattern toward his mother, whom he blamed for not giving him enough attention, care, and love. He did not resume affairs with women, but for a time lived with his wife as though he were a bachelor—in the home but withdrawn from it. The analysis improved this greatly.

\* \* \* \*

## NORMAL NARCISSISM MAKING A HEALTHY PERSONALITY

Celia was a young matron nearing 40. She had been a most delightful, happy, bouncy little girl with the best of relations with both her father and her mother. They in turn adored her, their first-born, but loved her wisely and well, not overprotecting or overindulging her. In adulthood Celia was still happy, bouyant, and secure. As her parents had once put it, Celia was born just right and had been just right ever since, a judgment shared by her wide circle of friends and acquaintances.

One evening at dinner, Celia's husband, Charlie, burst into tears and blurted out the following confession: "I can't stand hurting you or the children, but I am fed up with marriage and I am leaving tonight. I still love you all, and we can remain good friends." At the time Charlie revealed his feelings, Celia was anticipating emergency surgery for suspected cancer. Now she faced the added trauma of Charlie's sudden onslaught by quietly standing her ground, looking her husband full in the eye and saying, "Don't be absurd. We still love you, too. I hope we can work this out and save our marriage, but if you leave, then of course we can't be friends. Once we're separated, I won't ever see you again. Be friends after that? Don't be ridiculous, Charlie."

He did leave, but his dependence on Celia brough him back in a week (the usual dynamics). He went to a local analyst of reputation, and Celia went to another analyst about the whole situation.

Celia told a childhood dream she had of gently falling down the stairs of the back porch at an old house. Another childhood dream was of going to the toilet but finding that she had wet her bed, which she had not done in actuality. To the first of these dreams she associated her happy years in the family's old house, and her strong attachment to it and reluctance to leave it. She associated leaving the house with leaving her beloved grandmother, who had lived with Celia and her parents in the old house. The resentment for having to leave she could not express to her loving parents, but it caused her to dream of being back in the old house, in the mildly masochistic form of gently falling down the stairs.

At the request of Charlie's analyst, Celia went for an interview with him in which she explained her husband's childhood dynamics with more insight than the analyst had been able to elicit from Charlie himself. And still she was waiting patiently to see if any hope remained for reconstituting her marriage, meanwhile carrying on with the routine of home and children and preparing for major surgery. Wisely, she contacted a lawyer, not for action but for information, in order to be prepared to defend her legal and financial position and act wisely if the need should arise.

Where did Celia get this ability, strength, and understanding? Through identification with the adults of her childhood, because they loved her and she returned their love—thus allowing her to freely and strongly identify with them; they were relatively mature and loving themselves as models. Celia had become mature beyond her years, and could deal with husband and children with the same sympathetic loving understanding with which her parents and grandmother had raised her. Her needs to be secure and loved, while gratified by adoration, did not make her a spoiled brat but, through these identifications, made her a strong, loving adult. In this way, naricssism *strengthened* the maturity and in no way reinforced psychopathology, as it so often does.

Let us note in passing that psychodynamics continue to demonstrate that every motivation is affected by other motivations and reactions. Not all identification is so secure a force toward maturity as Celia's identification with her loving parents. In contrast, a relatively mature and loving father projected his narcissism on his adolescent son in a form which made the father overly controlling and dominating. He became aware of this and hated himself for it. He had worked out very reasonably, intelligently, and realistically a number of things which benefited himself and consciously he wanted to help his son utilize these fruits of his experience. However, he projected parts of himself onto his son so far that he could not tolerate the son's doing things differently from the way he himself would do them. For example, his son had worked hard one week in school and in an outside job to earn pocket money. One Friday evening the son lay on the floor to watch television. The father found the programs to be trash, a complete waste of time, he felt there were many informative and uplifting books to be read—why wasn't his son absorbed in books instead of TV? At this point the son phoned a friend. "Great," thought his father, "he has friends." However, after an hour of conversation the father's doubts began: "Is my son escaping from life? And why did he load the dishwasher the way he did after dinner? . . .He's so sloppy, not stacking and loading in a definite pattern like I do." Only then did the father bring himself up short, realizing that soon he would be constantly nagging and trying to direct and control his son, simply because the son's methods differed from his own.

### AN INTERMEDIATE CASE

Peter was an upstanding, highly intelligent, intuitive, loving young man of 30, engaged to a younger, bright, and attractive career girl.* His brother Dick, who was three years younger, had suffered a severely traumatic infection at age three, leaving some residual handicaps. "The squeaky axle gets the most grease." Thus Peter's mother turned most of her attention toward Dick, and so in his own eyes, Peter felt he must become the perfect son who does everything alone, while Dick, the sick one, got the major share of attention. Peter was too young to understand the family's emotional climate or his own emotions, and he reacted by gradually turning away from all members of the family. He could not cope with the situation at his tender age, nor could he accept his privileged position of winner in the sibling

---

*Peter was a graduate student who came to see an analyst just before he was to graduate from the University of Chicago, for advice on choosing a career.

rivalry. His reactions forced him into premature independence from his family; he accepted Dick's position as the "sick" one who received the most attention, and proceeded to accomplish everything on his own, from straight A's and an outstanding athletic record in school to his later triumphs with girls and in the world of business. Yet the sibling victory, because of his rejection of his family, created in Peter a certain bitterness and some guilt.

The storm broke over his parents' reaction to his fiancée, Stephanie. Both father and mother were critical, and Peter's response to them was: "I have done everything on my own, asking nothing of my family. I've put out and put out, and all alone I've achieved outstanding success. I've done everything alone, and now I've picked a wife. Who are you to question my judgment and ability to handle my life? I'm not a child any more, I've made my own way, I know something of the world and can make this decision alone."

What he said was true. Yet his parents loved him deeply, and he deeply loved them, realizing his great good fortune in having such unselfish, understanding, devoted parents. The narcissistic element included his need to prove that he could do brilliantly alone and the not fully abandoned sibling rivalry, with its need to prove that his parents did indeed see him as the perfect one. Were it not for these factors he might have introduced Stephanie to his parents with complete confidence in her being accepted totally, but this he could not do because of his reaction of independence and because of his narcissism which was stung by their thoughtless critical remarks when he mentioned marriage. Although he denied it consciously, unconsciously he had wanted his marriage and his choice of wife to be perfect in their eyes; to be the "perfect one" with his parents' full approval and preference in his sibling rivalry. He also had to make the "perfect" choice entirely on his own, independently. He had thought of himself as entirely independent of his parents and had not realized how strongly, unconsciously, he was still seeking his parents' complete approval as the "perfect" son—and he was still hostile to his parents for giving so much of their attention to Dick at a time when he, Peter, was too young to comprehend Dick's great need. Peter's identification with his strong, loving parents contained these adverse dynamics, which made a slightly less pure and wholesome relationship than that of Celia to her parents. Some psychodynamic psychotherapy could be expected, with a high degree of confidence, to solve rather quickly such a problem in a person so loving, talented, and mature as Peter.

## MORE INVOLVEMENT OF NARCISSISM WITH PATHOLOGY

The following illustrates a pattern of childhood dynamics familiar to all analytic therapists, that is, the effect on the children of an overly ambitious, hostile, fear-ridden, overly striving father.

Reid's story might be titled "An Episode in the Great Depression in Chicago" or "How Not to Fall off the Ladder." Where did he get his strengths despite the almost total emotional deprivation of his early childhood? The answer finally came in a visit from his older sister. She told Reid that, as the first boy to be born after three girls, his care was literally taken over by herself and the next oldest sister, both of whom lavished upon him much attention and love, none of which he got from his parents; this close relationship between Reid and his sisters still continued.

Reid's father was a pathologically exaggerated, narcissistic, selfish, self-centered man, with the shrewd brightness and the hyper-drive which would assure his success. He made his wife a slave, useful to bear and raise children, and to run the home with minimal expense and with minimum demands on his attention. He was free to further his career and had made a small fortune during a previous period of expanding economy. He imposed his own will on his family with little or no regard for their feelings, even bringing his mistresses into the home. He insisted on his son doing all sorts of chores in the house, demanding perfection but never finding anything done to his satisfaction. His wife escaped her sorrows by drinking wine with other neighboring wives of similar fate in life—"marital slaves." Her six children were raised to be prematurely independent and productive, serving the father. However, as the first son after three girls, Reid, while totally neglected by both parents, was expected to live out his father's frustrated ambitions. His father tried to make Reid achieve what the father himself wanted, namely, the social prestige of the right address, the right schools, and the right level of wealth. As this came through to Reid, he felt he must be perfect in all ways in order to achieve the admiration of both his father and society.

Reid suffered as a child from two main object relations: domination and deprivation. He also suffered from his early identifications. Programmed to be not only successful but perfect in all ways, he became an inventor who manufactured products that were financially profitable, but he lived always in dread of imminent ruin, as did his father. Reid's sisters themselves described their father as a psychotic personality. Reid and his wife traveled, as part of his business, to the great capitals of Europe, drove the best cars, and received the admiration and acclaim of their acquaintances for their success and wealth. Nevertheless, his wife, with bitter frustration, told how Reid would awake in the middle of the night in a panic of anxiety and depression, convinced like his father before him that his well-established business would collapse any day and leave him destitute, and that he would be abandoned by "the world." Only he and his wife knew that he left for the office every day convinced that he could not carry through the details piled up there and would be unable to pay off his debts. Sustaining this unremitting anxiety and depression made him feel his own death must be near.

Business people, in general, are as emotionally involved in their occupations as artists, scientists, doctors, and lawyers are in their professions. When business is bad, some businessmen react with severe anxiety and depression, coming for analytic help for their emotional problems. This Reid did instead of jumping out of a window like so many others did in the early 1930s. In one of his first analytic hours, Reid discussed how his extreme vanity, derived from his striving parents who expected perfection of him and thus made him feel superior to his sisters and all other people, in some part helped him in his own sales work, because of his conviction of the superiority of his inventions. This vanity also interfered with his judgment in the management of his business.

"Worse than that," he said. "I have thought I was so good that I did not have to operate on sound business principles like ordinary people." This showed encouraging insight. He was handicapped by not being able to run his business in the ways that "ordinary people" do; for example, even when threatened with bankruptcy, he could not borrow money from just any bank, but only from the most prestigious. When he got a large order, instead of feeling reassured he became so anxious that the customer might not pay for the order that he hesitated to fill it.

"But aren't there laws," he was asked, "to make the customer pay?" "Of course," he responded, "but I never use contracts—I operate entirely on faith. I send the man what he orders and trust him to pay." Reid was in a vicious circle: the more precarious the business, the more intense his anxiety and depression, and the less effective his running of the business. The more upset he was, the more threatened the business became. Having everything, enjoying nothing, fearing to lose everything, he struggled in anguish through the long days and nights of his life. He felt himself a total failure, a nonentity in the world of successful and wealthy artists, scientists, and businessmen, but simultaneously he felt the praise of what he termed "the multitude" and realized that in his halcyon days he had indeed done brilliantly, both scholastically and athletically, at one of the most prestigious colleges, chosen for him by his father as "the best."

His wife, however, denied that Reid had ever played football in college and told me that it was only one of his narcissistically gratifying fantasies. Although Reid complained bitterly about the expense of taking his wife on his business trips to Europe, she maintained with equal vehemence that she did not want to go, but went only because Reid was so dependent on her that he could not manage alone. His assertion that they stayed at the most expensive hotels only because of *her* needs for prestige were denied by his wife, who claimed that these were Reid's own needs to appear a great man in the eyes of the world and that she preferred smaller, less expensive hostelries.

In general, she was more realistic than Reid, less apt to be carried away by her imagination. He maintained that she was a typical, bejeweled, rich wife, making a vulgar display, but when she arrived for sporadic visits to the analyst, she was invariably dressed in understated good taste with no jewelry whatever. He objected to the time, money, and attention she constantly demanded of him, while she in turn said that Reid was incapable of giving affection, love, attention, or money. In reality, Reid was a considerate and pleasant man, tragically trapped into overwhelming narcissism in the form of having to be superior to everyone, and into an identification with his now long-dead, ungiving, anxiety-ridden, paranoid father.

Where was reality in all this? There was a psychotic element to it all, but exactly where? Reid was sweet, considerate, and well liked by all who knew him; only his wife saw his tantrums and rages, his nightly drinking to ease his psychic pain, and his insistence on dining out almost every evening at expensive restaurants, although claiming he hated it and went only because she demanded it. What eventually came out was that he suffered severely on empty evenings if they did not go out with friends.

The narcissistic element in Reid was clear, as was its form. The self-interest was evident in the cultivating of prestige, in the needs for high regard, admiration, position. Reid insisted that he resented the sales presentations he had to make of his inventions while away from Chicago on business trips, but when he told the analyst about them he glowed with pride at his ability to hold an audience fascinated and at how brilliantly his expositions flowed. He felt that in this field he was a recognized master. The cars, the home, the furnishings, the expensive restaurants, the exotic trips, the luxurious hotels, the shopping in foreign capitals—all this was narcissism in the form of winning recognition, status, prestige, and admiration. By all of these he sought unconsciously (1) to ease the sharp and painful deprivation and frustration of the dependent love needs; (2) to win his long-dead father's approval which he had striven for in vain as a child; (3) to ease the deeper feelings of inferiority from early rejection, deprivation, and depreciation by his father; and (4) to cling to some human contacts in his extreme emotional remoteness from people. This pattern in childhood came up clearly and repeatedly in his associations as the therapy progressed.

Reid had grown up severely deprived, as did his sisters, who all had profound personality problems and serious difficulties in their marriages, with their children, with their friends, and in all areas of personal relations. The sources were unmistakable. Their father, completely occupied with his own personal anxieties and desires, had given no consideration to the needs of others. He gave his wife nothing but made huge demands on her for housekeeping, cooking, laundry, children. She, getting no satisfaction, reacted by escaping to a neighbor's house to drink and bemoan their mutual fates. So frustrated herself, she did not have the inner resources to give enough of herself to her children.

Reid was reared with almost no warmth, affection, concern, or emotional interest from either parent. His stability was saved only by the attention of his two older sisters. With no other libido coming in, nevertheless he was forced to give out by helping with the mechanics of the household. He was forced by his father prematurely into responsibility for all the out-of-doors maintenance, and this was beyond his capacities as a child. However, he continued struggling to do well in the hope of getting some crumbs of recognition and appreciation. It was mostly to win this paternal love that he strove manfully with tasks that were beyond him and which he came to hate. This was the source of his fear and hatred of responsibility and of giving which had plagued him throughout his life. With the magical thinking of the small child, he came to believe that if he performed perfectly all that was demanded of him, he would reconcile his parents to each other and to him, his father would quit bringing home mistresses, and his parents would give love to each other and to himself and his sisters. Thus were generated the roots of much of Reid's ineffectual over-conscientiousness and exaggerated perfectionism, his intense inner resistance to responsibility and to giving, his sense of inferiority to those who could work and give freely with enjoyment and without inhibitions, his reactions against this sense of inferiority with needs to demonstrate his adequacy and superiority to others, and his needs for status, acceptance, admiration. His fantasies began to supply these needs when reality did not, slightly confusing his sense of reality.

As Reid spoke about his wife, she seemed like a character created by a writer of fiction: "My poor wife, how I wish I could give her everything she wants—a beautiful apartment at the right address, a fur coat, jewels, and a condominium in Florida to escape these Chicago winters! But I just don't have that kind of money. And I awake at night trembling lest I lose what I've got. All I really want is a little house in the country, with a dog and a few chickens." This sounds noble enough, but "my poor wife," as she tells it, is Reid's way of endearment, instead of "my dear wife." These desires are projections of his own mind, of what he wants for himself—all the symbols of the success and status his father demanded of him, the need to be the best in everything. The little house in the country represented escape from it all, but it suddenly dropped from his associations after a remark to him by his sister: "Do you have to tell us of your yearning for this house in the country which you really don't want at all, just because Papa was always moaning about getting it?" Reid's sense of reality was dominated and distorted chiefly by his object relations and identification with his father. It was a triumph that he had been able to hang onto his wife and his business this long in spite of it.

In many psychotic personalities, it is very difficult to get sufficient details of the patient's 0 to 6 to understand the childhood emotional pattern. Only gradually did this emerge for Reid. The father had set his heart on having a son and was disappointed with daughters until Reid arrived, the son who would achieve everything that his father, with all his financial success, had not. In school Reid was expected to be the best at everything, the unsurpassable scholar and athlete. Suddenly, in the middle of his four years at college, he felt this expectation as a compulsion forced upon him and he went into a rebellion. He deliberately decided that he would no longer lead his class in every activity, but would make a point of being in the middle of it. That was a conscious choice, but the ingrained need to be best did not vanish, it was only repressed by the hostile rebellion.

All the demands for perfection, status, prestige which Reid attributed to his wife become fully intelligible as the repressed demands of his father for the son who must be best and live out his father's ambitions. The realities of his childhood from 0 to 6 were living their own lives in the adult. Reid was feeling, thinking, and behaving exactly as he had once behaved toward his father. Once Reid began to realize this, his peace of mind and human relations began turning for the better, which was gratifying in a therapy that was so difficult because Reid, in middle age, was still so much the small, anxious, emotionally dependent child who could not relate to his parents.

Reid's normal, healthy self-interest in his own survival and maturing were warped during early childhood and developed into an excessive preoccupation with narcissistic needs, goals, and desires throughout his adult life. Persistent psychotherapy, with bulldog tenacity, over a period of ten years (at first three, and later one, meeting a week) put him on the road to reopen his development, to mollify his intense needs, and to make his existence bearable. He remarked that he had become somewhat more realistic, and *mirabile dictu*, one day his wife phoned the therapist to say that this was noticeable.

Reid was often depressed but, after starting treatment, never dangerously so. He never became paranoid. Reid felt put upon but soon realized that his blaming others for the plight of his business was only to excuse his own failures and save his vanity; his narcissism alone was sufficient to save him from the suicides which were not uncommon in those days of business bankruptcies, for how could he damage or do away with a being so superior as himself? However, Reid could not avoid inner rage, guilt, and self-blame in reaction to his frustrations, including his hurt narcissism, all of which contributed to his masochistic, self-generated, chronic unhappiness. His masochism was also a centrally important feature of his therapy.

Reid's vanity strongly resisted insights, and the analysis was difficult for him and the analyst. As the narcissism was reduced, over a period of ten years, he became much more comfortable emotionally and more effective in his business, which was saved. Except for the first year, he did best in treatment when seen only once a week.

Narcissistic preoccupation with self may be only an indication of the depth and extent of the regression to early childhood patterns of thinking, feeling, and behaving which form an important component of the psychotic elements. The predominant psychotic element remains the aberration or distortion in the sense of reality, which may result from trauma or may be part of the depth of this regression.

Once one is alerted to noticing narcissism in its many forms, there is no question of its universality and importance in human life. These manifold forms can be roughly divided into:

1.  the autistic or vanity type, in which the central feature is the person's relationship to himself, his own opinion of his superiority, his overrating of self, his self-love;
2.  the exhibitionistic type, in which the individual's chief desire is praise and admiration from others whom he must impress with his superiority.

Both types are portrayed in an anecdote which was popular when Mischa Elman, Fritz Kreisler, and Jascha Heifetz were considered the three greatest violinists of their time: Elman meets a few cronies after one of his recitals and pours out his own praises, e.g., "Didn't those trills come off beautifully, and wasn't the tone marvelous?" (his famous "golden tone"). Suddenly Elman interrupts himself with, "I'm sorry, I've been talking only about myself. Tell me about *you*—how did *you* like my concert?"

One of the very rich young women who drifted into the Chicago Institute was utterly self-centered. She could not be blamed for this—it was the inevitable result of the traumas of her childhood. Some of her friends were not so rich, but were more than comfortable financially. In them it was easy to discern the reason for their friendship with this disagreeable, hostile woman who had been divorced three times. The reflected prestige from her wealth fed their narcissism.

Other examples abound in creative fields: a highly talented young girl in the lovely sport of ice dancing had sacrificed much of her young life for a high level of perfection. Then, when she received the gold medal for passing the most advanced test, she stopped skating entirely. She had skated not for enjoyment, but to win acclaim from others or to prove herself.

Narcissism is not of itself pathological but can be so if fixated in the adult at a too childish, immature level or if too warped by early traumatic situations. In this it is just like infantile dependent love needs, sexuality, hostility, or any other urge, need, drive, or reaction— that is, a natural component of human psychodynamics, and it can only be understood in this setting and perspective.

* * * *

Jeannette, a middle-aged woman who had experienced a traumatic childhood, nevertheless had been superior as a wife to her physician husband and as a mother to their three sons. Now the sons were grown, and she served as a nurse and manager of her husband's center city office. She had much more than the average amount of interest, love, and energy to give wherever needed (object interest) and very little preoccupation with herself. Yet in her early childhood she had received almost no mothering. Her father was a highly respected but overworked country lawyer who could barely support his wife and six children. His wife had been "to the manor born," being a psychologically delicate, over-indulged aristocrat. Coping with all these children on inadequate funds was beyond her strength. She developed a severe stomach disorder, often accompanied by nausea and vomiting, and spent most of her life in bed. Jeannette, the youngest child, being least advanced in school, was trained to be nurse to her mother. When Jeannette as a small child returned from school, instead of having a mother waiting for her with milk and cookies, she had to bring a pitcher of milk to her mother and a basin in case her mother should vomit. Nature was reversed: the child was mothering the mother.

Jeannette's father down underneath was a good man, but he was strict and even tyrannical, not from ill will but because he was chronically exhausted and could not tolerate any domestic demands upon him. Jeannette was needed at home and therefore not able to visit her little friends. She could not tolerate the thought of being away from her mother, fearing that if she were absent her mother would die and leave Jeannette motherless. This fear revealed her resentment at the reversal of roles, as well as her narcissism in the form of satisfaction with her importance in being responsible for her mother.

Her dynamics were repressed but emerged in detail in her analysis. Her pattern in any crisis was to give out enormously, with no consideration for herself, and then afterward all but give up and withdraw completely, a long-delayed, "but what about *me*?" reaction. She never questioned in adult life her love, willingness to help, judgment, and capacity for responsibility. Her self-evaluation had come through satisfactorily, not exaggerated in her own opinion or needs, or by preoccupation with herself, or in needs for praise or recognition from others. She was not in disgrace with fortune or men's eyes, or in her own eyes. Her narcissism was healthy, and Jeannette was secure enough to have humility and a firm sense of reality. She suffered with neurotic anxiety but showed no evidence of psychotic personality.

Narcissism is an essential component in what appears to be a core of fundamental human dynamics (Saul, 1980): every human being has progressive and regressive trends. If the regressive ones are of such nature or strength that they impair the progressive growth to adequate maturity, then the individual feels to that extent like a child in a world of others who are, or seem to him, more mature. This injures the self-esteem, the self-evaluation of being mature, the adult masculine or feminine narcissism, and causes a sense of inferiority and frustration which stimulates a fight-flight reaction. In this way, narcissism is an invariable link in all psychodynamic understanding and therapy.

### MASOCHISM

Masochism means self-injury with the connotation of self-punishment, even though guilt may not always be an essential of its dynamics. It seems generally true, however, that "the punishment fits the source" of the hostility.

To illustrate: Ottilie, in her childhood, had lost her father in the war. Her mother was so occupied working for survival and finding another husband that she could give Ottilie very little care and demonstration of love. Ottilie's anger for this deprivation estranged any man or woman she tried to be close to, and made her even more rejected and deprived. Unfair as it was, she punished herself for her anger by directing this punishment at the *source* of the anger—her deprivation. Angry because of being deprived, she punished herself by depriving herself.

Similarly, a man who resented his mother's domination during childhood injured himself in adulthood by repeatedly getting into trouble with the authority figures, whom he saw as dominating. The dynamics may vary in the individual: in some the hostility causes guilt which, in turn, leads to masochism, but in others the hostility is taken out directly against another person or the self, without the intermediate step of guilt., i.e., without coming from the superego (conscience).

In the case of Reid Harman, the source of his frustration and anger was largely his envy and competition with those he saw as more successful than himself. Therefore his punishment was directed at this source of his anger and took the form of making himself fail (for further discussion of these dynamics, see Saul, 1979).

The following dreams of two other patients provide a glimpse into the unconscious dynamics.

* * * *

PATIENT X: I had a dream last night, I was on a road. There were many chairs. I feared that the oncoming cars and trucks might smash into them. I've been so unhappy. . .there is a change at work. I feel as though I am not handling all the problems well. I feel as though I'm doing something wrong but can't find out what it is. Why am I making myself unhappy?

ANALYST: What do you associate to the road?

P: I used to struggle to come here to see you right on time. . .I did not know where to wait if I came early for my appointment, but I did not want to be late. I guess that may come from Mother. She was so strict. . .I feel that I had a happy childhood but it was hard to please her. And it was hard to please my husband although I tried to fill all his needs and keep him happy.

A: What do you associate to the chairs in the road in your dream?

P: They remind me of all the pews in the church and all the chairs in the Sunday school. My mother was very strict about our growing up to lead good Christian lives.

A: We all have animal impulses. Did you feel conflicts over yours?

P: As I said, I think my childhood was happy enough, but when I got old enough to have sexual feelings, then the guilt and blaming myself began. It was then that I began to feel so inferior because I never could live up to what I ought to be. Mother's principles were probably all right—if she had not been so strict. I guess my feelings of depression and unhappiness really do come from guilt for not living up to her high principles. Maybe she is why I have made so many bad decisions and kept myself so unhappy, like picking a husband just because I thought he needed me and then flirting with another man and losing my husband.

A: And what do you associate to the cars smashing into the chairs?

P: I did not handle my marriage in the best way. When my husband did not live up to perfect behavior, I could not stand it.

A: Does that element of the dream perhaps represent your wish to smash some of these too strict principles?

P: Yes...I think so. And possibly the underlying resentment against Mother which I've now been realizing I must have had for many years. I still take the best care I can of her, but I do not really like her. She is very difficult and we do not get on well together. My brother and sister do not take care of her so I have to do it, because she is an old lady now, but I don't enjoy it.

* * * *

PATIENT Y: In this dream I am held hostage by two men; my body is all broken out and sore, and my arms hurt so. I try to run away, down a long corridor that is glassed in. I see policemen in the distance and I hope they will help me.

ASSOCIATIONS: I've been miserable, so unhappy. I hurt so that I feel I am crazy...I fight with my husband and have been in a rage at him twice. I felt that I could not enjoy my vacation, but

I talked to myself: "Why do you make yourself so miserable? What terrible things have you done?" I reviewed my whole life and I never did anything bad at all, so why do I make myself suffer so?

ANALYST: What associations do you have to being held hostage in your dream?

P: The night I phoned you and said I was so upset that I thought I was going out of my mind, I had to talk to someone about a situation with my children, and you were the only person I had. And what did you say? You said, "Your husband and children are fine and behaving in reasonable and realistic ways. If you are so upset about them, the problem is not in them but in your own neurosis." I was so mad at you. . .my husband said I should have hung up on you. Here I had told you I was so terribly upset and had to talk with you, and you told me it was my neurosis that was stabbing me in the heart. But I said nothing to you. . .I took it out on my husband. Some day you may see that I am not a dummy. I began to see what was going on and talked to myself: I said I would not let you spoil this vacation, so we went and had a grand time. I think that as a child I had too many people to please: there was mother, so often sick; and father, so stern and always busy, who would close the door on me with "I'm busy now, you can see me later." That's how I felt when you told me it was my own neurosis. And there was my older brother to please, and my older sister; everyone told me what to do and not to do. It was too much.

A: But the present reality is that you now have fine, loving children and a loving husband and countless friends, and no one tells you what you must do and not do to please them. Can it be, then, that it is you who keep yourself so unhappy, even in your dreams? And where you feel held hostage and trying to escape?

P: Of course. I see what you are hinting at: the transference, because I am so mad at you. This must be it, because I have also been thinking that I'm too dependent on you and that we should cut the frequency of visits. Do you agree?

A: Yes, I do, provided that we analyze this thoroughly to be certain that it is a healthy move toward independence and not too much an escape from analyzing.

Whatever the current excitement over abstract theory, we cannot question the importance and power of human narcissism in all its forms, nor can we question the importance of human masochism, and the interconnections between narcissism and masochism. They can be understood and clarified by assiduous study within the area of basic psychodynamics without changing the fundamental concepts or establishing new schools of thought.

In every patient there is a question of the extent to which his mental and emotional state is *reactive* to the *external* life situation, or is *internal* and relatively independent of the environment. Analysts in practice since the 1930s can compare patients seen during the Great Depression with those seen during the present inflation. Many businesses collapsed at both times, bringing reactive tragedy and even suicide to their families. However, it is not always so simple as it first appears: Arthur illustrates an interconnection of narcissism and masochism.

Arthur's wife called the analyst, indicating that she wanted to make an appointment for her husband, and asked if she should accompany him. When questioned about the nature of the problem, she replied, "He is depressed about his business." The analyst suggested seeing him alone for the first time, to which she agreed, and two days later Arthur rushed in punctually but somewhat breathlessly. At 55 he was of medium height, well-knit, with graying hair and keen but rather remote black eyes.

PATIENT: I have been a success. . .I made enough money to retire in comfort with my wife and children. That was just a few years ago. Then I did something stupid: I saw an opportunity to make a lot more money although I did not need it. I worked for two years setting up the whole thing. . .it would take a week to explain it to you.

ANALYST: Can't you give me just the main points?

P: It meant investing over a half million dollars in manufacturing 30 or 40 items, all related to each other but each salable as a unit. Now it is operating but this depression will prevent businesses from buying it. And then I will lose everything.

A: Are you speaking of bankruptcy?

P: Yes, but my credit is still good. I could borrow a quarter million from the bank right now.

A: Then are you realistic or are you only seeing the pessimistic side of this?

P: [Vigorously defensive] Of course I'm realistic. The depression will go on and the boys in Washington won't help any.

A: [Realizing that it is like pulling teeth to get the facts] When are your notes to the bank due?

P: [Hedging some] In 60 to 90 days.

A: How much must you sell to meet them?

P: [A little off guard] Three or four units.

A: [Wondering even further if the patient was doing so badly in his business not because of the depression but because of his own masochism and personal emotional depression, which were interfering with his usual effectiveness] Could there be an emotional element in you that is keeping you from solving this to the best of your ability?

P: Yes. . .I'm not at my best. But now it's becoming an emergency.

A: Is it correct that your business situation makes you upset, maybe depressed, and this upset prevents your solving the business problems with your usual effectiveness?

P: Yes, that is it.

A: Shall we start with the more mechanical, external problem of your business and then go to the matter of your emotional upset?

P: OK.

A: A close friend of mine is an expert business consultant, who has saved some very large and complicated businesses. How about looking into whether he could help you with yours?

P: [Even more defensive] No. I couldn't do that, I couldn't renegotiate these bank loans.

A: I never mentioned that. Have you always run the business all alone?

P: I had a partner who died two years ago, just before I got into this present deal.

A: [Recalling a businessman who became depressed upon losing his partner] Then why would it not be worth trying? You know your business much better than anyone else. But we cannot see ourselves. . .maybe with the consultant's broad experience he would pick up things that would help you see elements that you now miss because you are so close to the problem. And if you are handling the business all alone, wouldn't it be well to have an experienced expert in your corner, on your side?

P:  [Adamant] No, I couldn't do that!

A:  One more question on the business. . .I know a manufacturer's representative who I'm certain could sell those two or three units within the 60 day or at most 90 days. . .how about your phoning him?

P:  [Obviously unable to accept help from anyone] No. . .that would only add complications.

A:  [Realizing that patient seems unable to accept help and wondering if it is mostly because of his narcissism or of his masochism, and whether he can accept any help psychologically from the analyst] Let us now try to understand a little about your psychology. You seem to see only the dark side, the pessimistic. Are there no other aspects?

P:  No. . .I've been successful, I was ready to retire, and then I got myself into this. . .and I am not doing well solving it.

A:  Why do you seem not to be at your best?

P:  It's physical. I think of the business all the time—all day and all night. My regular doctor has given me pills to help me sleep, but I don't want to take them. I'm afraid of getting, oh, hooked on them. But he says I won't and that at this time the sleep is more important.

A:  Even if you do not immediately see any connection, would you please tell me a little about your early background, your childhood?

P:  There is nothing at all there. My father lost his money when I was about 12 years old and gave up completely. He died two or three years later of cirrhosis. Mother supported my sister and myself until we could work. I started working at about 15 and have worked hard ever since.

A:  Then can you tell me a little about your present feelings?

[As the analyst questioned Arthur further about his childhood and present emotional relationships, he was unable to gain any insight. His probing was cautious because some depressed patients react to any probing negatively and the analyst was not sure of this man's emotional state. Arthur's strong resistance against revealing himself or accepting any kind of help was obvious. The analyst wondered if he could risk discussing the resistance openly—would that diminish it or increase it? Would Arthur feel threatened by mention of his narcissism, masochism, or both—however indirectly, gently, and gradually—before he made a positive transference or achieved any insight? Was there possibly a latent tendency to suicide which could not be risked by interpretations? If he does not feel understood, will he give up and refuse to return to the analyst? Or, if he should feel understood, will this feeling threaten him?]

A: [Deciding to shun any interpretations and keep only to reality, while hoping Arthur will return] All I will say to you is that I think you should be in the best emotional shape possible to solve your business problem. I understand why your wife suggested coming with you, and I would like to hear her version of your problems.

P: I certainly am not now in the best condition to work effectively...but I don't know when it will be convenient for my wife to come in and I see nothing to be gained by your speaking with her.

A: [Recognizing Arthur's resistance to the suggestion of speaking with his wife] I can see both of you or her alone tomorrow evening.

P: Then I will ask her and let you know. . . .

[Whereupon Arthur left, refusing to make another appointment. He did, however, phone the analyst later to say an appointment for his wife was not convenient, nor did he want to commit himself to an appointment. He asked if he could phone the analyst at a later date.]

A: Of course, there is no commitment. If you do not like me, or do not like the idea of working with me, just let me give you the name of an excellent man who is experienced in your kind of problem.

P: Thank you, but I will not do anything now. . .may I call you if I want to later on? [Again he was assured of the analyst's willingness to help in any way.]

Arthur's response was not surprising. He exuded the feeling, although not intellectually, that his narcissism was the major cause of his resistance. He simply could not stand the idea of great, successful Arthur showing poor judgment, getting himself into trouble; nor could he stand the thought of anyone else knowing it. The result was severely masochistic: first, by reducing his successful business to this predicament, and then by refusing all help, whether directly (saving the business) or psychologically (getting himself into a better emotional state to run the business). His mental preoccupation with the business seemed to be only a nonproductive, compulsive symptom that paralyzed his action instead of making it effective. Why was he so masochistic?

His analyst wondered if Arthur suffered from some guilt deriving from behavior against his grain, such as an extramarital affair or, more likely, (since "punishment fits the source") some business dishonesty in this basically honest man. Arthur seemed hostile, but whether for mostly reactive or internal reasons could not be explored.

Accurate, careful analysis can penetrate even the silence which a patient might use as resistance, but the refusal of a patient even to begin treatment robs the analyst of his task. Absence is the most difficult of all resistances.

Arthur never returned for treatment, nor did he call the experienced analyst whose name he had been given. He lost his business, but that seemed to satisfy his masochism to an appreciable degree. He did not take to drugs or alcohol, nor did he commit suicide. However, the final irony came a year later: business conditions in his line improved, and if Arthur had accepted therapy it is not too much to suspect that he might have hung on to his business and realized a fortune, instead of losing it. From the little he revealed, he either was in a transient, borderline state or was a psychotic character.

\* \* \* \*

A few remarks are in order here on therapy for psychotic personalities. Arthur's resistance may have been rational—he may have been right not to undertake therapy or even diagnostic exploration at this critical point in his business. There was no doubt of his defensiveness and the probable difficulties that might have arisen in therapy had the evaluation led to it. Such difficulties often arise in the treatment of psychotic personalties. With Arthur, the patient's view of reality was so set, so fixed, so *compulsive*, that, as with many paranoids, the analyst feels he is being compelled to share it, however distorted, but there is no leeway or flexibility to allow new elements or angles.

Another common difficulty in treating psychotic personalities stems from the regressiveness and fixations of the psychopathology to a very early level. Reid Harman exemplified this problem; he was strongly bound on the level of deprivation and domination at about the age of 0 to 3. Thus most such patients cannot be expected to do well in a relatively short time.

Early traumata and what patients lacked so early in life obviously are not cured by insight alone: many of these persons suffered so severely and lacked proper caring at such an early age that it takes many years of analytic therapy to achieve reasonably satisfactory progress. What does seem to help is the analyst's sympathetic understanding, faith, and encouragement—those qualities never supplied by the patient's parents. It is better for the individual to get as an adult what he lacked and should have had as a child, than never to get it at all. This does not imply any overt activity on the therapist's part other than a silent attitude of sympathetic understanding and support. Obviously, diagnosis is important. In reaction to this same sympathetic support, another personality, barely holding his own in life despite his difficulties, may be tempted to give up the struggle and regress into extreme, passive dependence. When a psychotic personality is recognized as such, the analyst must accept the fact that the therapy may go on for many years and must consider all the implications, including the practical ones of his own and the patient's time and money, and of how and when to discuss this prognosis with the patient and perhaps with his near relatives. Usually it is far better to have a reasonably satisfactory life even though much time is spent in therapy, than to live without therapy and suffer a failed marriage, loss of one's job, or a breakdown. This evaluation can only be made on an individual basis. In most cases, the therapy soon shakes down to only one meeting every week or fortnight.

In a first interview, it became evident that the middle-aged man was a psychotic personality, mishandling his high level jobs so as to get himself fired from every one, mistreating his beautiful, devoted wife and his children, clinging to a desperate existence, and fighting off suicidal urges. He had seen at least six psychiatrists, none of whom had the training or experience to deal with this man's deep problem. He said, "I need help desperately. I have no interest in anything and no pleasure or satisfaction in life, but I do not want to spend the rest of my life in therapy."

The reply was prompt, sharp, and realistic: "Why not, if it gives you what you want? If—with proper, effective psychotherapy—you can hold a job and continue your life, getting and giving satisfaction in both areas? Would these not make your presently masochistic, futile life worthwhile, even gratifying? What if the price *is* to continue in therapy for the rest of your life? Would it not be worth it compared with this suffering and fear of suicide? Wouldn't it be a good bargain?"

Our series of vignettes is not long enough to draw conclusions but only *indications* that the distortion of the reality sense is difficult and often impossible to correct by psychotherapy; yet with persistence, some reduction of hostility is possible and some overall improvement does take place in most patients, especially those who have the therapeutic urge and patience with long-term, bulldog tenacity. We have seen some excellent results in about 20 patients who first seemed hopeless and unanalyzable.

## REFERENCES

Freud, S. (1914): On narcissism, an introduction, *S.E.* 14, p. 67.
Kohut, H. (1971): *The Analysis of the Self.* New York: International Universities Press.
Saul, L.J. (1979): *The Childhood Emotional Pattern and Maturity.* New York: Van Nostrand Reinhold.
_____ (1980): *The Childhood Emotional Pattern and Human Hostility.* New York: Van Nostrand Reinhold.

# 6
# REVIEW OF THE LITERATURE
# AND DIFFERENTIAL DIAGNOSIS*

Hitherto we have tried to describe observations and concepts in everyday language. The literature, however, is written mostly in technical terms, and its flavor can only be conveyed and accuracy maintained by using this "jargon," which we do reluctantly.

The psychotic personality disorder (PPD) combines characteristics from two major psychiatric diagnostic categories, namely, that of a psychosis and that of a personality disorder. We must therefore define both terms to understand what we have when we combine them. "Psychosis" has been defined in the standard psychiatric dictionary (Hinsie and Campbell, 1970) as:

Loosely, any mental disorder (including whatever is meant by the obsolete terms, "insanity," "lunacy," and "madness"); more specifically, the term is used to refer to a particular class or group of disorders, and particularly to differentiate this group from neurosis, sociopathy (or psychopathy), character disorder, psychosomatic disorder, and mental retardation.

While there might be general agreement that the term "psychosis" should be used in a qualifying sense to refer to a particular group of psychiatric disorders, use of the term in fact has not been so precise or definite. Instead "psychosis" (and its adjectival form, "psychotic") has often been used in a quantifying sense to indicate severity of disorder; thus a person with the psychosis, schizophrenia, may be labeled psychotic only at certain times when the

---

*This chapter is by Silas L. Warner, M.D.

symptoms of his disorder reach a certain intensity and/or adversely affect his mental competence.

As a result of conflicting usage, there is no single acceptable definition of what psychosis is.

The term "psychotic" is not precisely defined but generally refers to a mental disorder of some severity. Our psychotic personality disorder (PPD) has some psychotic-like qualities but is not fully psychotic. There are some gradations from being very psychotic to showing only a few psychotic-like qualities. These can be more or less repressed.

A psychotic *disorder* or state is of such a serious nature as to impair the adjustment to reality. There are two major psychotic features: (1) loss of control of feelings, as in manic-depressive states; and (2) severe impairment of sense of reality—at the extreme, illusions, delusions, and hallucinations as well as bizarre thinking and behavior, as in schizophrenia. In *psychotic personality*, on the other hand, there is less impairment in the adjustment to, or testing of, reality, and this distortion may be partly repressed so that such an individual may appear to be in good contact with reality. Hinsie and Campbell (1970) define personality as:

The characteristic and to some extent predictable behavior-response patterns that each person evolves, both consciously and unconsciously, as his style of life. . .the personality, in other words, is a set of habits that characterize the person in his way of managing day-to-day living; under ordinary conditions, it is relatively stable and predictable, and for the most part it is ego-syntonic.

Because the personality is ego-syntonic, it is rare that a person will recognize his own personality as being deviant or abnormal (even if, in fact, it is). Any such evaluation is ordinarily a social diagnosis and an outgrowth of the effects of that personality on the people about him who may view his behavior as destructive, frightening, non-conforming or otherwise unacceptable.

We can simplify this to: "personality is an individual's accustomed way of thinking, feeling, and behaving."

Personality disorders are defined as "deeply ingrained, chronic and habitual patterns of reaction that are maladaptive in that they are relatively inflexible; they limit the optimal use of potentialities and often provoke the very counter-reactions from the environment that the subject seeks to avoid." (Hinsie and Campbell, 1970)

A *psychotic personality* results when personality traits are seriously inflexible and maladaptive and not in keeping with generally accepted reality. Such personality traits have become a more or less permanent part of the individual's character structure and are both ego-syntonic and anxiety-binding, so that subjective distress tends to be minimal. Because the psychotic personality traits are acceptable to the individual's own sense of reality but not in keeping with the world's accepted reality, they are kept secret most of the time but *traces* of them show up in everyday behavior. Such individuals tend to externalize inner conflicts and experience problems with the outside world (interpersonally) rather than as intrapsychic conflicts.

Psychotic personality traits are outgrowths of faulty emotional and cognitive maturation from infancy to adulthood which may have been normal at an early phase of development but, if they remain in the original infantile state within the personality, create areas of disturbance in the adult's world. This results in an excessive self-preoccupation, selfishness, and a lack of empathy for others. These traits are most often the result of a fixation at an earlier stage of childhood rather than of regression. Because of the stability and permanence of the psychotic traits within the character structure, there is lessened chance of a total personality breakdown into psychosis. Such stabilized character structure is in contrast to the borderline personality's shifting moods and changes in sense of reality. Also, because most anxiety is bound by the ego-syntonic psychotic character traits, psychiatric treatment is generally not sought out, although psychiatric evaluation may be called for by outside authorities. When the psychotic personality's life is studied longitudinally, one can observe various starting points such as a personality disorder, a neurosis, a borderline personality, or even a temporary psychosis which led to the psychotic personality. Having arrived at this end point, the personality structure will probably not be altered appreciably by psychiatric intervention except over relatively long periods, e.g., ten years or more. Attempts at psychoanalytically oriented psychotherapy usually result in a psychotic transference or a special form of transference in which the analyst is not experienced realistically, often resulting in ineffective autoanalysis.

Our brief definition of *mental health* is simply: Emotional maturity plus adjustment.

\* \* \* \*

Let us briefly review the origins of the term and concept "borderline personality disorder" (Stone, 1980). From about 1900 to 1930 as psychoanalytic theory was expanding, analysts became increasingly aware of clinical cases which were "borderline" between neurosis and psychosis. A well-known example was Freud's "Wolfman" (1918), who showed paranoid and obsessional traits, but was not considered to be schizophrenic. There emerged new diagnostic categories to fill the void between neurosis and psychosis. Reich (1949) introduced the term "impulsive character" to describe patients with severe personality disorders as well as a grotesque quality to their symptoms.

Stern (1938) was the first to coin the diagnostic term "borderline," claiming these were office patients "too ill for classical psychoanalysis." The term, informally used by many analysts, did not reappear in the literature until 1954, when Robert Knight defined it more methodically. In the interim, other terms were introduced: Gregory Zilboorg (1941) described the "ambulatory schizophrenic" as having mild clinical signs but being reasonably aware of reality and functioning socially, at least marginally; Helene Deutsch (1942) then described another group of patients as having an "as if" quality to their personalities. These patients were characterized by depersonalization, narcissistic identifications, a poverty of object relations, a masking of aggressive tendencies, but with a fully maintained grasp on reality. This description was the first to emphasize a pathology of internalized object relations. Deutsch described how these patients "adopt the qualities of the other person as a means of retaining love," and therefore their own personalities act "as if" rather than in a genuine fashion. Later, Fairbairn (1944), Melanie Klein (1952), and Kernberg (1967) amplified our ideas of these disturbed internalized object relations.

By thorough psychological testing with special emphasis on the Rorschach, Rapaport, Gill, Schafer (1945-1946) found a group of unclassified patients whom they labeled as "pre-schizophrenic"; under stress, these patients could become actively schizophrenic, but under favorable conditions they remained pre-schizophrenic and nonpsychotic. Paul Federn (1947) added a new diagnostic terms "latent schizophrenia," while Hoch and Polatin (1949) described another new syndrome which they named "pseudo-neurotic schizophrenia." The latter term was differentiated from the "borderline" syndrome and thought to be part of a larger schizophrenic spectrum.

Rado (1962) added a new dimension by describing certain patients as "schizotypes," that is, phenotypes with a hereditary predisposition to schizophrenia. He conceptualized stages in schizotypal adjustment from the compensated to the decompensated, and finally to schizotypal disintegration (full-blown psychosis). Today this would be seen as environmental stress and "genetic loading" interacting to create less severe to more severe clinical forms along the spectrum between personality types, from neurosis to psychosis.

Robert Knight (1954), working with hospitalized young adults, used the term "borderline" to describe (from an ego-psychology approach) a small group of patients showing psychopathology somewhere along the spectrum between neurotic and psychotic. He stressed the marked weakness in their ego functions which led to secondary process thinking, inability to plan realistically, and the impairment of defenses against primitive impulses, and he pointed out the value of the psychiatric interview in showing the more subtle manifestations of the borderline individual's psychopathology. His clinical description of the borderline would seem to be close to the schizophrenic end of the psychotic spectrum.

Bychowski (1953) elaborated on Federn's concept of "latent psychosis," describing five clinical entities which he felt could be included under the diagnosis of "latent psychosis": (1) character neuroses and (2) symptom neuroses that under stress temporarily become psychotic; (3) severely socially deviant behavior (e.g., perversion, addiction, delinquency); (4) an "arrested" psychosis which later shows the psychosis; and (5) psychoanalytic patients who become psychotic during analysis. When he speaks of screening these analytic patients, Bychowski points out that psychological tests do not satisfactorily differentiate between active and latent psychosis.

John Frosch began defining impulsive character disorders in the mid-fifties, continuing to clarify the borderlines and related clinical syndromes through the 1970s (1960, 1964, 1970). He proposed the term "psychotic character" as a substitute for such descriptions as "borderline," "pseudo-neurotic schizophrenia," "ambulatory schizophrenia," and "latent psychosis." His "psychotic character" showed the following: (1) satisfactory reality testing; (2) object relations on an infantile level, but not as primitive as psychotic individuals; (3) the capacity for clinical reversibility, or quick recovery from a psychotic episode; (4) primitive defense organization. Frosch's descriptive framework includes modern ego-psychology and object relationships. He points out that although psychotic characters have the potential for psychotic episodes, some live their entire lives without any such occurrence, much as the neurotic character may never develop a symptom neurosis.

Additionally, Frosch (1964) makes a special point of distinguishing between the contact with reality of the psychotic and the psychotic character: "In examining the position of the ego and its functions toward reality, there are three areas which must be differentiated. . . these are the relationship with reality, the feeling of reality, and the capacity to test reality." The psychotic character may show transient and reversible disturbances in the relationship with reality and the feeling of reality, while more severe and enduring disturbances characterize the full-blown psychotic in his relationship with reality (e.g., hallucinations) and in his feeling of reality (e.g., depersonalization). In his capacity to test reality, the psychotic is impaired, while the psychotic character retains this capacity. Frosch sees the psychotic character as a counterpart to the neurotic character and a representation of "a specific and recognizable clinical entity." He emphasizes that "it is not a transitional phase on the way to or the way back from symptom psychosis, nor is it a latent or larval psychosis which may become overt, any more than we define neurotic character as a transitional phase on the way to or from full symptom neurosis. Like the neurotic character, the psychotic character is a crystallization into character structure, reflecting predictable modes of adaptation and response to stress." He elaborates further: "The psychotic character bears the same relationship to psychotic symptoms as the neurotic character does to neurotic symptoms. Under certain circumstances, stresses and strains, for instance, during analysis, decompensations or regressive adaptations may take place and psychotic symptoms and features may become manifest, just as neurotic symptoms become manifest under similar circumstances in the neurotic character. But it is equally possible for an individual to go through life without showing such psychotic symptomatology, preserving all the while the identifiable features of the psychotic character. Just as the modes of adaptation and response to stress, internal and external, in the neurotic character are characterized by a pattern which we have designated neurotic, the psychotic character's response to stress has a psychotic patterning, albeit with some fundamental exceptions." Frosch sees in both the psychotic and psychotic character "a propensity for regressive de-differentiation and an underlying fear of disintegration and dissolution of the self." Both can show "psychotic reactions of fragmentation, projective identification, ego splitting, etc., " but in the psychotic character they "have a transient quality and can be reversed."

Frosch (1970) also sees object relations in the psychotic character at a higher infantile level than in the psychotic. He describes "a push toward establishing contact with objects, though the simultaneously existing fear of engulfment by the object frequently leads to complications in the psychotic character." With respect to the ego's relation to the other psychic structures in the psychotic character, Frosch sees it as "characterized by poor differentiation and a lack of harmony and equilibrium. The ego is constantly threatened by breakthroughs of id-derived impulses as is also the case in psychosis. But in contrast to the latter, the psychotic character is capable of reversing these phenomena. The superego frequently appears in the form of regressive and archaic precursors, has an alien quality, and a marked tendency toward externalization and projection."

Frosch (1970) proposes that "the ego defects seen in the psychotic character are derived from real and actual severe traumata that were experienced in the late symbiotic and early separation-individuation phases of psychic development. In contrast to the psychotic, however, the psychotic character shows many progressive features, e.g., a push toward differentiation and maturation, in part inherently derived and in part via identification with reality-oriented love objects. The psychotic character has therefore actually evolved some degree of object and reality constancy in contrast to the psychotic. These factors contribute to the clinical features which differentiate the psychotic character from psychosis."

Frosch (1964) makes specific points of difference between the psychotic character and the psychotic, but is not as clear in distinguishing psychotic character from the borderline. He states: "It is the more crystallized borderline personality that in many instances I have chosen to designate as a psychotic character." He seems to be describing the borderline who has stabilized into having a stable and consistent ego. This fits our own concept of the psychotic personality who has externalized his projections and thereby experiences his conflicts as existing in the environment, not within himself. This is particularly true in the paranoid type of psychotic personality. In the usual borderline, there is more instability within the ego, with uncertainty as to whether the problem comes from within or from without, and the uncertainty causes emotional volatility in the borderline with accompanying subjective discomfort. The projection and externalization of the conflict in the psychotic personality binds anxiety ego-syntonically and allows him to focus his anger at the outside "enemy."

Frosch (1964) indicates that the psychotic character retains a capacity to test reality even though the relationship to reality and the feeling of reality are impaired. He defines testing reality as "the appropriate evaluation of the reality of external and internal phenomena," and adds that in studying the capacity to test reality, one also has to assess the patient's relationship to reality and his feeling of reality. The boundary between a distortion of perception or a feeling of depersonalization and the patient's evaluation of it has to be delineated: a patient can have a hallucination without a loss in the capacity to test reality if he is aware that the hallucination comes from within him. It can be very difficult to test reality in special situations.

Otto Kernberg (1967, 1975, 1976) has written extensively about the borderline personality and pathological narcissism, both of which are closely related to the psychotic personality. Kernberg (1975) describes patients with narcissistic personalities as having:

Excessive self-absorption usually coinciding with a superficially smooth and effective social adaptation, but with serious distortion in their internal relationships with other people. They present various combinations of intense ambitiousness, grandiose fantasies, feelings of inferiority, and overdependence on external admiration and acclaim. Along with feelings of boredom and emptiness, and continuous search for gratification of strivings for brilliance, wealth, power and beauty, there are serious deficiencies in their capacity to love and to be concerned about others. This lack of capacity for empathetic understanding of others comes as a surprise considering their superficially appropriate social adjustment. Chronic uncertainty and dissatisfaction about themselves, conscious or unconscious exploitiveness and ruthlessness toward others are also characteristics of these patients.

Kernberg explains these characteristics as resulting from "the pathological nature of their internalized object relations." This leads to "chronic, intense envy and defenses against such envy, particularly devaluation, omnipotent control, and narcissistic withdrawal."

Kernberg also has a thorough and in-depth analysis of the borderline personality organization. He starts his description with the words "patients' suffering." From this syndrome, he goes on to list the different symptoms that motivate these patients to seek psychiatric help. As we have noted, many psychotic characters do not have symptoms and do not seek psychiatric help. The symptoms are "presumptive" diagnostic signs of borderline personality organization; the presence of two and especially three such symptoms "strongly points to the possibility of an underlying borderline personality organization," according to Kernberg. He hastens to add that "the characteristic ego pathology" is what becomes essential in making the diagnosis, rather than the descriptive symptoms.

Kernberg's list of *symptoms* and *symptomatic categories* includes the following (1975, pp. 8-45):

1. Anxiety
2. Polysymptomatic neurosis
   a) Multiple phobias
   b) Severe obsessive-compulsive symptoms
   c) Severe conversion symptoms
   d) Certain dissociative reactions
   e) Severe hypochondriasis
   f) Paranoid and hypochondriacal trends

3.  Polymorphous perverse sexual trends
4.  The "classical" pre-psychotic personality structures
    a)  The paranoid personality
    b)  The schizoid personality
    c)  The hypomanic personality and the cyclothymic
5.  Impulse neurosis and addictions
6.  "Lower level" character disorders
    a)  Hysterical personality and infantile personality
    b)  Narcissistic personality
    c)  Depressive-masochistic character structures

Kernberg then goes into the meat of his concept by detailing: (1) structural analysis, (2) pathology of internalized object relationships and, finally, (3) genetic-dynamic analysis. Since these descriptions tend to be complex, abstract and full of metapsychological concepts, we will try to summarize them.

The borderline personality disorder (Kernberg, 1975) is characterized by "certain defensive constellations of the ego, namely, a combination of non-specific manifestations of ego weakness and a shift toward primary-process thinking on the one hand, and specific primitive defense mechanisms (splitting, primitive idealization, early forms of projection, denial, omnipotence) on the other; a peculiar pathology of internalized object relations and characteristic instinctual vicissitudes, namely, a particular pathological condensation of pre-genital and genital aims under the over-riding influence of pregenital aggressive needs." It is evident that Kernberg's criteria require a complete diagnostic evaluation of the patient, including psychological testing. Some of these formulations also require that the patient undergo psychoanalysis, during which the analyst can observe first hand the state of the internalized objects and the transference and countertransference positions.

Kernberg's descriptions are more easily understood when he uses clinical terms, such as in the following description of a borderline personality organization (Kernberg, 1975):

Patients who present serious difficulties in their interpersonal relationships and some alteration of their experience of reality, but with essential preservation of reality testing. Such patients also present contradictory character traits, chaotic co-existence of defenses against and direct expression of primitive "id contents" in consciousness, a kind of pseudo-insight into their personality without real concern for nor awareness of the conflictual nature of this material, and a lack of clear identity and lack of understanding in depth of other people. These patients present primitive defensive operations rather than repression and related defenses, and above all, mutual dissociation of contradictory ego states reflecting what might be called a "non-metabolized" persistence of early, pathological internalized object relationships. They also show "non-specific" manifestations of ego weakness. The term "non-specific" refers to lack of impulse control, lack of anxiety tolerance, lack of sublimatory capacity, and presence of primary process thinking and indicates that these manifestations of ego weakness represent a general inadequacy of normal ego functions.

He suggests that most borderline patients are good candidates for psychoanalytic treatment, especially if his suggestions concerning technique are followed. Kernberg points out that "transference psychosis is a characteristic complication in the treatment of patients with borderline personality organization," and makes the following distinctions between the transference psychosis of borderline patients and the psychotic transference of psychotic (especially schizophrenic) patients: in borderline patients, the loss of reality testing is not evident in the patient's functioning outside of the treatment setting; the borderline's transference psychosis is usually temporary, especially if the analyst is skillful in handling it; in the psychotic patient, there is poor reality testing both in and out of the treatment setting; some boundary between analyst and patient is felt by the borderline patient even in the midst of the transference psychosis; the psychotic patient experiences himself as one with the analyst most of the time after the transference psychosis is activated.

An additional distinction between borderlines and psychotics is made by Kernberg: the borderline's defensive constellations "protect the patient from intensive ambivalence and a feared contamination and deterioration of all love relationships by hatred." In contrast, the schizophrenic's defensive operations "protect the patient from total loss of ego boundaries and dreaded fusion experiences with others." He restricts his concept of testing reality to the patient's ability "to identify himself fully with the external reality represented by the patient-therapist relationship."

It is beyond the scope of this book to give a complete review of Heinz Kohut's concept subsumed under his theoretical understanding of the psychology of the self. As he explains it, Kohut was a classical practicing psychoanalyst who noted that an increasing number of his analytic patients showed problems in regulating their self-esteem. These problems could *not* be explained by Freud's libidinal drive theory leading to an intrapsychic conflict and replicated in "the transference neurosis." He formulated a narcissistic personality disorder which, during analysis, showed characteristic narcissistic transference manifestations, such as idealizing and mirroring transferences, but different from Freud's structural neurosis and also from the borderline personality disorder as well as the psychotic. If, during an analysis, a transference reaction evolves which is irreversibly psychotic, Kohut felt that analytic treatment was stymied and post hoc, the diagnosis had to be either psychosis or borderline personality disorder. A clinician could suspect a borderline diagnosis initially, but the definitive diagnosis in Kohut's patients was made from the finding of a psychotic transference causing a therapeutic impasse. Kohut's version of a narcissistic personality disorder is treatable by a modified psychoanalytic approach, a technique outlined in his books (1971, 1977, 1978). He gives in detail his explanation for the occurrence of a narcissistic personality disorder: essentially, he sees such a patient as suffering from an early and chronic understimulation from his parents; this understimulation has led to the formation of an archaic grandiose image of the self, coupled with an omnipotent (transitional) self-object which corresponds to the idealized parent image; these unconscious narcissistic internalized representations are automatically activated by the analyst into characteristic narcissistic transference reactions. The patient's sense of self is sufficiently cohesive to insure reasonably good contact with reality during analysis. Kohut reports good results using his modified psychoanalytic technique to treat the narcissistic personality disorder. He differs from Kernberg in his finding that borderlines are not treatable by psychoanalysis, even in a modified form.

Using his clinical experience as a background, Kohut offers a theory of the psychology of the self to explain certain contemporary clinical observations. He speculates that in Freud's day the nuclear family was much closer in its interactions than are families of today. Larger families tended to overstimulate children, which resulted in the formation of the more classical neurotic disorders such as hysteria, obsessive-compulsive neurosis, and phobias. Many families today, according to Kohut, are smaller with less intimate interaction, so the child is understimulated and develops an inadequate or pathologic self. Kohut believes that his developmental observations are characteristic of our Western culture and should be given careful consideration in explaining modern-day psychopathology. He thinks Freud's libidinal theory of psychosexual development which leads to an oedipal conflict and a structural neurosis can only explain a few cases, and should be supplemented by his own concept of the development of the self to better explain the psychopathology seen in today's psychiatric patients.

Modern critics of Kohut complain that his theory is too simplistic, not sufficiently taking into account the role of hostility, aggressiveness, and conflict in creating a narcissistic personality disorder, and that his wish to supplant Freud's theory manifests the very Oedipus complex which he denies. Thus his writings tend to take Freud's theories too rigidly, instead of for what they were: initial exploration in a newly discovered area of the human mind. Little if any of Kohut's theory is not a natural extension of psychodynamics which was Freud's great discovery. The polemic tone only weakens Kohut's contribution. No experienced analyst would think of denying the enormous importance of human narcissism, on which Freud wrote the first paper (1914). It is interesting to note that Freud came from a large family with much interaction and stimulation, whereas Kohut is an only child who, midway in his life, had to move away from Vienna and all that was familiar to him. It is also tempting to speculate that Freud was experientially aware of sibling rivalry and competitiveness within his own family which led him to appreciate the oedipal triangle and to rate it as the most important psychogenic factor determining personality development. He was clearly his mother's favorite: she lived with or near him during most of his life (he was 74 and she was 95 when she died). He had a more ambivalent attitude toward his father, who died when Freud was 40. As a consequence, he clearly saw his own mixed feelings toward his father, while he sustained a close positive bond with his mother. This may possibly be connected with Freud's not studying the vicissitudes of the mother-child relationship, and may explain why only late in his career did he examine the oral phase, separation anxiety, and the pivotal significance of mother-child relationships, to say nothing of human hostility. However, he observed and contributed so much that it is not right to question why he did not do more.

Kohut, on the other hand, challenges some of the most fundamental aspects of Freudian theory: he demotes the oedipal complex to a less important place. Many of his observations on self-development and the importance of early mother-child relationships are valid; some of his own early experiences (including understimulation) may have sensitized him to these observations.

Some of our clinical descriptions of the psychotic personality show certain characteristics of Kohut's narcissistic personality disorder. However, most of our cases do not respond rapidly to analytic therapy, and those which do respond are often marked by ego-dystonic symptoms and oscillations between good and bad feelings toward oneself. Our cases have become more chronic and crystallized with a self-reinforcing, higher sense of self-esteem.

The following illustrates how our concept of psychotic personality differs both from Kernberg's borderline personality disorder, and from Kohut and Kernberg's narcissistic personality (Warner, 1980): Bob was a 28-year-old, single, unemployed man who had completed three years of college, had four years of psychoanalysis and three years of conjoint individual and group psychotherapy. He sought additional "post-analytic" help because he felt chronically depressed and periodically lonely, was unable to sustain close relationships with either sex, and feared being humiliated or too dependent. He had a problem with "ejaculatory impotence" but could achieve orgasms by giving himself an enema. Since he was fearful of becoming too dependent on his therapist, he dictated the terms by which he would enter psychotherapy; these were tantamount to his analyzing himself with his therapist being used to monitor or supervise the autoanalysis, and also acting as a resource for Bob to have access to psychoanalytic literature. These terms were reluctantly agreed to in the hope that Bob would eventually enter into the more traditional patient role. Bob retained control of the psychotherapeutic situation at all times, finally terminating the autoanalysis because he "was not receiving sufficient benefits from it." The therapist felt hog-tied by his conditions, which basically consisted of listening to Bob theorize about his own psychodynamics. Bob could not deal with the possibility of the therapist being in any role except that of a "supervising analyst."

Bob had already compiled a psychoautobiographical monograph, fastidiously written out in great detail in a style similar to Freud's manuscripts on the Wolf Man and the Rat Man; he had detailed descriptions of his birth, early feeding, bowel training, and an account of his psychosexual developmental stages, as well as a full description of all his interpersonal relationships, schooling, and other life activities. This included the various psychiatrists, psychoanalysts, psychologists, counselors, teachers, friends, and relatives with whom he had contact. After three years of analysis with a well-trained, reputable local analyst, he optimistically concluded that he had experienced "the apparent resolution of his Oedipus complex." He expressed this as follows: "Father, I am not interested in displacing you from (rivaling you for) your *normal* sexual role with mother. Instead I *am* interested in another (nonrivaling) anal relationship with mother." While "working through" the above psychodynamics, his analyst went on a two-week vacation, and on his return Bob felt the need for "additional reassurance" from him. He requested that the analyst write a letter to another analyst on "speech symptoms of those using enemas to masturbate." Of course the analyst tried to analyze the reasons for Bob's request rather than automatically writing the letter. Bob then asked the analyst to help him meet a female patient who might like a similar style of sexual enjoyment. When the analyst said that he could not honor this request, Bob angrily claimed that he was already aware that the analyst could not ethically grant him such a request. This incident resulted in a therapeutic impasse: Bob felt himself losing confidence in the analyst and slowly experienced increasing antagonism and anger toward him. He abruptly discontinued the analysis "after the debacle," promising himself that "never again" would he trust a therapist. He described himself as feeling like a patient who awakens on the operating table only to find he has been operated on by "a clumsy butcher." This psychotic-like transference reaction could not be resolved.

Bob then sought out group and individual psychotherapy with a female social worker. He hoped that by working with her he could "substitute a good mother image for his own bad mother image," but soon Bob complained that his new therapist wanted to talk about such irrelevant topics as his current lack of a job and friends, his poor health habits, and his passive attitude toward life. Bob further complained that he was receiving no emotional support and consequently stopped looking for a job. His hypochondriacal symptoms increased. A major tranquilizer was prescribed for Bob as his paranoid feelings toward this therapist accelerated and he accused her of incompetence and malicious intent.

At this point in his life, Bob entered into therapy with a new and experienced analyst. Because his previous attempts at therapy ended in disaster, he felt justified in rigidly setting one-sided conditions under which he would work. These conditions seemed to doom his new treatment to failure, but also protected Bob from being traumatized by the therapy.

A look at Bob's life-style made clear that he was defensively living out a path of least resistance; he had convinced himself that his main aim in life should be to satisfy his curiosity about how his personality had been formed. This egocentric obsession took precedence over any practical life considerations, and since he had sufficient independent income he was not economically obligated to obtain a job. He lived frugally, book purchases being his greatest expense. His few friends had dwindled down to one or two people who would phone him occasionally, and although he wished this were not the case, he would do nothing positive to reach out toward anybody. If one knew nothing about him and were to talk to him or ask him questions, he would answer appropriately and correctly and appear to be in good contact with reality. He was never given psychological tests. From his psychoautobiography and his introspection during therapy one could see that he clearly felt himself to be a helpless victim whose only pleasures were his narcissistic and relentless pursuit of psychoanalytic insight and his enemas. He preferred his psychological understandings to be framed in "deep metapsychoanalytic terms." Practical, everyday, common sense concerns that all of us experience were of little interest to Bob. Attempts to get him to find solutions to his problems were swept aside as superficial, naive, and not worthy of his efforts.

That he had some elements of a narcissistic personality disorder (as delineated by Kohut) was unquestionably true: his grandiose self often showed its presence and had become a part of his normal facade; his transference reaction was initially idealizing and/or mirroring; and only later did he develop a psychotic-like transference. His feelings of anger and disillusionment toward his therapist became so strong that he could no longer tolerate being in the therapist's presence. There was indication that murderous impulses toward his parents had been activated by the therapist, and were too frightening for him to endure, so he took flight. In his termination he expressed considerable disappointment and a hostility which was only slightly diluted by being filtered through his intellect. His main criticisms had to do with the therapist's not adhering to his conditions and not abdicating the traditional doctor-patient role and treating him more as a colleague. The therapist acknowledged these difficulties but told Bob that he thought he could better help by being in a professional role. He felt friendly toward Bob, saw his potential for a happier life, and made a point not to be patronizing. Bob appreciated this, for in fact *he* was the one who structured the relationship in an impersonal framework. The analyst believed that Bob could only accept a certain amount of help from any one therapist and hoped that the accumulated benefits from different therapists might improve his quality of life. In his differential diagnosis, the analyst saw Bob as an individual who had gone through different adaptive stages and ended up a psychotic personality.

Bob went through an infantile neurosis and undoubtedly had an early (preoedipal) ego defect. He had originally remained psychologically compensated at home, probably because of the protective network which his parents had established for him, but when he went away to college his symptoms became so severe that he sought help. He saw a highly experienced analyst in consultation and complained of emptiness, depression, lack of purpose, poor work habits, and an unsatisfactory sexual life. He was referred to another experienced psychoanalyst and underwent four years of analysis. Bob dropped out of college, held a couple of menial jobs, and slowly sank into a withdrawn, self-absorbed existence; he wrote his psychoautobiography, spending innumerable hours in its preparation; he scanned the psychoanalytic literature, especially looking for cases resembling his.

By this time Bob was the "complete narcissist." He had become exclusively self-centered, closed to outside interests, ideas, and people, which culminated in his being his own analyst. His "autoanalysis" proved to him his superiority over his parents and all analysts. This extract is from his psychoautobiography: "In sum, I believe I have, after some 15 years of analysis and other experiences, learned something. I find I can predict myself better than any therapist, despite the idea that I am supposed to be the patient, and despite the 'expertise' of therapists. I find myself, consequently, less interested in therapy—e.g., 'ventilation' and analysis of what is ventilated, or attempts at 'conditioning' based on too simple models—and more interested in understanding cooperation by the therapist in acting on what is now known." Bob transferred onto his current analyst his feelings of helplessness and rage from infancy. He sought narcissistic revenge by depreciating all analysts while proclaiming his superiority over them. This transference reaction could be termed "psychotic-like." He saw the analyst as identical to all analysts, and therefore incompetent. This was more a prejudice against the analyst than a transference psychosis. This kind of transference distortion fits the psychotic personality.

Bob was living as if he were an adult who had been so psychologically crippled by his parents that he felt justified in his introspective self-absorption and social isolation. He was constantly preparing to live a fuller life after achieving a better understanding of himself, but never came close to this goal. Bob does not fit into the DSM-III narcissistic personality disorder, even though he showed a grandiose sense of self-importance and uniqueness and a preoccupation with fantasies of unlimited success, power, and brilliance; he was too regressed and withdrawn to be exhibitionistic, and he lacked any relationship with another person, so that his interpersonal relationships were not disturbed. Neither did he fit the DSM-III criteria for borderline personality disorder: he was not impulsive, lacked interpersonal relationships, and was not affectively unstable. Bob shows many similar personality characteristics to Freud's Wolf Man. He did not, however, have his own narcissistic and dependent needs directly gratified by becoming a vital, living historical relic of the early days of psychoanalysis as did the Wolf Man, he too might have slowly blossomed. Perhaps Bob intuitively hoped for this solution but could not adequately communicate it to his therapists. Perhaps they were unduly fearful of harming him by indulging him excessively, thereby creating a malignant dependency. Instead, he responded to what he thought were his unnecessary frustrations by regressing and withdrawing to a point near the autoerotic stage.

Grinker (1968) and his Chicago colleagues studied 60 hospitalized patients using an ego-psychological approach to establish criteria for the borderline syndrome. The following is a resume of their criteria*:

### Criteria of Grinker et al. for Borderline Syndrome

1. Common characteristics
   a) Anger is main or only affect
   b) Defect in affectional (interpersonal) relations
   c) Absence of consistent self-identity
   d) Depression characterizes life
2. Characteristics of the four sub-types
   a) Type I: The psychotic border
      (1) Behavior inappropriate, nonadaptive
      (2) Self-identity and reality sense deficient
      (3) Negative behavior and anger expressed
      (4) Depression
   b) Type II: The core borderline syndrome
      (1) Vacillating involvement with others
      (2) Anger acted out
      (3) Depression
      (4) Self-identity not consistent
   c) Type III: The adaptive, affectless, defended, "as if" persons
      (1) Behavior adaptive, appropriate
      (2) Complimentary relationships
      (3) Little affect; spontaneity lacking
      (4) Defenses of withdrawal and intellectualization
   d) Type IV: The border with the neurosis
      (1) Anaclitic depression
      (2) Anxiety
      (3) Resemblance to neurotic, narcissistic character defect in affectional relationships

---

*Adapted from Perry, J. and Klerman, G. (1978): *Archives of General Psychiatry* 35: 141-150. Copyright 1978 A.M.A.

(4)   A deficient sense of identity
(5)   Depression usually experienced as loneliness

In discussing the two fundamental traits of the borderline—anger and inability to achieve affectional relationships—Grinker et al. (1968) speculate that "in the borderline the aggressive component is related to defects in ego-development rather than regression." The borderline's "lack of [a] sufficient amount and constancy of affection prevents the control of aggression." The deficient sense of identity seems to be a product of the borderline's "excessive anger and deficient love." We note that this last point is true and excellent, but not limited to this particular condition.

Grinker continues that the borderline's depression is sometimes of an anaclitic type in which there is an "anxious search for a mother figure." The more usual depression was a "loneliness" described as a "secret feeling, difficult to communicate and...terrifying." Some borderlines oscillate between trying to be close to another person, with resultant anger, then distancing themselves and feeling the loneliness.

One distinction between our group of patients (whom we call "psychotic personalities") and those described by Kernberg, Kohut, Grinker, and Frosch is that many of ours are not in psychiatric treatment, while most of theirs are. This is highly significant in selecting representative cases for each category. Many of our psychotic personalities were seen in consultation, refused or were not suitable for psychotherapy, and rarely required psychiatric hospitalization. This is because their impulses and conflicts had become a permanent and ego-syntonic part of their character. Thus their defense mechanisms, object relations, and cognitive style are all served within the framework of their character and of society. They frequently use projection and externalization to bind anxiety and convert it from intrapsychic conflict to interpersonal conflict. An efficiently functioning psychotic personality is asymptomatic, but apt to be under internal pressure to seek out and resolve conflict with the environment. For this reason, they are slow to seek psychiatric treatment. The borderline patient's ego seems more in a state of flux, with ego-dystonic symptoms creating a need for psychiatric treatment; he not infrequently decompensates into a temporary psychosis and requires hospitalization. In contrast, the psychotic personality represents more of an end point with a more crystallized and stabilized personality structure which can hold up against all but the most severe stress and would only rarely decompensate into a psychosis. It seems probable that some actively psychotic patients requiring hospitalization can clinically improve and stabilize into chronic psychotic personalities, no longer requiring hospitalization and denying any need for psychotherapy.

It should be noted that all of Grinker's original series of patients from whom he gathered data about the borderline syndrome were hospitalized patients. It stands to reason that these patients were toward the symptom-psychosis end of the hypothetical spectrum. Frosch and Kernberg base their conclusions on clinical information drived from patients mainly in outpatient psychoanalytic therapy, although a few of their patients had brief hospitalizations. We started with analytic patients in whom we observed certain clinical patterns which led us to formulate the psychotic personality. Some were patients seemingly in good contact with reality who developed a negative transference which was hard to resolve because of its psychotic quality. In some cases, these transference problems could not be resolved and the patient left treatment, but we were able to follow the case. Others switched from an analytic-interpretive procedure to a more emotionally supportive one, somewhat similar to that described by Kohut. We found that even though these patients at first appeared neurotic, or certainly nonpsychotic, there was an underlying psychotic cognitive style leading to a distorted perception of the world or part of it which had become a part of their character and to which they tenaciously clung as it fed their narcissism. Having been sensitized to this pattern in the psychotic character syndrome, we began to look for it elsewhere than in our clinical practice: we found that certain individuals whom we saw in psychiatric evaluation for legal or other special reasons provided us with examples of the psychotic character. Such individuals may cause other people great distress but feel no need to change themselves; they deny any internal problems. We soon discovered that many well-known or famous individuals who had never been in psychiatric treatment, with plentiful available biographical or autobiographical material, fitted into this syndrome. We further examined individuals with impulse disorders, addictions, and antisocial personalities and found that many of them also could be seen as psychotic characters. We decided to avoid the superego and moral implications and call them more broadly "psychotic personalities." We questioned whether the syndrome was too large and had become a waste basket for too many different types of psychopathology, and wondered how better to differentiate it from already existing diagnostic categories. There were certain hard-core, unquestioned cases that met our slowly emerging criteria of psychotic character, yet there was also a twilight area containing cases that overlapped the borderline syndrome, symptom-psychosis and symptom-neurosis, character neurosis, and severe character disorders. It was important to study these cases over as long a period of time as possible. Some of these cases have been followed for up to 30 or 40 years; they have settled into the chronicity of their psychotic personality, but almost all who have continued in treatment have improved steadily and enormously. For example, Letty (Chapter 9), is presented as "withdrawal type with masochism." She was originally seen over 30 years ago in the midst of a marital problem. Although at first it was thought that she had a neurotic personality, it soon became evident that she was so swamped by her disordered childhood pattern and it so distorted her perception of those close to her, that she was a psychotic personality. She was able to contain the consequences of her distorted cognition by limiting her contacts and withdrawing; she drove her husband and most of her friends away and was left living with her aged mother, toward whom she felt tremendous hostility. At times this broke through and she verbally (and rarely, physically) struck out at her. She also used her as an excuse not to move, socialize, or travel. Letty kept in touch with her analyst by phone periodically and continued to feel the need for his interest in her well-being. At times she became involved with various causes which fitted in with her own psychopathology: when welfare checks were being cut off to a group of severely crippled people she started a citizens' committee to help them. She became very emotionally involved in this noble cause, even arranging newspaper interviews and blasting certain politicians whom she believed to be accountable for the problem, accusing them of being Nazi storm troopers who enjoyed seeing innocent people suffer. Her position was doubtless correct and praiseworthy, but she was so strongly identified with the helpless victims that her attack on those whom she blamed became "overkill" and counterproductive. It did represent a sublimation of her own basic drives, and it took some of the heat off her mother. Her hostility was aimed at politicians in the world who could better absorb it. As she got older, Letty would still express heated interest in certain political causes which appealed to her and which fed her righteous indignation and narcissism, but she limited herself to talking about the situation or, at most, firing off a few caustic letters. Undoubtedly her character is still essentially psychotic, but she has mellowed a little and led her life free of the old acute psychic pain and suffering. Her mother is approaching 90, and it is hard to predict what her death will do to Letty. She has felt "held back" by having to care for her mother; without this excuse she may or may not search for her Utopia and move there as she always said she yearned to. She affirms that her analyst was important to her improvement and to keeping her life tolerable, and that her mellowing was not just the result of age and experience.

In contrast to Letty was a 30-year-old single woman, Mildred, with a lifetime full of psychiatric care and problems, who perhaps would have been better off if her psychopathology had stabilized into psychotic personality. Mildred was the older of two siblings born to a beautiful but extremely self-centered woman and a passive-submissive and not very successful father. She was a rather average child, a mediocre student, and an embarrassment to her glamorous mother. She was neglected and ultimately rejected by her mother, who left her hapless husband for an affluent, strong-willed, self-made man. The husband also felt rejected. He took Mildred and moved back with his own parents, while Mildred's younger brother moved in with the mother and stepfather. There was clearly a family division, with the "winners" on the mother's side and the "losers" on the father's. Mildred grew up with a stammer, awkward physical movements, and a very poor self-concept. Although her mother paid for special tutors, piano and skating lessons, these did not improve Mildred's self-concept, and she started using hard drugs at 15. She had her first psychiatric hospitalization at 16 with a drug psychosis. Subsequent years of irregular outpatient psychotherapy were of no avail. Drugs were the only thing which made her "feel decent." Her stepfather finally put her into an expensive special psychiatric facility providing active treatment to very disturbed patients based on trying to make them feel so uncomfortable with their symptoms and drug use that they would be forced into a "flight into health." Mildred improved only slightly in her year under this regime and finally went to a half-way house at the age of 28. There she was very isolated and with-drawn, developing some compulsive, ritualistic habits. Her mother and stepfather were disappointed that she wasn't "cured" and had not become "a beautiful person." They told Mildred that they would henceforth send her a small monthly check but otherwise would not have any contact with her. However, her father and paternal grand-parents stood by her and tried to encourage her. While at the halfway house she met an unemployed former truck driver who had been married four times, and when he showed interest in her, she recipro-cated and soon found herself pregnant. He said he wanted to marry her and she initially consented, until she became aware of another side to him that was mean and cruel. She believed he wanted to ex-ploit and destroy her; there may have been some truth to her fears. She went into a panic, left him, and returned to her father, who ar-ranged a therapeutic abortion. She then became increasingly para-noid about escaping from his clutches. At first she agreed to go into a psychiatric hospital but then refused to because "he might find her there." She fled to a nearby large city and spent about a year on the streets—confused, taking drugs, and cohabiting with unsavory characters. She was picked up by the police a few times and even put into a psychiatric hospital, but rapidly signed herself out only to return to her driven, self-destructive life on the streets. She finally returned home and was rehospitalized, where she was confused and fragmented in her thinking but gradually expressed certain paranoid themes: everybody was against her and she felt it necessary to fight her (alleged) abusers; she constantly complained that everything in the hospital was wrong—food, personnel, medication, etc.; she de-manded immediate changes and became verbally threatening, un-reasonable, and very unpleasant to be around. When the staff avoided her, Mildred accused them of being indifferent. She had a plethora of daily complaints and accusations toward her attending psychiatrist. She had previously joined a national alliance of former mental pa-tients who complained about the atrocious treatment in mental hos-pitals and she backed up her complaints with alliance rhetoric, phoning them about every "indignity" or "mistake" perpetrated on her by "the pigs in the hospital." She was, however, unable to sustain her interest in their crusade for the improvement of mental health facilities. She could not share ideas and work cooperatively with others. Her need to parade herself as having been victimized by everybody became so strong that she even turned against the alliance. This was her opportunity to join a group with similar views so she could put her energy into a cause which, even if exaggerated and fanatical, would have offered her some structure and given a meaning to her frenetic and aimless life. This is the same stabilization and direction offered by other cults and fanatical groups. Many cults do provide individuals who may be borderline with a total life-support system which helps to stabilize their weak egos, albeit at the tremendous price of sacrificed maturity. Many of these individuals may then become psychotic personalities, easily fitting in with their cult's claim to be the "only true way of life."

Mildred appears as a paranoid psychotic who, with periods of hospitalization, was able to remain precariously ambulatory most of the time. She never diffused her psychotic tendencies into the defense of a well-functioning, stabilized psychotic personality.

The American Psychiatric Association has recently revised its official diagnostic nomenclature of psychiatric disorders under the title DSM-III (1980). Its most remarkable change is a "multiaxial evaluation" which requires that each case be classified on several "axes." Each axis contains a different class of information. There are five axes: the first is for clinical syndromes, conditions not attributable to a mental disorder that are a focus of attention or treatment; the second axis is for personality disorders and specific developmental disorders, and this encourages the use of multiple diagnoses to give a more in-depth picture. Axis II can be used to describe personality traits when no personality disorder exists. There are eleven specific categories of personality disorders listed in DSM-III and a twelfth category for atypical, mixed or other personality disorder. In the twelve years since DSM-II came out (1968), six new personality disorders have been added. These are the schizotypal, histrionic, narcissistic, borderline, avoidant, and dependent. Missing from the previous list are the following: cyclothymic, explosive, hysterical, asthenic, and inadequate. The additions reflect the extensive observations and writings on the subject of the borderline and narcissistic personality which have resulted in a sharper delineation of the boundaries in the differential diagnosis. This applies also to the categories of schizophrenia and manic-depressive psychosis where considerable refinement in diagnosis has recently been found in the literature.

We propose that the psychotic personality disorder (PPD) be added to the other personality disorders in DSM-IV with the following description.

## PSYCHOTIC PERSONALITY DISORDER (PPD)

*Differential diagnosis:* Borderline personality disorder, narcissistic personality disorder, schizoid personality disorder, paranoid personality disorder, schizotypal personality disorder, antisocial personality disorder, undifferentiated schizophrenia, residual schizophrenia.

*Diagnostic criteria:* A psychotic personality can be diagnosed if the following modes of thinking, perceiving, experiencing oneself, and behavior are relatively definite (the limitation of this list lies in the fact that *quantitative* features always distinguish all the disorders, including those in the psychotic personality disorder; we must therefore rely on the psychiatrist's expertise and judgment):

1. Disturbed interpersonal relationships with an inability to establish intimacy, but with social withdrawal and shallow or insufficient feelings for other people.

2. Self-preoccupation, selfishness, with or without grandiosity and/or exaggerated sense of self and accomplishments.

3. Impoverished ability to love or care about others accompanied by basic mistrust of others, suspiciousness and looking for faults in others.

4. A significant cognitive disruption with reality without a total loss of reality testing. This area of cognitive disruption can be subtle or blatant, but it colors most other ego functions such as perceptions, interpersonal relations, self-concept, and the experiencing of external threats.

5. A personality dominated or flooded by a certain theme or need. These themes set the pattern for most behavior and can be broken down into patterns of fight and flight. The fight patterns involve

hostility, aggressiveness, mistrust, and actively scanning the environment for enemies with an externalization of these feelings onto the environment. Subjective symptoms are minimized, but anger is the predominant feeling. The flight pattern involves avoidance of external threats, social withdrawal, depression, and subjective distress felt as fear, anxiety, and tension. Relief can occur if appropriate emotional support such as that provided by certain psychotherapies can be offered and accepted by the patient.

6. A social adaptability or veneer which superficially looks "normal" and would allow the individual to pass a mental status examination as well as structured psychological tests.

7. A fairly strong sense of identity which may incorporate some aspects of the dominant life theme. This strong self-concept may involve psychological distortions, but provides a certain security. At times this identity may be part of a fringe group's identity such as a cult member would experience. This sense of identity may be threatened from the outside world, but such threats only tend to strengthen the identity and group unity.

Furthermore, we would like to suggest in DSM-IV that the category of psychotic personality disorder have an Axis I category with such sub-types as criminal, paranoid, masochistic, diffuse, hostile, regressive, withdrawn, etc.

In the differential diagnosis of the psychotic personality disorder (PPD), we must clearly distinguish it from the borderline personality (BPD) disorder. In DSM-III, the BPD must show at least five of the following characteristics:

1. Impulsivity or unpredictability which can be self-damaging
2. Unstable and intense interpersonal relationships
3. Inappropriate intense anger
4. Identity disturbance
5. Affective instability
6. Intolerance of being alone
7. Physically self-damaging acts
8. Chronic feelings of emptiness or boredom

The PPD would probably not show the characteristics of numbers 4 through 8, whereas numbers 1, 2, and 3 might be present.

In the DSM-III category of the narcissistic personality disorder (NPD), the following characteristics are present:

1. Grandiose sense of self-importance or uniqueness
2. Preoccupation with fantasies of unlimited success, etc.
3. Exhibitionism
4. Cool indifference or marked feeling of rage on being criticized
5. Interpersonal relationships marked by feeling of entitlement or special favors and by exploitiveness and self-aggrandizement; Shift between over-idealization and devaluation of others, with a lack of empathy

This category could be included within the PPD, especially if the individual is prone to express and act upon his narcissistic thoughts and impulses.

The schizoid personality disorder could become a psychotic personality disorder, schizoid type, if his behavior was extreme enough to have a profound effect on those around him. Sam is an example of this: at 28, Sam had still not "found himself." He was committed to writing as an avocation, but he had totally ignored his withdrawal from life and his grim economic prospects. He had not made one cent from anything he had written; his only published piece was a brief news story in a local newspaper owned by his mother's friend. All his rejection notices from literary magazines were form letters—politely acknowledging his literary attempts, but diplomatically pointing out that only a small percentage of material received can be published, and suggesting he try elsewhere. Sam had long since toughened his reaction to these rejections: instead of lamenting his plight, he gave himself a pep talk to try much harder to improve the quality of his writing. He increased the quantity, and if practice alone could improve the quality, he would have achieved his goal. His preoccupation with writing short stories and a novel was so strong that he gave up all social life and reduced his contact with the outside world to an occasional phone call or letter.

He was seen in psychiatric consultation to determine if he was psychologically disabled to the degree required to receive Social Security benefits or welfare funds. During this diagnostic interview he remained in good contact with reality, giving no evidence of faulty thinking other than his obsession with writing. He was even given the Whitaker Inventory for Schizophrenic Thinking test (1980) and showed no sign of schizophrenic thinking. If one accepts Sam's initial premise that anybody with some natural ability can become a commercially successful writer on his own, then Sam's giving up everything else for the sake of developing himself as a writer makes sense. If Sam had an independent income, he could live comfortably and be known as a dilettante writer. In reality, Sam lived with a mentally disturbed father who received just enough "salary" from a family business to keep a family of four alive. Sam's father had been an engineer with great promise but always anxious around people; he covered this up with an increasing dependence on alcohol and tranquilizers. When Sam was about ten, his father was hospitalized as an alcoholic, lost his job, and decided to become self-employed. He was able to give up the alcohol by living at home and using Thorazine as prescribed by his family doctor. He had a basement filled with his own special equipment and spent all his time working on new inventions, some of which were patented and seemed like clever ideas, but he never was able to sell any of them. He became a confused and irritable hermit leading a totally self-centered life, never leaving home, and avoiding everybody except his family.

Sam's mother was a long-suffering woman with saint-like qualities. She was a devout Catholic who had long ago decided it was her duty to stand by her husband and two children. Sam's younger sister had talent in ballet and had taken lessons from an early age, which put an additional strain on the family's meager income. She gave up an opportunity to go to college and instead joined a ballet group that provided her with room, board, and occasional work.

Sam had been a B student in parochial schools and graduated from a large state university, where he received a B.A. degree in marketing. He took a few English courses and wrote adequate, but not outstanding, papers; however, he never submitted any writing to the university literary magazine, nor did he write for the college newspaper. He seemed to have his fair share of male friends in college but was considered shy around girls and never had a date. He drank beer at the fraternity parties, and by his junior year was aware that he needed more and more beer to feel comfortable around people. He consulted the university counseling service and was told that he was an incipient alcoholic and must stop immediately. At first this only spurred him to drink more, until he began having blackouts, getting into fights, and having traffic accidents while intoxicated. He also slept through an examination and was put on academic probation. Realizing the seriousness of his situation, he "went on the wagon" and did not touch a drop of alcohol in six years. After college he had a couple of jobs—as an insurance salesman and then as a car salesman. He was unsuccessful in both jobs, presumably because he lacked the drive and extroverted personality of most successful salesmen, but he did manage to save about $4,000 from his two jobs because he was living at home with his parents and had few expenses. He then decided to become a writer, having been impressed by the lives and books of both John Cheever and James Michener. His mother welcomed his decision at first because he could then help her every day with the delicate management of his father.

He bought a typewriter, taught himself to type using two or three fingers, and set up a schedule for writing in his room each day from 8:00 A.M. to 4:00 P.M. His mother would bring him a sandwich for lunch and they would have a short chat at noon, but this was his only distraction in an eight-hour working day. After two years of this self-imposed writing program without any financial reward, his mother became concerned and consulted an analyst. Attempts were made to bring Sam into psychotherapy, but he absolutely refused; the only way he could be interviewed was in connection with possible Social Security or welfare benefits.

In formulating Sam's psychodynamics, we have collateral information from other family members but we do not have detailed information from Sam himself about the inner workings of his mind. He must have had various neurotic traits in childhood which showed up mainly in his being a rather shy, passive, and anxious young man. His father did not provide a good role model for him so he necessarily became too dependent on his mother, this combination must have inhibited his psychosexual and social development. He was bright enough to do well academically and appeared to have some friends. The transition to college, where he was away from home for the first time, was very difficult for Sam emotionally. His increasing dependence on beer at first eased his inner tension but ultimately became life-threatening to him so he abruptly stopped it. His personality problems surfaced more during his unsuccessful attempt at sales. He apparently decided that he was unable to deal with the outside world and withdrew to his own room at home to write stories about people who were able to succeed in the outside world. The world of his stories became a world of fantasy, which gave him enough hope and gratification to continue his life. He also had his caring, ever-present mother, and he must have known that she preferred his company to that of his father. He had won his oedipal battle over his father, but he lost the war of life by not being able to survive in the world of reality. If by any remote chance one of Sam's stories were accepted or were to earn him some money, would this change anything? Probably not; he has already totally withdrawn from life and regressed to being completely dependent on his mother. Furthermore, he is unable to tolerate everyday frustrations or to sustain any relationship outside of his family.

Sam fits our diagnostic category of psychotic personality. He had the capacity to cover up any "loose thinking" when he was seen in a fairly structured psychiatric interview. When he was asked about getting a job, he had two objections: (1) he believed that he was just beginning to gather momentum in his writing career and it was essential to devote all his time to it; (2) he feared that he would get too anxious and uncomfortable in any job situation. He preferred to receive whatever disability benefits he could rather than take a chance on working. He even put up a notice at a local school that he was available to type students' term papers because he could do it at home and would be able to spend as much time as required by his hunt-and-peck system.

Sam also refused to consider getting any kind of help to improve his life or his writing. He had to conserve his savings (which had dwindled to about $1,000) so he did not wish to enroll in any advanced courses in literary composition. He felt his time could be better spent by reading good books, which he did each evening. As long as he remained within his writing and reading schedule he felt "reasonably normal" and did not have anxiety, tension, depression, or fear. His rigid and compulsive schedule and isolation apparently protected him from other symptoms. What will happen to Sam when his money runs out or when his mother and father die? He denied any conscious self-destructive ideation. In many ways, Sam was leading a remarkably similar life to that of his father, who could also be called a psychotic personality. Sam's psychodynamics were sufficient to account for his condition. We know too little of hereditary factors to completely rule them out of consideration.

Peter's case provides a useful contrast to Sam's, as it shows a similar but different type of psychotic personality. Peter was a large, awkward 40-year-old man with a shuffling gait and a pair of thick eyeglasses that highlighted his unusual appearance. He lived with his 78-year-old mother and had been employed by the Municipal Street Department for 16 years. It was his job to locate and map out the city's potholes so they could be repaired. He was conscientious in his work; the only time he missed work was after his father's death when he went into a psychiatric hospital for a month. He was upset by his father's death and felt anxious and tense, but with supportive psychotherapy and chemotherapy he was able to return to work.

When Peter was first seen in psychiatric evaluation, he complained of being anxious and tense and having a recurrent fear that he "might do something silly" or "act in a crazy way." He used to do some drinking but stopped because he felt uncomfortable with less control over himself. His family had complained that he "giggled a lot" and "acted like a child" when he drank. Peter had become increasingly dependent on his parents, both of whom were retired from their jobs. Although he had finished a parochial high school and had two years of engineering in college, he had never made any lasting friends. His sister was five years younger, better adjusted, and had a good job in another city.

Peter was the oldest child born to parents who lived in Hungary and escaped from the Russian occupation in 1936. Despite language problems, both parents obtained steady jobs in the United States. Shy, quiet Peter was usually the largest boy in his class, and was often teased about his excessive size and awkwardness, but it never seemed to bother him. Although he would talk to girls, he never had a date. He had enjoyed attending horror movies ever since his teens. He also secretly had a supply of pornographic magazines hidden in his room, which his mother soon discovered and destroyed, warning Peter about the dire consequences of "reading such filth." Peter brought others and became adept at hiding them from his mother. He looked at them during his attempts at masturbation, but this would fill him with guilt and he would then have to confess it at Mass. At college he continued the masturbation but gave up confession.

When he first took his municipal job he became painfully aware of the men boasting about their active sex lives and how they suspected men who were not heterosexually active of being "faggots." These comments turned into ideas of reference so that at times he believed some of the men were actually referring to him as a "faggot." He thought he could spot those men and was usually able to avoid them. He would take his coffee break alone, or if he had to be with a group, he remained mostly silent. Probably because of his large size, the other men did not openly confront him, but he felt there were frequent innuendos about his being a homosexual. He decided to throw away all his pornographic magazines and felt less guarded around his mother, but still experienced the ideas of reference. It was not clear whether or not Peter's fellow workers were actually saying something to him about being sexually different.

After his father's death, when he was temporarily hospitalized, he complained that other patients and members of the staff were whispering that he was a "faggot"; in this instance it clearly represented a projection from his own conscience. When he returned to work, these accusations slowly disappeared as he began to feel better about himself and was helped by a major tranquilizer.

Peter remained very vulnerable, however, and totally dependent on his mother emotionally: he could drive a car and chauffeur her, but she initiated any plans they had and told him what to eat, how to dress, and what to say. The only break from this dependent, submissive existence was his eight-hour workday and his sister's visits home two or three times a year. When he was in the hospital, his mother brought in a suitcase full of clean clothes which remained in the suitcase throughout his hospitalization because he was unable to take them out of the suitcase and place them in his chest of drawers.

Psychological testing done during his hospitalization indicated that he had a personality disorder of a schizoid and paranoid type. He was having difficulty holding onto reality; some of his Rorschach responses were felt to have been so strained as to indicate a slight ego break with reality. There was a bottomless-pit need for protection and nurturance openly shown, with poor sense of self-worth; he felt insecure and immature, and was preoccupied with his sexuality;

anger, frustration, and sexuality were merged in his thinking so that appropriate action seemed impossible. It was felt that his father's death had led to a decompensating of his defenses. Peter was both relieved by, and frightened of, being in the hospital. He feared losing his job and improved by showing "a flight into health."

He continued to function on this level of schizoid-paranoid personality disorder, however. Although it was a marginal level, he managed to support himself economically and coexist with his domineering, but fearful, mother. He had problems in remaining separate from her emotionally and had to become an isolated "loner" to keep his own ego boundaries. She protected, directed, and took care of him, but he was not psychologically engulfed by her. She remained in good health, but at her death his schizoid type of existence would again be sorely tested.

Peter can be called a schizoid personality with paranoid trends. If his projections were stronger and he believed he was being constantly threatened by being called disparaging names, he would withdraw more from the world, quit his job, and remain safely at home. This further regression and belief in his own projections would make him a paranoid schizophrenic. But he ignored this basic paranoid position enough to keep his job and appeared to be in good touch with reality. Peter was unusual in having to enter a psychiatric hospital, but he was reactively upset and depressed by his father's death. He felt so threatened by being in the hospital that he made a speedy recovery from his temporary depression. He seems to fit best the diagnosis of PPD paranoid type.

* * * *

Glover (1955, p. 254) is one of the few psychoanalysts who has commented on the psychotic character: "For the striking feature of most character cases is the operation of alloplastic systems of defense, meaning thereby that abnormal patterns of reaction are displayed in object relations, whether sexual or social, the aim of which is to modify the environment to suit fixed instinctual needs and demands of the patient. The aim corresponds to the reaction of the psychotic, with this essential difference, however, that whereas the psychotic abandons his most important object-relations and substitutes for reality a fantasy system of relations, the psychotic character maintains an extremely tenuous system of relations and persists in his attempts to modify his objects, thereby maintaining his hold on reality." He goes on to say that in some psychotic characters, "regressive features predominate." In these, "the main symptoms include a reduction of already tenuous contacts, together with an exaggeration of personal idiosyncrasies of thought and behavior." He summarizes thus: "In short, the character groups illustrate a character continuum varying from extremes of regressive and introjective disorder to extremes of projective reaction, presenting in a larval form all the varieties of pathological reaction that can be demonstrated in a gross clinical form in the classical psychoses."

Glover (1955) attempts to distingush the "systematized" psychotic character groups, based on their resemblance to standard psychoses, from a group of psychopathic characters which may manifest a few of the features of psychotic character along with many others that by no stretch of the imagination can be called "psychotic." He emphasizes that the purely psychotic character must be excluded from the psychopathic group and that the psychopathic group can be subdivided based on characterological considerations. He suggests that to make such a differential diagnosis the clinician must note "the predominating types of defense, the scatter of ego-fixations and the focal point or points of instinctual frustration both past and present." Unfortunately, Glover does not provide any case material to illustrate his concept of the psychotic character. He does make some suggestions about analytic treatment of the psychotic character: "Only when a relatively durable but still acutely ambivalent transference has been established it is possible to press against the alloplastic defenses of the patient." He closes with an acknowledgment of the extreme difficulties found in the psychoanalytic treatment of psychotic characters: "Provided the technique has been carried out to the best of the analyst's ability, the failures so frequently experienced, though by no means so frequently recorded, are honorable failures."

The term "alloplastic" (in contrast to "autoplastic") appears in the early psychoanalytic literature. Eidelberg (1968) defines alloplastic as "a form of adaptation directed toward altering the environment rather than the self." He sees it as "a successor to the autoplastic developmental stage in which affect is discharged inwardly." He points out that "initially dominated by the pleasure principle, the individual's motility evolves into purposeful action under the guidance of the reality principle. Pathological manifestations of alloplastic adaptations are found in cases in which motility retains its more primitive and magical functions as in acting out, compulsions, impulse disorders, flights into reality and psychoses." Freud (1924) makes the point that "in neurosis a piece of reality is avoided by a sort of flight, whereas in psychosis it is remodeled." This alteration or remodeling of reality is an alloplastic adaptation.

Peter Giovacchini (1975) has written extensively about severe character disorders or borderline conditions which present ill-defined clinical features. He does not attempt to pigeonhole such cases diagnostically but instead focuses more on their psychoanalytic treatment. He does point out that these patients have a disturbed sense of identity, regress readily, and may show various affective states and/or symptoms. Often they show no specific symptoms but complain of vague dissatisfactions in their lives which lead them to wonder how futile or without purpose their lives are. Some of these character disorders would come under our category of psychotic personality disorder, but since Giovacchini does not offer specific diagnostic criteria we would have to look at each individual case to determine whether or not it fits our criteria.

Mention should also be made of Karl Menninger's concept of the regulatory devices of the ego under major stress (1959). This concept is based on Menninger's point of view that all clinical phenomena can be placed on a continuum between a state of good adjustment with good mental health and the opposite extreme of severe illness or complete disintegration. This continuum makes such terms as neurosis and psychosis unnecessary. It is worth noting that in DSM-III there is for the first time no such category as psychoneurosis.

Menninger proposes that the functions of the ego be compared to a homeostatic regulator which ideally permits the individual to function comfortably and effectively. Any stress requires the ego to make adjustments which may be appropriate to the stressful situation but which at times can be excessive, insufficient, or too persistent. These regulatory devices are categorized according to orders, with the first order being the most healthy and adaptive, and the fifth order representing "the ultimate and irreversible catastrophe" or even death. We can apply this concept to the psychotic personality disorder and note that our cases show maladaptive regulatory devices which are the third and sometimes even of the fourth order. What first may have been temporary emergency reactions to stress become incorporated into the psychotic personality's permanent repertoire of behavior which is maladaptive.

An attempt has been made by a group in New York City to define "psychotic ego function patterns" (Bellak, L. et al, 1969). This group arbitrarily chose 12 ego functions from the psychoanalytic literature and developed a scale to rate their functioning in individual patients. These ego functions included:

Reality testing
Judgment
Sense of reality
Regulation and control of impulses and affects
Object relations
Thought processes
Adaptive regressing in the service of the ego (ARISE)
Defensive functioning
Stimulus barrier
Autonomous functioning
Synthetic-integrative functioning
Mastery—competence

A profile is made of each individual patient which becomes valuable in diagnosis, treatment, and etiology of the condition. We feel that when this scale and approach are better defined and refined, they will be useful in studying the psychotic personality disorder.

### REFERENCES

Bellak, L., Hurich, M., and Crawford, P. (1969): Psychotic egos, *Psychoanalytic Review* 56: 526-541.
Bychowski, G. (1953): The problem of latent psychosis, *J. Am. Psychoanal. Assn.* 1: 484-503.

Deutsch, H. (1942): Some forms of emotional disturbance and their relationships to schizophrenia, *Psychoanal. Quart.* 11: 301-321.

Diagnostic and Statistical Manual of Mental Disorders III (DSM-III), American Psychiatric Association (1980).

Eidelberg, L. (1968): *Encyclopedia of Psychoanalysis.* New York: The Free Press, p. 25.

Fairbairn, W.R.D. (1944): Endopsychic structure considered in terms of object relations, in *An Object-Relations Theory of the Personality.* New York: Basic Books, 1952, pp. 82-136.

Federn, P. (1947): Principles of psychotherapy in latent schizophrenia, *Am. J. Psychotherapy* 1: 129-137.

Freud, S. (1914): On narcissism, *S.E.* 14, p. 67.

_____ (1918): From the history of an infantile neurosis, *S.E.* 17, p. 122.

_____ (1924): The loss of reality in neurosis and psychosis, *S.E.* 19, p. 185.

Frosch, J. (1960): Psychotic character, *J. Am. Psychoanal. Assn.* 8: 544-551.

_____ (1964): The psychotic character, *Psychia. Quarterly* 38: 81-96.

_____ (1970): Psychoanalytic considerations of the psychotic character, *J. Am. Psychoanal. Assn.* 18: 24-50.

Giovacchini, P. (1975): *Psychoanalysis of Character Disorders.* New York: Jason Aronson.

Glover, E. (1955): *The Technique of Psychoanalysis.* New York: International Universities Press, p. 254.

Goldberg, A. (1978): *The Psychology of the Self, a Casebook.* New York: International Universities Press.

Grinker, R., Werbel, B., and Drye, R. (1968): *The Borderline Syndrome.* New York: Basic Books.

Hinsie, L. and Campbell, R. (1970): *Psychiatric Dictionary,* 4th ed. New York: Oxford University Press, p. 620.

Hoch, P. and Polatin, P. (1949): Pseudoneurotic forms of schizophrenia, *Psychia. Quarterly* 23: 248-276.

Kernberg, O. (1967): Borderline personality organization, *J. Am. Psychoanal. Assn.* 15: 641-685.

_____ (1975): *Borderline Conditions and Pathological Narcissism.* New York: Jason Aronson.

_____ (1976): *Object-Relations Theory and Clinical Psychoanalysis.* New York: Jason Aronson.

Klein, M. (1952): Notes on some schizoid mechanisms, in *Developments in Psychoanalysis,* ed. by J. Riviere. London: Hogarth Press, pp. 292-320.

Knight, R.P. (1954): Management and psychotherapy of the borderline schizophrenic patient, in *Psychoanalytic Psychiatry and Psychology,* ed. by R.D. Knight and C.R. Friedman. New York: International Universities Press, pp. 110-122.

Kohut, H. (1971): *The Analysis of the Self.* New York: International Universities Press.

_____ (1977): *The Restoration of the Self.* New York: International Universities Press.

Menninger, K. (1959): *A Psychiatrist's World.* New York: The Viking Press, pp. 497-515.

Rado, S. (1962): Theory and therapy: the theory of schizotypal organization and its application to the treatment of decompensated schizotypal behavior, in *Psychoanalysis of Behavior,* Collected Papers 2. New York: Grune & Stratton, pp. 127-140.

Rapaport, D., Gill, M., and Schafer, R. (1945-46): *Diagnostic Psychological Testing,* 2 vols. Chicago: Year Book Publishers.

Reich, W. (1949): *Character Analysis,* 3rd ed. New York: Farrar, Straus & Giroux.

Stern, A. (1938): Psychoanalytic investigation and therapy in the borderline group of neuroses, *Psychoanal. Quart.* &: 467-489.

Stone, M. (1980): *The Borderline Syndromes.* New York: McGraw-Hill, pp. 5-33.

Warner, S. (1980): A clinical note on auto-analysis as a narcissistic resistance, *J. Am. Acad. Psychoanal.* 8(2): 279-286.

Whitaker, L. (1980): *Objective Measurement of Schizophrenic Thinking: A Practical and Theoretical Guide to the Whitaker Index of Schizophrenic Thinking.* Los Angeles: Western Psychologic Services.

Zilboorg, G. 91941): Ambulatory schizophrenia, *Psychiatry* 4: 149-155.

# SECTION II
# SOME EXAMPLES OF THE
# CLINICAL OBSERVATIONAL
# DATA

# 7
# IN THE TRANSFERENCE

Most phenomena in the emotional life can only be understood quantitatively. Small wonder then if the problem of the psychotic personality should turn out to be solvable only in quantitative fashion. In his brief papers (1924a,b) Freud states: "The ego's conflicts with the various powers ruling it. . .will assuredly depend upon. . .the strength of the forces striving with one another. And further, it is always possible for the ego to avoid a rupture in any of its relations by deforming itself. . . .Thus the illogicalities, eccentricities and follies of mankind would fall into a category similar to their sexual perversions for by accepting them they spare themselves repressions." It is doubtful if all the abstruse presentations and abstract theorizing in the expanding literature have added substantially to this succinct paper. In this book, we have tried to provide clinical descriptions to be sure we are discussing the same clinical picture. It is to be hoped that these clinical descriptions will also extend our insights and concepts in defining and understanding the psychotic personality.

\* \* \* \*

The following vignettes are all from extensive notes written after analytic hours with patients seen many years ago who are no longer in analysis. The main reason for this is discretion: it is unthinkable to write of recent patients without radical disguises, and to make such disguises risks too great changes and distortions in the observational data, which must be the basis for all our theoretical ideas, formulations, and working hypotheses. Although not current cases, the patients discussed here remain vivid examples of the points to be made.

\* \* \* \*

Some individuals manifest psychotic feeling, thinking, and behavior almost only in the transference, while moving in and out of relationships with psychotherapists. Many cannot tolerate closeness although they long for it. When they reach a certain degree of closeness, even only professionally with the therapist, they take fright and leave for another therapist. Usually this is an unconscious repetition toward the analyst of an early childhood traumatic relationship; at the same time, the individual is unable to tolerate consistent analysis—thus presenting a fine challenge to the therapist. Alberte is an example. The most central element of her personality seemed to be very early and severe rejection by her mother, before Alberte's reality sense was well developed. If the psychiatrist was sympathetic, as of course he must be, she attached to him her dependent love needs, just as when small she had directed those love needs toward her mother, but she also experienced the rejection, frustration, and consequent rage she had felt toward her mother. Just as the rejected young child often clings all the more to its mother, so the patient clings to the psychiatrist. Ten years after she first contacted the analyst, Alberte phoned him again three times in one evening to rage at him for referring her to another analyst, although she had previously of her own accord seen three or four others. Her combination of infantile clinging, feelings of frustration and rejection where no rejection actually existed, and feelings of inferiority and rage which took the form of all manner of accusations formed a paranoid transference that had remained uninfluenced by all the analysts she had seen during the ten years. She repeated the same pattern toward each one in turn. She would start talking in the office or on the phone in an amicable, realistic, and rational manner, but after about 20 minutes would drift into intense complaints of being abused, then would rage about these abuses and make impossible demands upon the listener. It was impossible for her to grasp the reality. Alberte was swamped in a sea of her rationalizations and did not even hear what the analyst was saying. Yet she could hold a job and run a home— therefore, she was not an overt paranoid, but a psychotic personality of paranoid type, or possibly a latent compensated paranoid, except in relation to the therapist to whom she tried to be close and, therefore, against whom her paranoia became overt.

* * * *

A less extreme example of such reactions was Dorothy, a diagnostic challenge. Dorothy was a "glamazon" with raven black hair and intense shining black eyes. She came to the Chicago Institute sincerely seeking therapy, but also for whatever education would improve her effectiveness as a psychiatric social worker. Over the years she was in analytic therapy at different times with three analysts, all of whom agreed that she was not an everyday neurotic but a psychotic personality. However it was difficult in the extreme to define her psychotic features. No one was able to say, "There, that thought, feeling, behavior is psychotic."

At that time, few analysts were categorizing patients as psychotic personalities. At the Institute, it was the application of psychoanalysis to physical symptoms that intrigued analysts, and their studies helped initiate psychosomatic medicine. Dorothy was obviously "needy" emotionally, although to mention this in her presence was to risk her wrath; it meant she needed the therapist emotionally. Her initial interview revealed nothing psychotic: in her earliest years, there was much deprivation and rejection, domination and control. She complained that her parents did not allow her when small to express any emotion, especially not anger. She was forbidden to cry. It was difficult for her therapist to deny her enormous dependent love needs toward him for time and attention, but his patient schedule was overflowing and other commitments filled his time far beyond any possibility of taking her into psychoanalysis, acutely as Dorothy seemed to need it. Therefore he referred her to a colleague connected with the Institute, Will Norton, an able, conscientious, dedicated, experienced, and handsome psychotherapist.

Dorothy immediately fell madly in love with him. She was of the "dumplings and gruel" type, described by Freud (1915), and never accepted being a patient in therapy with a skilled, experienced physician—no, her love for Dr. Norton was not neurotic, not resistance, not transference, not connected with treatment, but was a real-life, elemental passion. Her narcissistic prestige needs mounted in dimensions and intensity, until Dorothy insisted that she was not his *patient* but his *colleague,* and certainly his equal in love. She knew Norton had a wife and three children, but still demanded that he get a divorce and marry her. He was of a reserved nature and strictly professional with his women patients. Confronted by her passionate onslaught which did not yield to analysis, he wished to be rid of her as a patient, but as a conscientious analyst he persevered in trying to analyze this uncomfortable transference in order to turn it into therapeutic help. Many patients fall in love with their analysts in the course of treatment of everyday emotional problems, but Dorothy's ego and sense of reality were so utterly swamped that this particular transference love was beyond the bounds of reality. When her feelings were strong, she plagued Will with telephone calls. Eventually, of course, he had to defend himself and his family against such demands and interruptions. As could be predicted, Dorothy then felt the rejections and deprivations of her childhood pattern (which probably occurred before age three because of the extreme nature of her reaction) and began accusing Will of mistreating her. She insisted that they must be "equal" and that if he analyzed her feelings, he must submit to her analyzing his; if she told him all, he must tell her all.

Probably no more clear example could be found of Freud's description of the use of "transference love" (1915) as a resistance than Dorothy's unconscious use of her passion for Will to obstruct and then terminate the therapy. Yet Will helped her enormously, as she admitted to him years later. During the decade she was seeing Will for treatment she survived rejection by her husband and divorce, and supported herself and her two children in her position as social worker, proving herself no less than heroic.

It is doubtful, however, that Dorothy could have come through all this without Will's help. She saw situations as flattering as her needs required, but only a strong ego could have supported herself and her children, even at the price of some warpings of reality. These warpings were diffuse and hard to pin down. Her own emotional stresses and problems even seemed to help in heightening her perception of the unconscious of others.

Once Dorothy got the idea that abuses in childhood cause reactions that continue into adult life as emotional disorders, she revealed an outstanding talent for this kind of insight. Also it gave her a rationalization for her anger and demands: "Look what my parents did to me!" Will was an excellent analyst with keen, accurate psychodynamic understanding. Dorothy caught on quickly, and her narcissistic prestige needs and competitiveness drove her to try to prove that she had better insight than Will. Introspection, with the specific weaknesses of her repressions, revealed to Dorothy the rejections and deprivations of her early childhood by both her mother and her father, their preferences for her siblings, and their insistence on running the family in a dictatorial manner. They were too busy earning a living to give each of their children individual attention. Occasionally Dorothy was nearly overwhelmed by her anger, which in part sought drainage by sex.

One could only respect Dorothy highly for supporting herself and her children, raising them with love and understanding if also with turbulence and turmoil as the result of her insights and anger. She was a dedicated and effective mother and a superior social worker. In fact, she had more insight into her clients than many psychiatrists and even many analysts. The very intensity of her own feelings, almost at the bursting point, supersensitized her to the feelings of her patients and gave her close identifications with their sufferings, frustrations, sexual starvation, and anger (Saul, 1953).

Her hypersensitivity of feelings did not, however, facilitate her own personal relationships and Dorothy led an emotionally needy existence. She clung to her children and to her analyst, through occasional phone calls and rare visits. He respected her deeply for surviving and contributing against great odds; she felt his admiration and was supported by it.

After she had broken totally with Will, she was referred to another analyst, Frank. She quickly fell in love with him, but he had been forewarned by Dorothy's original analyst, and she had been through one such experience with Will. Consequently, her ego was not so swamped this time, and two years later she reconciled with Will. As Frank expressed it, "Dorothy declared herself cured and then phoned me to say that now she was no longer a patient but a 'colleague.' " This was true in that she was busy and earning enough to curtail phone calls with the first analyst, with Will, or with her new analyst, Frank. However, in her years of treatment she had won genuine respect and had succeeded in making the crucial compromise adjustment of accepting transference dependence upon the three analysts. This gratified somewhat her childhood pattern without offending her narcissism too strongly.

What in an individual's dynamics makes a strong healthy, realistic ego, with full control and excellent judgment, and what are the characteristics of a neurotic or psychotically colored ego? Although we have no effective tools available for measuring ego qualities, such as those used by mathematics or physics (Saul and Sheppard, 1958), there seems little doubt that this problem is mostly, if not completely, quantitative. If the ego qualities of reality sense, judgment, and control—i.e., perception, integration, and executive direction—are unmistakably disordered, then we readily agree that the condition is neurotic or psychotic or, to some quantitative degree, so tinted. If the distortion of these functions is subtly pervasive but beyond the bounds of neurosis, then we tend to view the ego or even the *total personality* as *to some degree* psychotic or so colored.

We are faced with the following question: If the subtlety and pervasiveness of a psychotic quality of the ego characterizes the psychotic personality, then is uncertainty of diagnosis inevitable in the present state of our knowledge? Is not this very uncertainty itself a diagnostic criterion? Overt psychosis, even if borderline, is usually discernible. So is neurosis. But does not the very concept of the psychotic personality imply a subtlety, pervasiveness, and lack of specific psychotic features that make uncertainty an inevitable characteristic of its diagnosis?

For a while, Dorothy's only contacts were her children and Dr. Norton. Upon them blew the full force of her passionate dependence, love needs, prestige needs, frustration, and rage. She so strongly identified with her children that she could treat them as she demanded to be treated herself and so obtain vicarious satisfaction. Apart from her emotional demands on them, she gave them enormous love and interest, and did a good job of rearing them. Sex is apt to be a great release and is often a channel for draining all kinds of tensions (Saul, 1979, p. 207). This pathway was mostly cut off for Dorothy by her divorce. Like most divorced women, she could not readily meet new men of her high level, so she suffered from the lack of a sexual love life. Her demands and her anger kept her from tolerating most human relations. Never daunted, in her desperation Dorothy tried everything and almost always did come up with some male companionship for a brief period. She only chose to meet professional men of high standing. She managed to live and to feel the gratification of helping others, and conscientiously earned enough to support herself and her children.

It is unusual to be able to check a patient's dynamics by repetition under controlled circumstances. Here, however, the initial transference to Will was repeated exactly to Frank. As described above, Dorothy was deprived and dominated in some degree and combination as a child, especially by her father, although she must also have been rather well loved for she had no strong complaint on that score and has had much love to give her children, as well as having been able to support them and herself against the odds in the long years since her divorce. As her dependent love needs developed toward her analyst, Dr. Norton, her frustrated sexual needs also began to focus on him; that is, the transference became eroticized as she experienced it—she "fell in love" with him. She accepted these feelings only as reality, refusing to see them as anything to be analyzed. All her sense of rejection, deprivation, and control by her father now came forth in full force toward Dr. Norton. Unrealistically, she felt that he reciprocated her feelings in full, and would indeed divorce his wife and marry her. When he instead analyzed and refused to respond to her demands and objected to her frequent phone calls, she felt deprived and rejected, and justifiably enraged. She rationalized this as his leading her on, only to reject her. It was beyond her sense of reality to accept the position of Dr. Norton's "patient." She saw it as only fair that she should analyze him just as he analyzed her, confident that she could help him enormously to grow through insights which she could give him, insights to which she believed he was entirely blind. When he refused to permit this, she felt it was attempted domination instead of a fair one-to-one relationship.

The following conclusions are justified: (1) The understanding of the dynamics of the initial transference to Dr. Norton was correct because it was subjected to prediction and confirmation twice—with Frank and, in a more restrained form, with her original analyst. (2) There was some emotional learning (after-education, as Freud called it, or corrective emotional experience, Alexander's term) for she was able to handle the termination with Frank which had almost destroyed her with Will Norton. In addition, she was able to maintain a relationship with the original analyst on his own terms (rare phone calls and visits). Thus we were able to observe dynamics and their subsequent confirmation through repetition in a closely similar situation.

Certainly Dorothy was not psychotic. Yet one often sensed a slightly unreal quality in her perceptions and feelings in the transference, although not in her actual behavior in life. Perhaps this is another diagnostic criterion: the actual behavior, the final common path, comes out as relatively normal, although the intensities of the feelings warp the perceptions. If this is true, then the diagnostic lable indicates chiefly distortion of the ego in its perception and in its integrative rather than its executive functions, at least in certain types of cases.

Diagnosis is difficult because it lies in the ego and not in the general dynamics. The psychodynamics are identical in the classic neuroses and the neurotic character—the difference being that certain of the dynamics which cause symptoms in the neuroses are *acted out* unconsciously in the neurotic character, while in the psychotic personality they are of such an intensity that certain of the ego functions are distorted, especially the reality sense. The emotional intensity in Dorothy caused suffering but contributed to her drive to survive and to support her children and herself.

This all fits into our basic concept that all emotional disorders manifest a failure to mature adequately. In general, most people are still very much the children they once were, and the question becomes in what mixture of age levels and of emotional trauma? Many a "successful" man or woman is seen, on closer scrutiny, to be a combination of a two-, three-, four-, or five-year-old child and an adolescent. Insofar as this is true, the earlier the fixations, the greater is the chance that perception and integration will be as remote from reality as in the mind of a young child. Generally the younger the mind, the more unrealistic and poorly integrated and less able it is to cope with the exigencies of adult life, i.e., the more near it is to psychosis or psychotic personality.

Certainly most people are not mature. Freud said that the child we once were lives on in us all. A child of what age, then, and how disturbed? This varies from person to person. Each individual's thinking and behavior usually fluctuate between a mixture of ages: in some instances he may seem like a two, three, four, or five year old; at other times his behavior is that of an adolescent. Moreover, this child within is not always a happy child, with good feelings toward others. Indeed, the child within exists so strongly in the adult personality because it is fixated at a very early age by improper treatment that caused unhappinesses and proved traumatic since the child could not resolve his reaction to it, and continued to struggle internally and unconsciously with this fixation.

The severity of the psychopathology in the psychotic personality, as in the neurotic personality, is determined by at least two factors or variables: (1) how early in the child's life the emotional patterns were formed which are not outgrown and (2) the degree of abnormality—of psychopathology—of the patterns, i.e., how severely disordered the feelings toward self and others are. Before the age of about three, and particularly before mastery of speech, the child's capacity for comprehension of its feelings is severely limited. The ability to deal with emotional problems is a function of (1) age, but it is also a function of (2) the nature, (3) the intensities of the emotional pressures which are generated within the child, and (4) the kind and amount of loving support given the child in dealing with these pressures. The pressures of these reactions strongly affect the development in kind and intensity of (1) the child's dependence upon others, (2) his needs and ability to get love from others, (3) his sense of self-worth and of competitiveness, (4) his ideals and standards, (5) his conscience, (6) his fight-flight reaction, (7) his sexuality, and (8) his grasp of reality (Saul, 1979).

This is exactly what we should have anticipated because, in general, everyone lives under the strains on his ego of his emotional forces, especially of his emotional pathology. From these strains, as we know, can come a whole gamut of psychopathological symptoms: psychosomatic disturbances; classic neuroses; anxiety; depressions; perversions; psychoses; and every form, extent, and degree of acting out (including the neurotic personality) from self-injuring masochism to all forms of hostility—crime, torture, murder, and sadism. If the motivations express patterns from too early a period in life or if they are too intense, too pathological, or all of these, then the distortions of the ego, which constitute the essence of emotional disorder, may take the form of spotty, diffuse psychotic variations in the person's accustomed thinking, feeling, and behavior (i.e., some form and degree of psychotic personality). No wonder this condition is so common. Also, the earlier the age and stage of the regressive motivations, the more prominent is the self-centeredness (and, therefore, usually the narcissism) and the weaker is the perception of reality. Every human shows every kind of residual childhood reaction (Saul, 1979) such as excessive or disordered dependence, love needs, inferiority feelings, egotism, competitiveness, superego motivations, and all manifestations of the fight-flight response. When we diagnose headache or depression or paranoia, we only indicate the *most prominent* of the childhood patterns of reaction which everyone has in some degree.

The pathognomonic point in the psychotic personality usually lies not in an individual's main psychodynamics, but in the ego and especially its sense of reality. Thus, a woman who had been deprived and dominated during childhood sooner or later felt deprived and dominated by everyone she tried to be close to. Either rapidly or gradually she came to make demands on someone, usually a man. He would respect her for her fine qualities and many superior abilities but, in time, would lose patience with her demands upon him, feeling that he must protect himself from her. She would not realize this but would feel frustrated and rejected, and blame this all on *him—his* lack of understanding, *his* hostility, *his* unfair and groundless mistreatment of her.

As her rage at the rejection she had provoked mounted, she accused him of mistreating her in every way that fit her rationalizations, introducing some degree of paranoid coloring. This formed a familiar pattern which kept repeating throughout her life as a regular part of her personality.

In failing to recognize her own provocation of rejection and her paranoid projection of her rage because of it, this patient's sense of reality is *partially deficient. If it were completely deficient, she would be paranoid, but its failure is only partial and she can rightly be called a psychotic personality rather than a psychotic. This forms the crucial quantitative distinction.* This is just as frequently the reaction of a man to a woman: same dynamics, same ego distortion, same deficiency of reality sense, same diagnosis of psychotic personality disorder (PPD).

## REFERENCES

Freud, S. (1915): Observations on transference love, *S.E.* 12, p. 157.
_____ (1924a): Neurosis and psychosis, *S.E.* 19, p. 149.
_____ (1924b): The loss of reality in neurosis and psychosis, *S.E.* 19, p. 183.

Saul, L.J. (1953): Telepathic sensitiveness as a neurotic symptom, in *Psychoanalysis and the Occult*, ed. by G. Devereux. New York: International Universities Press, pp. 192-196.

_____ (1979): *The Childhood Emotional Pattern and Maturity*. New York: Van Nostrand Reinhold, p. 207.

Saul, L.J. and Sheppard, E. (1958): An approach to a systematic study of ego function, *Psychia. Quarterly*, 28: 237-245.

# 8
# PSYCHOTIC PERSONALITY OR NEUROTIC CHARACTER?

Bobby, long, lean, and blonde, slouched in the chair and blurted out: "I can't stand living with my wife any longer. She is so distant that we can't discuss intimate things anymore, only objective things. It is beginning to affect my work."

"But how," the analyst asked, "can you expect to tell her that you have other women, women with whom you have opened up completely and who are good in bed, and then tell your wife she is too fat and expect her to forget it all and greet you with open arms?"

"I don't want her to greet me with open arms," he replied. "I can't stand it any more—I want to live separately." Was this because Bobby's wife was really so bad, or because he could not stand any emotional closeness, or why?

It quickly appeared that he had one of the most extreme, egotistically ambitious drives encountered in the analyst's office. He was ruthlessly self-promoting, and this took the form chiefly of social and financial climbing. He strove to be best in high social and business circles. This was reflected typically in his characteristic recurrent dream of winning a race, while gloating in triumph. Bobby's egotism was also represented in his childhood repetitive dream of climbing up the stairs, symbolizing his climbing in life. Appearance was important to him, as seen in his childhood repetitive embarrassment dream of being naked, a fear of being seen for what he really was. In real life, Bobby's huge, expensive house, his ultrastylish, ultraexpensive, made-to-order clothes, and his insistence on being addressed as "Mr." by both his secretary at work and the maid at home were part of his same drive to show himself as a great man. He had "made" the most expensive clubs in town: his egoistic striving for prestige and status and their exhibitionistic components pervaded his life.

Also evident was his tendency to be a helpless child. For example, at home he loaded every detail onto his wife, Marge, who had to do everything for him. As is usual, this childish dependence hurt his vanity and contributed much to his efforts to compensate by displays of superiority in all ways. His was close to the ultimate in narcissism, short of psychotic delusions of grandeur.

His regressive drive back to early childhood reflected a falling away from his self-imposed, vicious, hopeless struggle to be first in life, which he saw as a race to be won or as a ladder to be climbed. His anxiety was mostly from his hostility and guilt, which were the most repressed of his drives. He sacrificed himself and everyone else, especially his wife and children, to his own ambition. One simple example was the dangerous way he showed off in driving his car with the family in it, putting them in such a state of panic that they sometimes felt nauseated, while he tried to show off his superiority by counterphobically acting "masculine" and brave, demonstrating that he was heedless of danger—"Macho." Part of the ambition and exhibitionism were "masculine protest" denials of the feelings of being a helpless child, based upon his father's excessive ambitions for him since his birth.

These sharp contrasts between excessively strong forces of egoistic striving and being a helpless dependent child created a conflict which prevented Bobby from finding a consistent, stable, secure *identity*. The two trends were exaggerated by childhood dynamics which caused *a deficiency in the capacity to love and an intensification of repressed hostility*.

Seeing life as a race involved hostility because Bobby viewed everybody as hated competitors. Thus from Bobby's current picture we noted:

1. excessive striving for his own personal, egoistic advancement—socially, financially, and in every way—sacrificing himself and others, especially his wife and children, and exhibitionistically showing off his superiority;

2. the opposite drive—to be a helpless, dependent child, waited on by others while being played up to as a strong man;

3. the conflict between the two which resulted in a failure to find his identity and, from his childhood dynamics, a *deficiency in loving* and intensification of repressed hostility.

Bobby was miserable—unhappy, depressed, anxious, seeking relief in drugs. After leaving his wife he began an affair with another beautiful girl but, typically, after a year he asked his wife to take him back. She had by then endured too much and, in spite of his financial success, refused him. He would tell Marge what wonderful girls he was meeting and having affairs with, just as some adolescents confide in their mothers. Bobby's 0 to 6 was similar to that of Reid (Chapter 5): his father had been overly ambitious and driving, treating Bobby's mother like a slave, as well as insatiable in his sexual affairs, bringing his women into the home. Like Reid's father, Bobby's father wanted perfection and superachievement from his son. Like Reid, Bobby felt neglected and rejected, rather like an outcast in the family, always hoping that if he achieved perfection he might then be accepted by this father.

Bobby refused analytic help for a number of unconscious reasons: he might see defects which would offend his needs to be perfect; he could not spare even one hour a week from his frantic struggle for success; he also feared a breakdown with total withdrawal if his repressions weakened and his warped infantile motivations became mobilized.

Meanwhile, the drives that tormented him also drove him to phenomenal financial success. Was it not at least a little psychotic to live a miserable, isolated existence when young, handsome, sexy, and rich by deserting a warm, beautiful wife and three attractive children, refusing help even though he could afford it, and making himself an outcast from life (as he was in his family during childhood)?

It seemed so, but an essential element in this became evident only as related to the analyst by Marge; although not in treatment, Marge kept in touch with the analyst over the years: Bobby never married any of the girls he boasted of having affairs with, nor did he return to Marge and the children. What he did instead, unconsciously, was return to his adolescent pattern, having sex but no closeness. It seemed he could not tolerate closeness with anyone. This repeated a deep pattern of early childhood toward his mother, who was so badly treated by Bobby's father that she could not be warm and loving herself. Bobby grew up identifying with his father's hostility to, and rejection of, his mother. In his six hours with the analyst, Bobby did glimpse this pattern; when he left Marge and the children he attempted to expiate the guilt toward his mother by giving her money. Basically he was living out toward his wife and other women a pattern of hostility, rejection, and emotional distance toward his mother. Marge was attractive, intelligent, loving, devoted, beautiful, and sexy: the trouble lay in Bobby's inability to tolerate closeness. He would rationalize by saying Marge was a trifle overweight, but he could offer no realistic complaint.

Bobby's inability to tolerate emotional closeness (his problem in separation-individuation) kept him isolated, hostile, tense, and anxious—seeking surcease with drugs. It was this depth of regression that was the main source of the element of psychotic personality. Quantitatively, the condition was a little too severe to be referred to as a "neurotic character."

# 9
# FOUR TYPES OF PASSIVE-REGRESSIVE WITHDRAWAL

## IRMA: MASOCHISTIC REGRESSIVE WITHDRAWAL

Irma was 28 years old, slightly below average height, blonde, and pretty. The outstanding characteristic of her personality was withdrawal. Her withdrawal was *from* life and *toward* complete isolation. When she was five years old, she felt that the other children did not like her and she tended to stay home. Her first memory was of being sick in bed and looking out through the window at other children playing. Soon after entering kindergarten, when she was not quite five years old, she was running as fast as she could to her father who had called to her, and tripped, falling quite hard on her forehead. These were her only early memories. Irma graduated from high school and went to a college about 200 miles from her home which was on Chicago's North Shore. At college she felt unpopular and was so homesick that, insufficiently reassured by frequent phone calls to her parents, she gave up and returned home to live. She then entered a college near home as a day student. Irma came to see the analyst because of anxiety and study inhibition as graduation neared. The symptoms came mostly from her fears of graduating and leaving college to go out into life. She revealed occasional traces of protest against her dependence and submissiveness toward her parents; occasionally she would have a fleeting idea of going to California with a boy. However, Irma's *thrust to life* was too feeble for independent action. It was probably just as well, because she was ill-equipped to care for herself and might easily have been victimized.

She responded but little to insight, and it was mostly by moral and emotional support and appeals to her willpower that she was helped to graduate from the local college. In other words, the analyst supplied the strength of ego and superego which she herself lacked. During her last year at college, Irma began going with a boy named Harry. According to Irma, all he wanted was sex, and he had no feeling or use for her otherwise. Also, he himself was very selfish and "neurotic." He did eventually give Irma an engagement ring when he graduated and moved back to his hometown about 100 miles away. Harry had an apartment and a few acquaintances there; yet he too, like Irma, did not make close friends. She paid her own train fare to visit him, purchased the food she cooked for them in his apartment, paid for half the meals they ate out together, and adapted to his wishes in everything. Yet she was certain that if they married it would never work out. Irma continued this one-sided relationship almost entirely because it was "an ego trip"—she could feel that she was engaged and therefore present herself to others in a satisfactory status. She also felt demeaned and exploited by Harry and built up a rage against him that eventually exploded. It took a year for the inevitable break to come. Harry did nothing to heal the breach. Irma felt rejected (as indeed she was), completely alone, and desperate, but at that critical point she reported that her parents refused to let her see the analyst. The result was that Irma had no support during the rupture of this last exogamic libidinal tie, her last bond to a human being other than her parents. Her anxious, tentative probing out into life had met with frustration and rejection; she recoiled from it back into her bed at home and again was almost literally a shut-in, looking through a closed window at her peers out in life, just as in her first memory.

Over a year later she was chronically exhausted but unable to sleep, eat, or exercise. Irma persuaded her parents to let her see the analyst again with regularity, once a week. He strongly supported her ideas of taking a secretarial course. She finished the course and got a job in a small company. Here she felt that no one liked her and she would be fired. She never was but continued with the job until she resigned after five months. She made no friends with either sex. She said that people always asked about her life but lost interest when they found she had only a menial typing job with no other interests and was not even engaged or married. She spent most of her time in bed at home.

In Irma's view, the whole world consisted of (1) older people whom she wrote off, having no interest in them whatsoever; and (2) her own generation, most of whom were married and therefore to her mind outside the sphere of any mutual interest. Those of her generation younger than Irma were also excluded from any mutual interest; those men whom she saw in dating bars, where other girls managed to attract men, she felt unable to attract because they would find out she only held a menial typing job and therefore she felt they looked down on her, especially since she was not engaged, married, or even divorced. They all expected her to go to bed with them the same evening or else they rejected her.

Irma felt totally inadequate—unable to do anything worthwhile, unable to make friends, and unable even to date. She did take up with another boy who wanted only sex and had no consideration, let alone feeling, for her. She realized that she was not attracted to "square, substantial young men" like her father, who might make reliable husbands, but only to those "sadistic bums." A girl she knew suggested sharing an apartment conveniently located on Chicago's near North Shore; this Irma tried. For a period of time, then, she was out of the parental home, living in an apartment with another girl and earning a steady although sparse income with her typing. However, in her feelings, nobody at work or whom she knew anywhere had any respect for her (which is of course how she felt about herself), and Irma felt isolated, ineffectual, and close to no one. She hated her apartment mate because of the girl's success in work and also in attracting men, and as a reaction to this Irma became deeply depressed. The analytic task was to prevent suicide or gradual deterioration into a condition requiring hospitalization, i.e., total withdrawal from life.

This was not merely an incapacitating neurotic character, acting out neurotic patterns, nor was it a normal personality incapacitated by circumscribed depression and paranoia. This was so severe as to be a different category altogether. Irma might be called a "simple schizophrenic," but there was nothing obviously bizarre or primary process in her thinking or symptoms. She seemed to fit the category of a psychotic personality. She was as withdrawn as an ambulatory schizophrenic, but it was not possible to pin down definite psychotic symptoms. When the analyst talked to Irma's parents, they told him of a girl who had responded dramatically to a drug. This was before the great advent of numberless psychotropic drugs, but seemed worth trying; however, it turned out that the girl they mentioned was an overachiever, successful in a difficult, highly competitive field. This girl was a normal or, at worst, a neurotic personality with the drive to overachieve in contrast with Irma who felt that she could do nothing, that she was valueless and inadequate in every way, and therefore that everyone shared her dislike and lack of respect for herself.

Irma summarized the situation herself: "I am going to give up my job; I can't stand it, it is so boring. I see no one, I am not allowed out of the office to talk with anyone, and if I were allowed out there would be no one to talk with anyway. I want to get away from Chicago where everybody knows me for a loser, where they have no respect for me and I can't make any friends. But there is no place I can go alone. I wouldn't be able to do it alone and probably would break down completely or commit suicide. It is too late, I am over the hill. I would like to take a trip and get away from here and see some new scenes. But I can only go with my parents. I could not cope with anything alone. I am pathetic."

As to Irma's childhood dynamics, the main features seemed to have been physical illness plus some rejection and overcontrol, both interfering with her growth into independence and responsibility. She said that on an auto trip with her parents, they ordered her to stay in the back seat and say nothing. Of course they would not consider letting her do any of the driving. She related to older people slightly, but hardly at all to her peers, never having emerged from the parental nest. Yet a few people did phone her, and there seemed to be no complaints about her work on the job.

The vagueness of this clinical picture is not entirely due to the deficiencies of the authors' descriptive powers. In part, it represents the quality of Irma's personality. It is like trying to come to grips with fog: nothing sharp or definite, no steady object interest, self-identity, determination, or certainty.

This patient suggests that one way of judging whether a diagnosis of psychotic personality is correct is to consider the *end result*. If the characteristics that seem amiss became much worse, would the end result be only neurotic patterns or would it be psychotic manifestations? In Irma's case, it would be total withdrawal, most probably schizophrenic in nature with paranoid elements.

Irma exemplifies the absence of a tangible clear-cut severe disorder of the psychodynamics, and represents an apparent overall failure of development beyond the infantile passive dependence upon her parents into life among her peers. This is depicted by her first memory of lying ill in bed, looking out the window at the other children playing together.

Irma's psychopathology is of the type that suggests a *prenatal* regression—a psychology similar to that which occurs just after or even before birth. In effect, she seemed less able to form any human relationships than a newborn baby. Some infants are cuddly and responsive from birth, while others not only refuse to respond but even resist their mothers' attempts at fondling. This may antagonize the parents into reacting with anger and rejection, and a vicious circle develops. Some babies are born with a well-marked difficulty in making the psychological transition from intrauterine life to an emotional relationship with the mother, no matter how loving the mother might be.

Irma illustrates in extreme form the impairment of closeness which is illustrated in other vignettes and which we note is a characteristic of the psychotic personality. Warping of the sense of reality in Irma was unmistakable although less prominent than the incapacitating passive dependence and inability to tolerate closeness to others, including her own parents.

Therapeutically, Irma was kept going and even held simple, undemanding jobs, but she never achieved marriage or an adequate social life or career—she had to accept herself as she was.

Exhaustive medical studies revealed no physical abnormalities, but her analyst felt that some organic impairment could not be ruled out even though it could not be proven.

### FRANK: SWORD OF DAMOCLES

Here is an individual with psychodynamics similar to Irma's but quantitatively so much milder that he was able to function in society, although not independently. With dynamically based psychotherapy, he made much progress.

Frank was born to parents with marital difficulties. They loved him, however, and in trying to shield him from the tensions between them the parents unknowingly overprotected him to the extreme. Everything was done for Frank, everything was given him. This made him excessively passive and dependent, and also impeded the development of his sense of reality. Because the central reality of their troubles was shielded from Frank and because life never required him to come to grips with tasks or problems, he never fully recognized the reality or developed the responsibility for accomplishing tasks or solving problems. This was purely in his emotional orientation and not a matter of deficiency in intellectual comprehension, which was demonstrated by his excellent school record, including graduation from a college of high academic standing.

However, Frank was unable to make his own way in the world and was welcomed back home to relatively high position in his father's business. His father felt that he was saving Frank by giving him the job, doing only what a good, loving father should do for his son. In reality, Frank had been struggling to get along alone, far away from home, and needed only a small financial supplement while trying his own wings. To come home and draw a high income (almost without working) in a high-level position with his father tempted him into regression, into returning from trying for independence to more childish emotional dependence upon his parents, and it confronted him with tasks beyond his abilities. This increased his inferiority feelings, and he built up a whole area of his personality to deny these. If a sale amounted to a few hundred dollars he would increase it in his mind to a few thousand. He would waste hours on expensive and unnecessary long-distance phone calls because they made him feel important. He would arrange his father's important business trips, but then would often schedule his father to be either in the wrong city at the wrong time or else in two different cities at the same time. Obviously he was not a great help to his father or the business. However, when I discussed with Frank the possibility of his leaving the nest for a position elsewhere, backed up by an allowance from his father, he explained that it would be letting his father down, but that in six months or a year he would have the business in good enough shape for him to consider leaving. Whatever his incompetence, he was a sweet, generous young man with, as already stated, a high intelligence although a deficiency in his sense of reality. Tragically, he intensely wanted a girlfriend but was not attractive to women. He knew a few and tried to impress one with what a "big shot" he was. If she admired something in a shop window, he offered to buy it for her. He invited another girl to accompany him on a business trip with which his father had entrusted him. He insinuated the boast that he could have all the affairs he wanted but did not pursue them and really wanted to marry, ignoring the fact that he could not support himself let alone a wife. It was sad. The whole superstructure of his personality was based on the denial of his actual helplessness in the world and on the distortion of reality to demonstrate to himself and others that he was a strong, effective, successful businessman, ladies' man, and man-about-town. These narcissistic defenses, by distorting reality, worked so well for him that his helpless, passive dependence upon his parents did not cause intolerable feelings of inferiority, which in turn might have led to unremitting rage, the usual consequence. The rage is then usually turned to anxiety, phobias, paranoid trends, masochistic acting out, or other serious psychopathology.

Frank managed to live with these dynamics because he was in equilibrium in his father's business, protected by his father but with his self-esteem maintained by his prestigious position in the firm. However, he was alarmingly vulnerable because he lived by relying on a distorted sense of reality. Truth was a sword of Damocles over his head. It was a therapeutic task to tactfully and gradually acquaint him with the truth, by interpretation of his behavior, and to encourage him to move out of his parents' home and business, thereby helping him see and accept reality so that he might learn to make his own way in the world. No mammal can live out its entire adult life while continuing in childish dependence upon its parents without paying an exorbitant price in emotional disorder.

The degree of the regressive-passive dependence and of warping in his sense of reality makes Frank a psychotic personality. He cannot be called a simple neurotic character, but neither does he have a definite psychosis.

## LETTY: WITHDRAWAL WITH MASOCHISM

A simple marital problem was the reason Letty gave for coming to see the analyst. She was 22, blond, and sexy-looking; yet the analyst soon sensed that something was wrong in Letty's relationships with men, an idea that was reinforced when she related her complaints about her marriage.

Letty's husband had been a widower when she married him; he was 45, handsome, gentle, kind, considerate, and still a strong, virile personality who through his success as a builder was wealthy. The analyst (in several later interviews) found him most intelligent and attractive, interested in everything and widely read, with innumerable successful and interesting friends, a veritable paragon such as one rarely sees. Letty seemed to be a sex object for him, but little else. She could give him youth, femininity, sex, a keen practical sense, and affection, but she could not share his esthetic, intellectual, political, and other interests. Nevertheless, he was satisfied with his marriage, which seemed to complement the rest of his life. He engaged an excellent cook and a gardener who doubled as chauffeur. His only dissatisfaction was his knowledge that Letty was unhappy, but her unhappiness was not definable. Evidently Letty saw her husband's excellent qualities, yet she could not appreciate them or tolerate the marriage. Her background was too different and her husband was too different from her father.

Letty was the only child of lower-class parents. Her father was hardworking, but the tyrant of his household. The mother had sided with her husband, leaving Letty to bear the brunt of his rejection, his chronic anger, and his restrictive dictatorship. Letty's anger at her mother was mostly repressed because her mother was Letty's only refuge. Letty did not become aware of this hostility to her mother until years later, but she was partly conscious of her anger and rebellion against her father. She expressed this anger by staying away from home as much as possible. As she entered her teens, Letty could more easily act out her flight from home; to this she added angry rebellion in the form of occasional sexual relations with boys. Such activities led in later years to an affair which developed into her present marriage. She had a few close girlfriends whose psychodynamic makeups were similar to her own, and these friendships continued for a few years after Letty's marriage, but then gradually dwindled away.

All she told in later sessions fitted the obvious initial impression that she was continuing unconsciously toward her husband the childhood emotional pattern to her father of fear and defiance, hostility and escape. Her husband could not have been more gentle or more loving; in all, he was the direct opposite of her father. But such is the human lot that Letty's life was dictated by her childhood pattern (not by her paragon of a husband), and therefore to her the role of wife was like being trapped, just as she had been trapped as a child in her parents' home. The marriage became increasingly intolerable to her. Yet she was in no way whatsoever equipped to support herself independently in life. Although her intelligence seemed normal and adequate, she was untrained and lacking in any sustaining interest. She possessed two things—youth and beauty—but by now she had turned against sex, probably because of its guilty connection with hostility and rebellion against her father. She had become aware of this hostility, for better or worse, through analysis, but could not separate it out or reduce it. Letty had been in therapy in an attempt to free her from her pattern toward her father sufficiently for her to continue the marriage. Her husband built her the dream house she desired; she had a garden and a gardener; she enjoyed a beautiful swimming pool; a superb cook provided delicious meals. Ample spending money was available and Letty had the time to use it—the material world, such as it was, was at her disposal. Yet her mind worked daily on fleeing from it, into what could only be destitution, loneliness, insecurity, and isolation. She seemed to be a neurotic personality with masochism, who could be much helped by psychodynamic therapy. However, although capable of insight, Letty did not improve. The analyst wondered what he was missing; he watched the transference like a hawk, analyzing exhaustively the few dreams she related. Letty reacted to the analyst as to her mother, her refuge (however inadequate), and the repressed pattern toward her father was dictating her anxious, resentful reactions to her beautiful home and her excellent husband. Her analyst knew this, she knew it, her husband could see it. It was all discussed frankly and openly. Daily meetings were tried. Interruptions of treatment were tried. Top-notch analysts were consulted. Letty was always cooperative and always pleasant, but at last her husband could take the strain no longer and wanted to obtain the divorce which Letty had manipulated him into desiring. His final expression was not one of anger but of love: he nobly and generously made provision for a modest but comfortable annuity for the wife who had given him so little; Letty was adequately appreciative. Divorces so often bring out the worst in both partners, yet Letty and her husband were that rare pair who separate amicably; they continued their relationship as though they had pledged eternal friendship. He remarried, happily this time, a woman closer to him in age, background, and interests—a marriage based more on identification. He and the analyst had liked and respected each other since their first meeting, but lost contact once he was settled in his new marriage.

Letty continued to keep in touch with the analyst by phone. The little 22-year-old blonde had kept her figure but was now silverhaired, still living in Chicago. She would phone the analyst about once every month or two. Her two girlfriends of her premarital days had drifted away; Letty lived alone in the city. Her father had long since died. Her mother had been self-supporting and had worked steadily through the years, but now was getting old. It seemed natural for her and Letty to save money and alleviate each other's loneliness by living together instead of in separate apartments, so Letty arranged this. Gradually her mother (in person) and the analyst (as a voice on the telephone) came to be Letty's only human contacts. For a while she had done volunteer work in a hospital where she was able to fight for the underdogs, but then this too ended. She knew that she should get a job to provide some income and interest in her life and should have a daily routine to get her out of the apartment. However, despite her adequate intelligence, Letty proved totally incapable emotionally of taking a job. A part of the reason was, of course, the childhood pattern toward her father: she always felt trapped in the job as she had in her parental home and in her marital home. She did some traveling, but before long her anxiety on ship, train, or plane became too great and she could no longer leave her home. Her life was shrinking so that her contacts were limited to her mother and to a few dentists and doctors that Letty began seeing every few months for various complaints. Now her new home with her mother began to be worked into the childhood pattern. Since her income was assured, she could just as well live in Florida, Arizona, California, or any locale with a good climate rather than in the center of a large, crime-ridden, polluted city, usually excessively hot or penetratingly cold. Letty determined to make such a move and looked at places here and abroad, but never did leave. Because she still felt trapped and unable to escape, her repressed anger now mounted against her aged mother and at times was so intense that Letty feared one day she might even injure her. Her childhood pattern of repressed rage at her mother was emerging under the pressures of intimacy. At age 60, Letty found her life contracted to no more than it had been from birth to age six: she was living with her mother, had no friends among other women, no relationships with any man or men except those rare professional ones with her doctors or dentists. Her analyst had been in touch with Letty for 40 years and had seen how she lived her life, manipulating herself into almost complete isolation despite the initial advantages of youth, beauty, health, vigor, and intelligence.

It seemed as though Letty was not just a neurotic personality but her ego had been so swamped by her disordered childhood pattern that her sense of reality could perceive only a constricted life and her object interest was so slight that she was incapable of such sustained responsibility as is required by even the simplest work. She appeared in actuality to be a psychotic personality of a withdrawn masochistic type. Insofar as psychodynamic therapy had helped her, it had prevented her having an overt psychotic breakdown or else committing suicide. She had endured an isolated, empty life, but it was all she could accept, and if the purpose of life is only to live—if "they also serve who only stand and wait"—then to that modest extent, therapy had succeeded.

Letty, as we have said, had almost no close, intimate human relations throughout her life. In youth she had experienced some contact with other girls, and some sexual contact with boys, which was all she could achieve of closeness; in marriage she had tolerated a little transient closeness. Now her only relationship was with her mother, which kept her in a constant rage, and she was trying to end this contact by attempting to put her mother in a retirement home. Occasionally Letty would call the analyst to talk on the phone.

Letty's sense of reality seemed intact so far as it went, but the analyst always felt that something was not quite sound about it. Once during a telephone call something inappropriate showed through: Letty phoned in a rage, ranting and threatening to give money to a terrorist organization. Of course she never did this and she phoned back to apologize for this call, but it may have revealed a glimpse into a warping of her reality sense, being so contrary to her usual outlook and personality. Her degree of withdrawal from human relations was greater than that encountered in a neurotic personality and would alone indicate psychotic personality. In sum, Letty's behavior was characterized at the deepest level by (1) severe impairment in the ability to establish close intimate emotional relations (emotional isolation) and (2) by a repressed and suppressed distortion of the sense of reality (disturbed reality sense).

## BILL

Bill arrived at the analyst's door for his appointment with the news that his cat had recently delivered two kittens, and he ceremoniously handed over snapshots of the proud mother caring for them.

As the interview progressed, Bill related his various physical ailments: his kidney stones had been few and relatively painless, his asthma was presently absent but the allergy season was soon to come, and his chronic back pain only bothered him if he moved too vigorously. He continued to lead a "cautious" life with his usual emphasis on reading and experimenting with new cooking recipes. His social life was pretty well confined to his immediate family members. His tyrannical and alcoholic 70-year-old father still kept Bill at his beck and call, demanding to be chauffeured here and there at his slightest whim. Bill often ended up carrying his father up the stairs to his bedroom so he could pass out with maximum comfort. The analyst had long since abandoned previous attempts to rescue Bill from remaining a prisoner of his sadistic father, who had recently been admitted to a psychiatric hospital and diagnosed as having a chronic brain syndrome due to chronic alcoholism, including severe confusion with paranoia and Korsakoff's syndrome (disordered orientation and memory with hallucinations). It was a marvel that this formerly proud, hard-driving tycoon could have slipped into such severe psychopathology and still have remained titular head of his internationally known business. Bill disclosed that his father bullied his employees and fired them on impulse, but still had a few loyal associates who covered up for him, composing the confusion he created and urging him to take off more time. Bill's father had completely intimidated his family and most of his employees. They tolerated his vulgar, uncouth outbursts because he retained total control of their lives. His wife did occasionally escape his wrath, but at a price; she was of hearty, self-sufficient New England stock and had learned to stand alone, aloof from her tyrannical husband. Although accommodating him at times, she usually waited out "Big Bill's" moods with stoicism.

Toward the end of this interview, Bill offered his usual morbidly hostile, sadistic closing vignette: he had read a newspaper account of a small boy who somehow was trapped in the powerful jaws of a garbage truck's grinder, and this recalled a movie in which an escaped convict crawled into a metal garbage can that was then fed to a grinder. Bill wondered how frighteningly close the child felt to being pulverized into nothingness. This picture of a helpless child being sucked into a garbage grinder was the way Bill felt toward his destructive father. All his life Bill had been helpless and dependent on this powerful and often evil man.

Bill was overcome by his father; he could complain of "Big Bill's" demands and indiscretions, but to stand up to this intimidation was futile. Bill's spirit had been crippled and rendered ineffective. At 45 his only pleasures were taking care of cats, talking to plants, and cooking new dishes. He pretended not to be engulfed in the psychological quicksand. Bill thought his vacuous life was due to faulty biochemistry, and he had consulted many noted psychiatrists with expertise in both psychoanalysis and chemotherapy. He had tried on every known drug. His father labeled Bill a drug addict and had threatened any physician or druggist who would give him medication. When Bill was put in special treatment programs at the best psychiatric hospitals, he would apparently get addicted to the hospital and its staff and make no sustained progress. Instead he increasingly enjoyed the hospitalization while slowly regressing.

Interpretations about his anger toward his father and the world met with cordial denial and a grimaced sigh which seemed to say, "Leave me alone, I've had enough. Don't add insight to already existing injury." To become independent, away from his family, appeared dangerous, threatening, and plain impossible to this pathetic figure. Bill held to one hope: a miracle drug would be discovered that would transform him into a successful person. He knew his father would not live much longer but felt unable to prepare for the father's death. Bill lived in a fantasy world of his own making, full of sugarplums,

Christmas tree ornaments, and pretty flowers. Yet his mental status showed no sign of psychosis; he answered questions accurately and relevantly. He revealed a timid, anxious, tentative nature with naive attempts to ingratiate himself with everybody.

Bill's life clearly showed the source of his problems in the pathetic, robot-like obedience to a tyrranical father. His emotional life had been so warped that Bill appears as a psychotic personality. His narcissism consisted of total self-absorption camouflaged as self-denial, sacrifice, and martyrdom, with shallow, barely existent, unsustainable relationships. Never having been able to derive enough strength from his mother, siblings, teachers, friends, or therapists to develop his own identity, Bill endured a wasted life as a mere survivor in a world he perceived as monopolized by his destructive father. He was unable to sustain enough interest in any area outside himself to systematically pursue a goal.

Bill was almost totally devoid of human relationships, his only one being the hated masochistic contact with his father. His reality sense was distorted by his feelings into the single hope that a miracle drug would be invented to transform him into a successful person.

# 10
# FIVE TYPES OF PARANOID-HOSTILE BEHAVIOR

## ELSIE: DIFFUSE PARANOID TYPE

Elsie was 40 years old; short, vital, and energetic; with olive skin and dark hair and eyes; alert, intelligent, and capable. She had been badly deprived in childhood. Her mother died and her father showed no interest in her. She came to see an analyst because she thought her husband needed help in getting over being so difficult to live with. When asked to tell a little about her own daily life she rambled on about as follows:

"There was a slight leak in a radiator. The plumber said he would come right over, but it was two days before he appeared. He at first gave me the idea that he only had to tighten a nut. But then he said that he had to replace a part. And the water in the house was turned off for three or four hours.

"I bought a dress. But when I got it home, it was a different shade than what it looked like in the store. The store really should have enough daylight or lights similar to daylight so that you can see what you are buying.

"My cousin, Wilma, and I used to be close. I wrote her a month ago and have not heard a word from her. That is no way to treat a friend and relative.

"My husband is supposed to be home in time to have a cocktail and eat dinner at six. But for the last few weeks he comes in late with all sorts of excuses about the demands of his business. How can I run a home that way?

"I read in the paper the other day that the hour when husbands are unfaithful is usually after work, while on the way home. Maybe he is late because he is having an affair with another woman. In fact,

I even have an intuition as to whom she might be. . .she is married and has children. That keeps it from being too hot and heavy. But just suppose her husband died. Then she would go for my husband and I would really be threatened."

The incongruity of fearing the death of the fantasied "other woman's husband" instead of concern with her own husband's health, since he worked long hours with little recreation or relaxation, provided a clue to the irrational elements in her outlook. She was completely rational and realistic in details but the trend was to feel abused. It soon became evident that this trend, only slight in the first interview, went deep, pervaded her entire emotional life, and at times reached such intensity that she attacked her husband physically. The start of analytic work seemed to mobilize this trend in a rather alarming degree, and it was found that her emotional intensity could be diluted if the analyst saw both Elsie and her husband (which also eased her narcissistic wound by her feeling that her husband needed help rather than she). The marital relationship improved, but the calm was like that of a quiescent volcano.

Elsie was strong and vigorous, very much in command. There was no overall withdrawal with regression to helpless, childish, passive dependence. What was prominent, rather, was the childhood trauma and its permanent aftereffects in her pathodynamics. These factors are similar to those in the cases of John Orbison (Chapter 11) and of Wynne (Chapter 13), but not so extreme, and they took a paranoid form which was subtle and diffuse, as seen in her feeling abused and put upon by not only her husband but also her cousin, the dress shop, and the plumber ("the butcher, the baker, and the candlestick maker").

It quickly appeared that Elsie had almost no warm feelings toward her long-suffering husband, but only much hostility, and no close relations with anyone. She stayed in the marriage for practical reasons of finances and her reputation, but also (unconsciously) because this was the only human relation she had, tenuous though it was. She cared about no one and nothing but her own feelings. Elsie's reality sense was warped by her paranoia, into which she had no insight, yet she had no psychotic symptoms. She could be diagnosed a psychotic personality.

## URSULA

In petite, raven-haired Ursula's particular mixture of rationality and flagrantly psychotic personality, these elements were so intimately entwined as to make them almost inseparable. She had come to see the analyst only once, but would then sporadically phone, beginning in a completely realistic and reasonable tone but, after 15 or 20 minutes of talking like a broken record, going over the same ideas endlessly, getting nowhere. It did not seem to matter if the analyst ended the call sooner or later, if he listened for 20 minutes or two hours, it was always the same: invariably she felt rejected and, at some point, would become enraged and hang up on him. Many times she was invited to come in for an appointment to see if a face-to-face meeting could help work through this pattern, but she refused. Finally the analyst told Ursula that he knew the calls were going nowhere and he was too busy to talk further with her. She phoned about three or four times a year. On one occasion, Ursula phoned and then made a repeat call, to tell the analyst that her sister had been listening in on another phone to the first call to find out the analyst's opinion of Ursula. He in turn reminded Ursula that he had been trying for a long time to tell her exactly what his opinion was, and her ruse was totally unnecessary.

One point was clear: *however realistically and reasonably she started off, as soon as the least emotion arose in her, Ursula's sense of reality was excessively distorted by it, in a psychotic, not neurotic, manner, so that rational conversation became impossible.*

Ursula had been making her phone calls to more than one analyst. One evening, after he had experienced a long, hard day, Dr. A was relaxing with a book before bed when she called:

PATIENT: Hello—this is Ursula. How are you?
ANALYST: [Greeting her with warmth] Hello! I'm just over the flu, and how are you? I'm glad to get caught up, but it is late and I am tired. So please try to fill me in in ten minutes. I hope you do not feel rejected by that request.
P: I do! Anyway, I have a new psychiatrist. [She had by then seen six or eight the analyst knew of and complained to each one about the other.]

A: Do I know him?

P: I doubt it. His name is Dr. T. He is away for six weeks' vacation and referred me to Dr. Jane Smith, a woman psychiatrist who is covering for him. She slipped up and let me know that she thinks I will not be helped by psychiatry. I think she may be right—I want your opinion. I've been seeing psychiatrists for 15 years and have spent a fortune, $50 per week. Now I'm 45 years old... give me your opinion.

A: Ursula I only saw you once, maybe twice.

P: Once.

A: And that was almost 15 years ago. I do not think it would be proper or ethical to give an opinion on that basis on the phone.

P: But what do you really think?

A: I really think that it is a very proper question...you have not been helped over all these years and you've made a large investment of time and money. . . .

P: And emotional strain.

A: That too. Now Dr. T must know Dr. Jane Smith well if he has asked her to cover for him. How about her raising this question you've asked with Dr. T, having a professional talk about it, as they both know you and are seeing you presently?

P: I've already asked Dr. T that. I even accused him of telling me that he can help me because he wants to hold onto me as a patient, to get my money.

A: How long does he estimate that it will take for you to improve?

P: He says nine months to a year and a half.

A: [Knowing the futility of trying to deal with the realistic, but also knowing Ursula's rage if he were to mention her anger at her therapist for taking a vacation] Then why not try to get his opinion of you, and if you are not satisfied try seeing him for another two or three months before coming to a final decision?

P: Well, I saw a loi of other psychiatrists and some were even analysts...they did not all turn out so well; Dr. T simply told me that he was going on vacation for six weeks and sent me to Dr. Jane Smith. Another analyst, Dr. Y, whom I saw 15 years ago, would have told me where he was going and to phone him if I needed him. He was a lot warmer.

A: That is why your question to me seems legitimate, although I cannot tell you any more about it now. You have already seen some very good, well-trained, dedicated, and able men.

P: But not Dr. Z! He was awful.

A: [Risking the interpretation] Ursula, there is no use arguing about Dr. Z, whom you saw ten years ago. We are getting away from your original point. . .perhaps you only phoned me after all these years because Dr. T is away. If so, I have responded.

P: Did you know about my childhood, how I was rejected by my mother? And abused sexually for four years? That is why Dr. Smith said I could not be helped. . .did you know that?

A: Ursula, you know I like you and respect you, but it is late and you know the trouble with our phone calls; they get off the point, which I think is your anger at feeling rejected by Dr. T, and go on and on. Even if I stay on the phone for two full hours, in the end you feel rejected and go into a rage at me. . . .

P: [Interrupts] That is the most insulting thing I ever heard in my life! [Bam! She hung up in a rage.]

It had never made a difference in what manner the analyst handled the calls from Ursula; he might have sympathetically interpreted her turning to him for help because Dr. T was on vacation, and because her feelings of rejection and rage toward her mother might make a woman psychiatrist intolerable as a replacement for Dr. T. Yet in the past, the most careful, tactful interpretation had never quieted her, any more than the opposite tack, shunning all emotion and holding assiduously to just the facts and the obvious reality. Unless Ursula met an analyst with a personality perfectly suited to her psychopathology, one especially experienced and skilled in the therapy of the psychotic personality, she would continue exactly as she had for another 15 years. Nonetheless, any bit of help she did not reject would enable her to carry on in society—without it, she might slip into an actual psychosis and require hospitalization. She seemed incapable of sustained office treatment, clinging only to the sporadic, angry phone calls.

The process of analytic psychotherapy is in large part the "analyzing out" of the transference relations to the therapist (the most disturbing of the patient's feelings toward the analyst—dependent, sexual, competitive, hostile, anxious, etc.). This could not be accomplished with Ursula. Her ego was not strong and realistic enough to maintain control of her feelings, and there were not sufficient good feelings between Ursula and any of her analysts (therapeutic alliance) to work on the realities of her dynamics. There must be some firm area in the ego, like an island of dry land, to be used as a reliable, realistic base for winning over more and more of the passions of childhood which are disrupting the feelings, thinking, and behavior of the adult. Ursula was 45 years old, and none of the analysts had succeeded in establishing such rapport as a base. It was swept away by every emotional tide; the disrupting feelings could never be "analyzed out," leaving a good easy relationship or even a tolerable one.

Ursula had little or no realistic grasp of her situation: with no good human relations in her life, she clung to the tenuous contacts with her analysts, and was absorbed with her own complaints and memories of past wrongs done her. She was not sane, rational, and responsible, but neither was she overtly psychotic, although this element was diffused in her thinking and behavior. While she was healthy physically, highly intelligent, and attractive, she was a tragic figure. Everything including hospitalization had been tried, but all was futile.

### DANIEL THORPE: PARANOID-PASSIVE-HOSTILE

Daniel Thorpe had always been suspicious of everyone, including his wife, son, and daughter. He was a successful businessman who had developed a large company. Although his company was to be left to his son, a mathematician at the University of Chicago, Daniel never let his son learn the business he was to inherit and operate. He forced his son to take his advice and hold on to some stocks and bonds instead of selling and diversifying. They declined and resulted in a total loss. Daniel's son lived near the university and had to waste untold hours traveling to the northern suburbs to keep in touch with his father, who not only distrusted his wife but was irritated by her; when he was ill at home, he was not above going into a pet and overturning a lunch tray she had brought him.

After an abdominal operation, Daniel was bedfast. His lawyer tried to explain the importance of his signing a power of attorney for his son so that the business could be kept running, but the old man refused.

His business was in danger of disintegrating completely before the doctor in charge of his case got Thorpe to sign.

Possibly impaired cerebral circulation had weakened his mental powers, but he was simply expressing more freely personality characteristics that had been present all his life. He eventually signed the power of attorney under skillful pressure from his physician and higher-ups in his business. Yet he had been a successful businessman who should have made arrangements long before and not waited until he was nearly 80 years of age. Now Thorpe's son did at least have power of attorney and could legally attempt to save the company, but he also could not jeopardize his meager income from his university position to grapple with a complex business he had been prevented from learning about in depth. Thorpe's suspiciousness and inaction had now brought the business and its hundreds of employees and their families to the brink of disaster.

A review of Thorpe's personality characteristics included: distant, suspicious, almost nonexistent human relations with his wife, son, daughter, and business managers; ignoring the welfare of his employees, as well as that of his immediate family, and deliberate rejection of appropriate measures to take reasonable care of those dependent upon him even in the event of his death. Thus it seemed that these and other lifelong idiosyncrasies really betokened a mildly psychotic personality of a paranoid, passively hostile type. Meager as the data are here, this case illustrates a certain type of condition. This person just barely misses (we hope) achieving his psychotic goals in his lifetime—that is, the financial destruction of his business and, through it, the destruction of his employees, his wife, his son and daughter, and their families. He provides a good example of rational process being used to serve definitely irrational, infantile, psychotic goals—goals that are hostile, paranoid, and destructive in nature. All his life he had been withdrawn, even from his wife, children, and business associates, excessively narcissistic and unrealistic, even in planning for the business. All this was a regressive part of his personality; the rest of his personality was aggressively efficient in his own self-interest.

## LUKE: CRIMINOID TYPE

Luke was 65 years old. In a way, his life had been a success. He had graduated from a high-ranking technical school and done well

enough with a big company in technical work. He was unspontan-
eous and even rather withdrawn socially, and had no conversation
except in technical subjects.

Luke met Rosemary, a social worker aged 45, who was raising
her two teenage sons alone, after a divorce ten years earlier. Luke
was also divorced and had been alone for ten years. His wife had had
a psychosis and been committed to a mental hospital, where she
died soon after. He was estranged from his daughter, a grown and
divorced woman. Luke lived alone in a large house cluttered with
the accumulated junk of decades. Here and there was an occasional
fine piece, such as a cherry wood cabinet, but mostly the contents
were valueless, the junk a normal person would have long since discarded to keep the house uncluttered. Luke claimed that all the
pieces had sentimental value, such as a rusted old dustpan and its
worn-out brush. Against one wall in the living room stood eight
rotting window frames. There were some sticks such as one might
pick up after a storm in clearing the lawn. There were three old,
cracked toilet bowls.

Luke courted Rosemary persistently. Although the most modest
of people, her feminine vanity had to be flattered by his courtship;
she hoped to assuage the loneliness she felt at being both father and
mother to two teenagers, nor could she deny the desire to have a
man in the house again and to be relieved of some of the burden
of breadwinning.

Yet Luke's courtship was unsettling: she would sometimes angrily
ask her friends, "Why doesn't Luke leave me alone and go away?
He's an ugly-looking, unattractive old man; I have my little family
and my job—life is difficult but we are content. Why doesn't he just
leave us alone?"

"Then why not end your relationship?" friends would ask. Rosemary had to admit she was angry with herself, because she was fighting the temptation to give in and marry Luke. In her naiveté and
need, she put down Luke's strange accumulation of junk and disordered house as mere idiosyncrasies, growing out of the poor man's
living alone for ten years.

Then summer was over, winter began to worsen. Rosemary's son
fell accidently and broke his arm; her daughter did brilliantly in school
but was unhappy: Rosemary herself came down with the flu. Luke
increased the pressure: Why should she struggle like this at age 45

when he had plenty of money? He insisted that she resign from her job, marry him, and let him support the family. She was sturdy of body, mind, and character, but only human. Close friends could see her weakening and advised her to at least make a premarital financial agreement if she remarried: "If you resign your job, you may never at your age get another. The social agencies can get a talented young woman half your age for half your salary. What will you and the children live on if the marriage doesn't work? . . .Get the agreement, hard as it may be for you." She mentioned this to Luke and he agreed, but Rosemary was too embarrassed to follow through on it.

She planned to finish out the year at work and marry Luke the following June. Her next step was predictable: winter set in early, she often had to work after hours, she could not prepare proper dinners for her children or for Luke, who spent all day at her house, although he went home at night to sleep. Why should she struggle on like this when they were going to marry anyway? So the wedding took place just before Christmas.

There are those who sincerely and stoutly maintain that marriage is no more than a brief ceremony of no particular consequence. Yet examples to the contrary abound: a pretty girl of high intelligence and superior ability "goofed" in her first marriage, then lived successively after that with two different men and had, she said, complete orgastic gratification. She then fell in love with a man for whom she forsook all others, living with him faithfully for over a year with complete sexual response and fulfillment. When his divorce became final, they married. No sooner was their union sanctioned by state and church than she felt a subtle change in her desires. Although they had been living together for more than a year, on her wedding night when she lay with this man she loved and who fully gratified her, she lost all desire. He was furious, but he loved her and wanted children, so the marriage rocked along.

As another example, a handsome couple went together and slept together for over a year, then decided to make the arrangement legal. They went through the conventional procedure with all the usual trimmings, but no sooner was the ceremony over than the groom lost his previously strong sexual interest and became a helpless little boy, regressing from independence and genital sex to childish dependence, unable to make a decision or take any action without his wife's direction and support.

In the case of Luke and Rosemary, it was not she who regressed, but Luke. No sooner had he moved into her apartment than Luke regressed into domination and miserliness. He "presided" at meals but in silence. He stuffed himself while complaining that the children ate too much. He took over all the shopping because he said he could do it more cheaply than Rosemary, but his method included purchasing food in damaged cans. Rosemary feared this risked food poisoning. Gradually Luke took over the whole of Rosemary's little apartment; he was retired and had no use for a desk, yet he moved his big desk into one of the rooms and then littered it with such useless articles as had once glutted his own home. The clutter spread to Rosemary's basement and then throughout the apartment. Now that Luke had achieved his objective of marrying Rosemary, he rapidly regressed into what he unconsciously wanted, namely, to be the little boy again in a family with a strong mother, but he could not bear the relationship.

Finally, Luke cluttered their bedroom to the point that Rosemary moved out, leaving her own bed to sleep on the couch in the living room, where she finally took her stand. Luke kept the four of them living on much less that what Rosemary and the children has been used to when she was working. It was more than they could stand, but when Rosemary voiced any objections, he threatened to leave. Once he did just that: he went back to his own big house still crammed with the miscellaneous junk. That was a relief to them all, but he stopped paying Rosemary's bills. She reasoned and pleaded with him and Luke did return, but now he felt he had the upper hand and became even more controlling, dominating, and miserly, filling the house with more and more useless clutter. When Rosemary again complained, he returned to his own home but left the mess behind. This time she did not try to get him back. She could stand him no longer.

Rosemary applied everywhere for aid but she got nothing. She saw a lawyer who tried to obtain a court order for support. Luke had written a letter to Rosemary's mother asking her to urge Rosemary to give up her job and marry him. This was solid evidence, but the Judge awarded Rosemary a meager few dollars a month. She was reduced to destitution.

While job hunting, Rosemary moved the worst of the junk, the ugliest and the dirtiest, from her apartment into the garage. Luke began to appear when she was not home to take things out, not just his things but hers too. She changed the locks. Then one day, Luke drove up accompanied by a van in which were a male sheriff, a female sheriff, and two other men. He had a court order for which he had put up a bond of seven thousand dollars. In his hand was a list of every item he claimed. Rosemary could do nothing. It was late afternoon, her lawyer was in court and could not be reached. Rosemary could only watch and weep, and ask the men carrying out her furniture, "We have so little. . .why must he take away even that?" They loaded up the sleeping bag which before marriage Luke had given her son, who now loved it, and the sewing machine to which she was now attached. Luke carried out the toaster, which he had picked up somewhere, persuading Rosemary to replace her own toaster with it. Therefore it was included on Luke's list as *his*. Then came a little table which Rosemary had scraped down and refinished, a chair she had reupholstered, and a small chest she had scraped down and polished, and so on—all on Luke's list as "his."

All the while, Luke's face wore a look of rage and determination. His victims were down and he was set on knocking them out. The two sheriffs were openly sympathetic with Rosemary, refusing to let Luke take some of the things whether they were on his list or not. They said loudly, "We sure hate doing this," while Rosemary whispered, "Can't I give him just one good punch?"

Several months later Rosemary could no longer pay even her most urgent bills and asked Luke to send money to tide her over the next few months. He refused a cent. Before they had married, he had told her that money was no problem, that he had plenty. Now desperate, Rosemary took one of the very few worthwhile pieces Luke had left in the apartment, a chest of drawers which she had stripped of paint and refinished, and sold it to an antique dealer to get money for food. Somehow, Luke found out about it and started a lawsuit against her to try to take the apartment from her. He could afford a lawyer but she could not. What vagaries of the law permit a husband to sue his wife and take her apartment because of a chest of drawers? Rosemary tried her best to locate the chest. Luke included in his charges "the anguish she has caused me."

All Luke's reasonableness, his wish for companionship in his lonely existence, his wish to relieve Rosemary of the burden of working and providing for her sons—all his rationality—was in the service of a malignant, infantile pattern of acquisition, control, hate, and destructiveness. He had always been a loner and had never sustained any good or close human relations. Perhaps he had been attracted to his first wife because she was a latent psychotic personality like himself, or maybe she broke down under his own psychotic personality, which is what was stated in her hospital record. Luke belonged to the same church as Rosemary, and during the year of their courtship and marriage he had suddenly volunteered many services for the care of the church. Now Luke used the church to talk against Rosemary, complaining of how she had "mistreated" him. He was committing crimes *within* the law—that is, he was a "criminoid" personality. His unimpaired reason was being used in every way to destroy Rosemary. His goals were infantile, irrational, hostile, paranoid ones. Was Rosemary a masochistic character? She may well have been, but if so, she was neurotic, not a psychotic personality.

Luke was the kind of man who seemed never to have been young. Rosemary spoke with his mother who told her that Luke was such a "good" baby. He would lie in his crib, never crying or causing trouble. Later, he saved every penny, but as he approached adolescence his mother said he became "so combative" that she worried he would have an unhappy life, and said that reluctantly she decided that she would have "to break him."

What is apt to happen to Luke if his symptoms intensify? Will there be more hostile, possibly paranoid or criminoid, behavior? If he should get worse, he would probably not commit suicide, for his self-love and self-absorption are too great. Would he attack someone then? Probably not, because his superego is too rigid, as seen in his life as a prudish goody-goody who never had a sexual adventure and never permitted himself or his wife even a glass of wine.

All Luke has permitted himself is his hostility, if he can rationalize it. Between the poles of fight and flight, probably all that is open to him is flight, and this most likely accounts for his withdrawal from all human relations into an eremitical existence within this big, messy house, overflowing with inanimate objects of "sentimental value" to him. This withdrawal might go so far as a schizophrenic type of regression with some depression, and although his defenses have held during his life so far, his repressed hostility, if events mobilize it further, might well generate some psychotic symptoms. He seems already latently paranoid toward Rosemary. If her financial situation improves enough for her to afford an aggressive lawyer and not be forced by penury to endure his technical legal attacks, he might go over the line. However, she (no doubt wisely) chose to forget about Luke and did get another position in her field; each of them returned to the same existence as before this marital misadventure.

Certainly Rosemary did not handle all this in the best way, but the picture of Luke is correct and clear: he was a man who made his way in the world but was partially fixated at an infantile level; he had twice attempted the intimacy of marriage but could not tolerate closeness and withdrew from all human relations into a miserly hermit-like existence. Perhaps the closest he came to human relations was in his fantasies connected with his "things" and the complete absorption with himself into which all his libido was drawn. His sense of reality was distorted, at least as to his goals. His eremitical existence was the only evidence for psychotic elements until they eventually coalesced under the pressures of his marriage to Rosemary and found expression in his feeling, thinking, and behavior.

## A CASE OF REHABILITATION

Molly is a somewhat atypical case of the successful rehabilitation of a 13-year-old, highly criminal, Caucasian, urban girl. She was institutionalized following two years of delinquent antisocial behavior which culminated in her being convicted of manslaughter for drowning a three-year-old boy. She admitted responsibility for the drowning but excused herself by saying that she had been under the influence of drugs. She spent 23 months in a correctional institution where she made progress in assuming more personal responsibility for her actions. She had weekly interviews with the consulting analyst at the institution and more frequent interviews with a mature, caring female social worker. She went to live with her mother, who had moved to a new community and settled down. Molly returned to school and seemed to have changed substantially. Then she met a young man of 20 who had a regular job and they were married when she was 17 years old. Their first child was born prematurely and died 24 hours after birth; Molly felt despondent but bounced back and a year later had another child, a son. He too, was born prematurely but managed to survive. Molly kept in touch with the analyst and in a letter reported that after five years she was happily married with two children. She described how her young family was doing such normal things as buying a car on time, taking a week's vacation at a lake, and bowling with friends.

There are some significant points about Molly: she was raised as an only child; her two older half-sisters never lived in the same home with Molly. Both her father and her mother had been married previously, and Molly was their only child together; she felt very close to her father even though he was in the army and stationed away from home much of the time. Her earliest memories were of happiness when her father returned home. He was killed in an accident when Molly was seven. Her mother was a large, earthy woman who was much given to drink and the company of men; after her second husband's death she and an old boyfriend moved into a trailer. Molly was fond of this man and he partially made up for her departed father, but he left them after a fight with Molly's mother, at a time when Molly was ill. Another man whom she despised then moved in with them. The mother and her new paramour would drink too much, argue, and then have physical fights in which Molly tried at first to physically protect her mother, only to find it made things worse, so she stayed away and avoided these daily clashes. She began playing truant from school and became involved with older teenagers who were experimenting with drugs and sex. Her personality changed to being a tough, aggressive street child with no respect for authority, and when she did attend school she was both rude and provocative to the teachers, even beating one up. The principal of her school wrote this a month before the drowning of the three-year-old boy: "Molly has been in a detention home twice already this year. She wants to be placed in an institution to get away from her mother and her mother's boyfriend. She literally hates her home and consequently has a terrible 'I don't care' attitude. She takes money from children on the street and hangs around with gangs of boys."

When she was institutionalized, Molly explained the drowning of the child this way: "I had been using some speed and LSD and had some bad flashbacks. That day I just smoked some pot and felt pretty good. I saw this four-year-old kid who I liked and offered to buy her some ice cream, but her three-year-old brother kept hanging around and I told him to get lost. He kept following us when we walked down to the river. I got anry and yelled at him and he started to cry, which made me madder, so I shoved him toward the river and walked away with his sister. Then things went blank and I just remember a lot of people and police and his body wrapped in a blanket."

At first Molly showed no feelings of guilt about the drowning or about anything else. Her affect was either flat or angry. She did reveal how she "always got beat up as a kid" which "made it OK to beat up other kids." Her psychological tests showed that she hated herself and everybody else, especially her mother. Her mother had always told her that she had a devil in her (a good example of resorting to fantasy rather than seeing the reality), and now Molly thought maybe that was really the case, so she either stayed to herself or physically fought with any of her peers who sought to intrude into her world. The little girl in her was never in evidence, and her facade of being tough, unfeeling, hateful, and vindictive was always predominant. Only very slowly and tentatively could she show another side.

Much to everyone's surprise, Molly asked to work with young children in the institution's summer camp. At first the staff was afraid to let her near the young children, but she persisted and finally was allowed to be a counselor under strict supervision: she did an excellent job, being strict but fair, and all the children liked being with her. Molly's anger then focused on how unfair it was to keep her institutionalized for so long and this anger led her to run away. She always turned herself in to the authorities after a few days. She became closer to her social worker, who was divorced with two children, and in time Molly felt herself a part of this family. As her anger and defensiveness lessened, she was taken on excursions by her mother (who had broken up with the despised paramour) and by the social worker.

She became more trusting as she was trusted more and learned to talk about her feelings other than anger and hate. During her AWOLs and visits home she developed a relationship with a tough, rather sadistic young man who everybody told her was undesirable. When she returned to live with her mother after 23 months spent in the institution, Molly showed definite improvement, but the staff agreed the prognosis remained guarded as to whether she would reestablish her criminal behavior. She voluntarily terminated the relationship with the undesirable and sadistic young man, and formed a friendly relationship with her mother. Molly wrote the social worker positive letters of appreciation for all that had been done for her, giving glowing reports of her better adjustment in the community and at school; in subsequent letters she reported meeting her husband-to-be, feeling love for him, and ultimately marring him when she was 17. Molly was young but determined to make the marriage work and to create a happy family. This she seemed to have accomplished, despite the death of her first child at birth and the lingering memories of what had occurred in her youth—the killing of a young child and being institutionalized as a hostile, angry, bitter, and hurt youngster. She might well have become a chronic criminal personality, shut off from any tender, caring feelings for others—the fate of other juveniles with similar experiences and attitudes who are so filled with hate that they never recover from it. Probably it was Molly's early good relationship with her father that saved her, and the fact that her mother, although she often disappointed and hurt Molly, always seemed to care for her. Without these good early relationships she could not have established the good feelings toward her social worker which led to her gradually feeling a part of her family, and to Molly's eventual marriage. Without such a caring and understanding woman who was not discouraged by Molly's resistance, Molly might have remained a psychotic personality, criminal type. A turning point may have been just after the child's death, when Molly thought she might have a "devil" in her, and stayed by herself or physically fought with any peers who sought to intrude into her world. Her relations with her parents in childhood, however, were close enough and good enough so that she did not continue or sink deeper into this regressive withdrawal, and therefore did not permanently remain a psychotic personality.

# 11
# REACTIVE, WITH PSYCHOSIS
# AND SUICIDE: JOHN ORBISON

John Orbison was a handsome young man. He had a fine athletic build, raven-black hair, and brown eyes, softened by an almost cherubic smile.

When asked for his chief complaints, he said, "Tension, anxiety, fears that I will lose my mind and what my doctor calls 'paroxysmal tachycardia,' and fears that I will die. Also drinking too much alcohol." He then stressed confidentiality, saying that his father was unaware of John's coming to see an analyst.

[At this point we must consider that if this patient is only a neurotic character, the fear of losing his mind and of dying are no more than common symptoms of anxiety which should be diminished and eventually should disappear with good, accurate psychodynamic therapy. Usually it is in part a reflection of repressed hostility and guilt. If, however, John Orbison is a psychotic personality, then these may be real fears and the patient may indeed break down into a psychosis and may in fact attempt suicide.]

The analyst said, 'Of course that cuts both ways. . .I will tell no one of your being here or what we discuss, but I think for the time being and until we discuss it and decide on something different, you also should not say anything about your visits to me."

John continued: "I have been under great strain since the age of 14. . .I am caught in the middle. Father leans on me. When I wanted to get work and be independent and make my own way, Father said, 'No you can do that later, you should spend a little time with me.' So I went with Father to St. Louis where he kept an apartment; he drank a lot, had women and fun, but I often saved Father from dying of exposure. Finally I just left. I got a job as a salesman here in Chicago and was successful. A friend and I decided to start a company

166

of our own; I held 43 percent of the stock. I needed 15 thousand dollars to get 51 percent of the stock, but Father, who would not have missed this amount, refused to give it to me, and as a result I lost it all. This was because of my friend! I almost had a nervous breakdown.

"This past week was terrible—there were two divorces in the family. My father had been fine about not drinking too much, but then about a week ago he and I were in the Loop and he insisted that I drink with him. I refused, and Father said if I did not, then he would really 'lay one on,' so I felt I had to drink with him. But I was attacked by the family for doing so; one of the women in the family actually hit me. I do not want to get into alcohol; I don't like it; I do not find it an escape except occasionally. I want and like to be sober; I like to play tennis and golf and go hunting.

"Then Father left town suddenly, but I knew where he was. I'm always the one Father turns to, 'Good Old John,' but Father never expresses one word of approval for my work or any of my successes, and never even inquires how things are going. He has never come to see my office. My job is a good one, and I think should start me on a satisfying career. My wife is a fine girl even though we have some problems in our marriage. But my tensions are mostly with Father. There is no emotional support or anything else from him, yet I feel a loyalty to him, as though I must take care of him."

The analyst discussed with John whether he was too involved with his father and his parental family to be satisfactorily oriented to his adult interests: his job, his wife, and his children. He was asked tentatively if it was not time now for him to be independent. He ducked this and said that the paroxysmal tachycardia started two years previously: his pulse jumps to over 200 and his blood pressure rises. The worst attack lasted four hours and he passed out.

"It seems," the analyst said, "that you excessively drive yourself, but if you take things easier you are bored and depressed. It is possible that you make yourself fail, and in this conflict you become tense, drink too much alcohol even though you dislike it, and your blood pressure goes up? Could an element in this be that, although you are now adult with a wife and your own business, you want more dependent satisfaction, more emotional support from your father than you get, and also more recognition and appreciation from him than you get, and these are all to some degree frustrated which makes you angry and you turn this pent-up anger on yourself as masochism?"

John said, "When my five-years-younger sister was born, my brother and I reacted strongly because she was on the scene and a girl—we all soon agreed that she was Father's favorite. Even today Father listens to her, respects her, loves her. If Father ever broke up with Louise, our sister, he would probably go to pieces. Louise was number one in his eyes and I was number two; Louise was terribly spoiled until the age of two. She was aggravated by Brother and me teasing her, and she cried to get attention. Then Father would hit Brother and threaten me. Of course, Louise learned to cry even if Brother and I were doing nothing to her. Father showed no interest in my sister Jean, who is three years younger than Louise. Jean knows he has no interest in her and it hurts her because it is so obvious. Louise has a personality like Father, completely independent. She doesn't care whether Brother, myself, or anyone else has guests present or not, she does whatever she pleases, tells anyone to go to hell if she feels like it. Father gave her a whole lot of parties from the age of ten on. Then he complained of all the money he spent on her. He gives her expensive jewelry, but he gives me no money at all. When I was a kid I used to ask for ten dollars to take a girl out on a date, and he wouldn't give it to me. . .I would have to explain who the girl was, all the details, and so on.

"Father, who lives in a northern suburb, tried to keep me with him in St. Louis. When I was young he objected to me being with boys and girls my own age; he objected to my working. I couldn't move without Father. Not until I went out and got my own job. . . .I gave up the drinking and women and got my own job, something every father should be proud of, but my father was hostile to me. I saw that I could not stay with him; I would be pulling him out of bars, that kind of thing, and for that I would get no thanks at all, but when he went on the wagon and did not drink he was crazy." [The needs for his father's love and the underlying rage at him were obvious.]

Asked for his first memories, John said, "The first one is at about age two or three. We were down at the shore. Father lit a firecracker and it exploded, hurting his hand. [Is this not hostility to Father?]

Second memory, also between ages two and three: I got up at night and groped for the bathroom and fell down a whole flight of steps. [Is this masochistic?] The third memory was probably between three and four: Father took us to a farm. He took me on the train, but not my older brother. He gave me candy and I got it all over myself and the train. [Is this wanting attention and affection from Father, plus hostility to him coming out masochistically?] My fourth memory is of the same age, in the country at a farm where Father was close to a woman there." [Is this oedipal envy of Father plus jealousy, plus feeling rejected by Father for a woman?]

In response to further questioning, John proceeded to give more of his history, "My mother was a wonderful, warm person, but she—or possibly my father—kept me in curls and dresses until I was age four, even though I objected. From the time I was born until about age five, I had much attention from Father and Mother, mostly Father, and I was much attracted to my nurse. But I had some resentment about being cared for by a nurse. I was dressed up and then brought down by her to play. I was extremely close to my brother. I am now 32 years old, and he is two years older than I; we slept in the same room. Brother had a problem with Father much more than I did. Now they are not on speaking terms, and what Brother feels for Father is just pure hate.

"I was moody even then; either very gay or depressed. I would cry and Mother or Father would come, but I was afraid of Father even though I loved him a great deal. He was big and strong, and the way he looked and dressed I liked very much. The fear was because of his temper—when he was mad he was a different person, and looked as though he could kill me, which was terrifying. I felt a lot of insecurity because of all the fights between Father and Mother. Once, when I was between five and six, they had a big fight. Father asked me whether I loved Mother or him the best. I think Father had been drinking. I said, 'Father,' but my brother said, 'Mother,' because Father always beat my brother physically with a strap or later with his fists. It was really horrible. Father never beat me. When Father beat Brother, my mother would cry and say that Father loved only himself. Such a fight would go on until three or four in the morning. That is about the first thing I remember. When Father drank he would not be himself. He would fight and talk of divorce. It was a lousy childhood after five years old, because then we children first went to the movies and outside amusements and expected some participation from our parents, but then all we got were big, drunken brawls.

"I was close to Mother; I was great pals with Brother. Father was away much of the time, for maybe two weeks at a time. I think Mother pampered me. Even then, I tried to understand Father and couldn't see how he went from one extreme to the other. He would be kind and understanding and then suddenly violently harsh, cutting, and demanding. Mother would cuddle me excessively to express love. I would sit in her lap, but as I have told you, she kept me in curls and dresses, and I rebelled. I guess it was all right until I was about three years old; Mother was loving and also demanding. She would say, 'Come here, my little boy,' things like that. But later on I had a good relationship with Mother; she was not demanding of me and I was not demanding of her. She put the children's interests ahead of her own. She was consistent, but Father was and still is entirely inconsistent. If either one of them differed with me, Mother would not get mad but Father would. I think Mother was more attentive and loving to me than to my older brother, or to my two younger sisters. When I went away to boarding school, I was very homesick the first year. Anytime I went back there after a vacation, I would be homesick also.

"I told you my brother and I were close; I admired him; we had lots of fun together, pillow fights and things like that. But Mother showed more attention to me, and I think Father did also. I had no hostility against Brother.

"In a way, during those first five years, I did get along with Father, at least for periods. Because he was away a lot, I could not be close to him but I idolized him, I hero-worshipped him until I was nearly 20. I would fight anyone who criticized Father even though I never understood him."

John Orbison did not continue with the analysis, partly because he was out of town a great deal and also because he thought his father would disapprove and he was too afraid of his father ever finding out. Several years after this, John was in the locked ward of a mental hospital, and when the analyst found out he went to see him. John was most grateful and more or less clung to the analyst. Nothing could be done, however, because at that point he was under the care of a psychiatrist who was not analytically trained and was opposed to analytic therapy. After an hour's chat in the hospital, the analyst got the impression that John was making no progress with his basic problem (his father) because the psychiatrists were ignoring his feelings completely and only trying out some drugs. Five years later John killed himself. It should be added that between the time of his psychotic break and his suicide, he descended into the depths of alcoholism, so that even his older brother could no longer stand to be with him. It must also be noted that when his analyst visited John in the mental hospital, John was able to talk entirely rationally and was by no means then overtly psychotic. He was, in fact, reaching out for help. However, with an extremely prejudiced, antipsychoanalytic psychiatrist in charge there was no way to get him any help of this kind. This probably left John with alcohol as his only defense, the only remaining way to hang onto his sanity, but it was not adequate.

During the time he sought treatment, his severe psychopathology was well covered by a perfectly reasonable and charming exterior, in other words, by a strong and wholesome but superficial ego. John started his business and did well despite the odds against him. His relationship with his wife had its difficulties but was not too bad until his wife could stand it no longer and divorced him, thus precipitating his breakdown and hospitalization. However, his childhood pattern was kept alive by his father, and ultimately, while John was apparently perfectly sane and reasonable, he vented his anger (especially at his father) and escaped by a deliberate, well-planned, and successfully executed suicide. It was tragic. He could be labeled "compensated psychosis" but could also be considered a psychotic personality of a reactive type, because his father's treatment of him prolonged his psychopathological reactions and blocked his maturing.

John exemplifies the type of psychopathology which does not result from an overall fixation at a very early age (as seems to be the case with Irma) but rather from the occurrence in a largely mature person of a severe disorder of the psychodynamics, the roots of which were reactions to serious trauma in earliest life, in this case continuing into adulthood in reaction to abuse by his father.

This patient seemed to fit our original conception of psychotic personality, but once the criteria emerged, the fit became questionable.

However it is included here because the reactive element was clear. John strove mightily to free himself of his father and made an independent life for himself, but he was no match for his father. He was so beaten psychologically by the older man that he lost his business, his wife, and his children, and had a breakdown while still fighting to have a life of his own. The psychic pain of his defeat and rage and guilt toward his father was so great as to make him drink to excess for some relief. What was the immediate precipitant of his suicide? This act often occurs when the last libidinal tie is broken. Having lost wife, children, mother (by death), and siblings, it is likely that any rift in the precarious attachment to his father could do it. His pathology was largely reactive, i.e., forced upon him by his father, who blocked the object interest, causing the loss of John's business and family, which led eventually to loss of the reality sense that enabled him to make his way in the world. This was all without organized symptoms until the alcoholism developed. Therapeutically, the analyst did not handle him as well as he would have after more experience. Probably he should have "gotten out" into discussion the rage and guilt toward his father after the first meeting, as well as the love John experienced during the first five years.

If John were not a psychotic personality, his father certainly was. The latter had no close friends and fought to keep *his* sanity by alcohol, by clinging to John, and by an endless series of women, because distant, transient relationships were the only closeness he could tolerate. This was reflected in his two divorces. He had been overtly and seriously rejected from 0 to 6. He was entirely narcissistic, caring only about his own desires and whims. His view of others was a little psychotic—he felt they were only objects to serve his wishes—and, when thwarted, he felt violent, almost uncontrollable rage but this psychotic element was repressed under a superior intelligence. He seemed physically indestructible, continuing unchanged into advanced old age. "The good die young, and those whose hearts are dry as summer's dust burn to the socket."

# 12
# COMPULSIVE TYPE: ELLA LOWRY

Ella Lowry was 20 years old, a pretty and intelligent girl who held a regular job on a newspaper. She came to see an analyst because she wanted to know whether she should remain at the Illinois Psychiatric Institute with her excellent therapist or should return to her job in Pittsburgh, which would probably mean living at home. Ella had noted that her newspaper was offering a summer seminar to those interested in studying the news media, and was undecided as to whether she should participate. "I've got a lot of doubt and can't decide whether to take that course being offered. I am sort of immobilized by the doubt and have created havoc at home; I'm up nights trying to figure it out. My father and mother agreed to bring me to the Institute to Dr. L for evaluation. Now I think I would be much better off on the job than here in the Institute. The psychiatrists in Pittsburgh tell me that the hospital is no good for me; that I cannot solve my life's problems in the hospital.

"I did well in a girls' school, but then went on to the university and fell on my face. For example, I did not know how many weeks there were in a year. I was a desperate, frightened little girl who had been overachieving. Is this an emotional problem around an almost symbiotic relationship with my mother? We are mutually confiding. On the Rorschach I saw an injured chipmunk. Could this have been myself and Mother? Maybe I have been denying this basic problem. Dr. L has made me see that I am a sweet girl but that I irritate my father and mother and others by phoning all these people at all hours, asking all kinds of questions. Does the regression produced by the hospital help or hinder? I have been to six different psychiatrists in Pittsburgh; each one lasted only a week to a month. The classical ones said nothing at all. Should I try to keep with Dr. L for only a few more days? I could live in the Chicago area with my aunt and uncle, or maybe in a halfway house. The job in Pittsburgh is half-time, and I find it so simple that a monkey could do it; I am so verbal."

She surely was, it was almost impossible for the analyst to interrupt her, to discuss whether she could stay in the hospital at least a few days until Dr. L and her analyst had a chance to talk over her problem. She seemed to show a great deal of hostility toward her mother and father, unconsciously, despite her stress on all they had always done for her. She felt over-protected and, at the same time, pushed out. Her dependent love needs (if that's what her clinging was) developed in this first session with her analyst because she hung on verbally so that it was quite impossible for her to end the hour—she simply hung on and hung on with an uninterruptible torrent of talk. The session ran for nearly two and a half hours; she walked off with a box of matches and a pen.

At the second meeting she poured out the following: "I guess I was an ideal child and a great joy to both my mother and father; I have been hardworking and conscientious. I have a brother five years older than myself and another two years older. They have both graduated from college. I have been very close to Mother, but I felt Mother sent me off to boarding school and Father did not show a great deal of love and affection. Mother always wanted a daughter; then I came along and that was divine. I was accepted at several colleges and chose a big university because one of my brothers went there, and because it was away from home. I had a compulsion to get straight A's, self-instilled—to prove what? Maybe a high IQ, so I could be high on the Student Aptitude Tests. I graduated cum laude from a small girl's school. The first semester at the university I got a straight 4.0 average but had no outside activities and I spent almost all my time in the library with a boyfriend who came a hundred miles to see me. I thought my professors were awful, and I saw that I would not get an A in two of the courses. I talked with the dean and was given permission to drop the courses; I studied excessively until I lost weight and could not sleep nor eat properly, and felt terribly homesick. I went to the university hospital and saw a clinical psychologist, a woman. She said I should go to see a psychiatrist. My father did not understand why I panicked; I phoned him and

Mother 12 times in one day. I went to see the psychiatrist one time, and he said my parents should take me to Florida.

"In Florida I cracked up—I spent 20 hours a day, for five days, writing a letter to the dean at my college and to the psychiatrist I saw in Florida. A doctor down there admitted me to the hospital and administered sedation so I could get home, where I saw Dr. Stephens for about two or three months, but I could not get into treatment with him. Then I saw a Dr. Johns for about six weeks, but he only asked me about my sex life. I saw a Dr. H who was very nice, and brought in Mother and Father too. Three months went by and I was still not in treatment with him; then I suggested a woman, and went into treatment with Dr. J's wife, who was a social worker. I did better with her, but I hounded my mother with questions over what I thought was a major catastrophe, but was nothing. I made threats of suicide, and now Mother is all upset and on tranquilizers; Mother and Father are both upset in fact, because they are both exhausted."

Finally managing an interruption of her flood of talk, the analyst asked Ella what she thought were the main features of her life from birth to about six years of age. If asked a question, she poured out her thoughts and could not be stopped or interrupted by other questions. "My first memory was of not wanting to go to nursery school. I did not want to leave home and there were eight kids in a little Volkswagen. The most outstanding feature was my closeness to Mother and Father—really, my closeness to Mother. My father worked like a dog and now has an ulcer. I saw my father as a very hard worker; he cared about me and loved me, but there was little closeness because he was excessively busy making a living. The closeness to Mother was all comforting. As I got older, I felt that Mother lacked confidence in herself, but I got great grades and had much confidence in myself. Father was considerate; he was caring, but he did not like touching, he did not like to show affection. I think Mother was rejected during her 0 to 6 and has excessive needs, while Father can't satisfy them. Recently, Mother has been getting angry. My brother Robby has been busy with sports, and my parents had little emotional relationship with him but there was no hostility in it. We would play with the neighborhood kids together. My other brother, who was only two years older than me, was not close. My brothers shared a room, ate and played together, but they were not especially important in my life." With no pause, the flood continued.

"My 0 to 6 was rather idyllic, except for not wanting to leave home and go to nursery school. Father and Mother occasionally went away on vacation and I was extremely upset then, and would cry. They would hire a babysitter but I could not wait until they got back. Father said my IQ was very high, but I don't think so; the dean said I should have had a low B or high C average; the SAT was 660 verbal, 500 math out of a top of 800. Things were always very structured for me and I did well, when there were no decisions that I had to make. The first semester at the university had many more courses than I was used to. I did what I could and tried not to worry. The second semester I wanted a drama course but could not get it and was given poetry, which I knew I could not do; I couldn't understand the professor. It was full of juniors and seniors. I then got another poetry course that was very unstructured. We had to analyze poems on our own and I did not like the professor; I dropped one course and only carried four, but in the poems I never knew how I was doing. Then I would wake up with my heart pounding, scared and with insomnia.

"Most of my confidence was based upon handling school, but then when I felt the courses were going badly, driving me batty, I went to pieces. I guess I am still so upset today because I failed and ran home to Mother; since then I am trying to pick courses at the community college which I am capable of handling. I thought the courses would give me direction; I did badly at typing and at art. Last summer I was dating a French fellow, ten years older than I, whose wife had left him. We would go out and play tennis and have dinner, and I would forget my problems for the evening. Then he went back home, left the country, and I had no one. My parents took me to Florida and I was scared. Actually my parents went there first and I was to follow, but I got this job on the newspaper and worried about the job and the courses. I was afraid I would ask Father and Mother the questions again, but I managed to control this compulsion. I was OK when I went out with Phil, an old friend, and the social worker I was seeing for therapy told me I should not continue taking the courses at the community college. Later, she told me I could start the courses again; I had a choice between history or sociology and I could not decide. She told me I was using the courses as a resistance to therapy with her."

The analyst forcibly broke in, told Ella to be quiet a moment, and asked, "Could you reestablish the relationship to your mother for a while and for a short period do whatever might be necessary to be loved?"

"Possibly," she replied, "but I lost the structure of my life when I left college."

ANALYST: [Breaking in] It seems to me that all your doubts and indecisions are really a symptom.

PATIENT: Yes, I can see that is possible. I. . .

A: [Breaking in] Could they be a symptom of anger?

P: That's possible, too, because I have lashed out at Mother for her overprotection of me.

The analyst suggested to Ella that the continual questions she asked, and the unstoppable torrent of speech, sounded as though they might be a compulsive symptom and that, as usual, there could be anger behind it as well as anxiety.

This seems to be a compulsion neurosis in a girl who has sufficient sense of reality to handle, briefly, her job on a newspaper. In the above description of Ella, however, the *intensity* of her questions may not have been conveyed. Once she is seen in the office or calls on the phone, it is completely impossible to terminate the conversation without directly rejecting her. She keeps bringing up new questions with an unbelievable degree of insistence. By the test of projecting what Ella would be like if she were to get worse, one deduces that she would be unable to think because of the insistence of her questions, and her interminable talk would estrange all human relationships. It reveals an almost total self-absorption. Therefore, the core of her problem seems to be psychotic rather than neurotic. She controls her psychosis when she is able to control herself and do work. Also, the acute upset she feels over college courses she took more than a year ago is quite unrealistic. It seems proper to call her "a psychotic personality with compulsion neurosis."

This tragic young girl illustrates our remark that every urge, impulse, need, drive, and reaction exists in everyone in some proportion, mix, or condition. She must have serious *patho*dynamics which are also driving her into a deep and extensive regression from human relations and from life, into a passive dependence of early childhood and the narcissism of absorption in her own thoughts and questions. This impairs her reality sense and thereby her ability to make decisions. Her irritating, provocative, almost intolerable flow of questions and talk is like a drowning man clutching at a straw, her last desperate struggle to cling to some bit of human relations and not be swallowed up in a full-blown psychosis (which was why the analyst rarely dared interrupt her—she might not have been able to handle it). She was a psychotic personality heroically fighting against further regression into an overt psychosis. The most severe mental and emotional symptoms are often the final desperate defense against something worse.

The analyst persevered despite all difficulties and, surprising as it may appear, Ella eventually developed a transference to him of some of the closeness to her mother in her 0 to 6. Thus she became capable of analytic psychodynamic treatment and over a five-year period achieved a reasonably satisfactory life.

# 13
# SUICIDALLY DEPRESSED TYPE: WYNNE

Almost immediately after her release from a state mental hospital, where she had been committed for suicidal depression, Wynne came to see an analyst. She looked rigid and under severe tension. Wynne was 40 and divorced. She was completely rational in her first interview, and made two points. First, she understood clearly that she had been committed to the mental hospital for the purpose of preventing her from killing herself. She had agreed to try to work her problem out analytically, in return for her release from the hospital. However, she was also determined that if she were ever again committed, she would give up all attempts to solve her problems and make a successful suicide her sole goal. This would be her revenge. She felt sure that she knew the hospital ropes well enough to accomplish this; if something should cause her attempt to fail, nothing would prevent her committing suicide once she was out. "What will they do?" she asked, "keep me locked up all my life for fear that I will end it?" Her second point was not uncommon: "I am totally unable to see or even talk on the phone with either of my parents, especially my mother, without its stirring up these suicidal impulses. I have seen some psychiatrists and I think I can improve and have a reasonably satisfying life, but only if I have no contact whatever with my parents."

Of course every psychiatrist is aware that the period of greatest danger for a person contemplating suicide is during *emergence* from a severe depression, but the hospital staff took this risk at this time. Now if Wynne were again committed, in spite of her threat, would it not end all hope of her attempting a psychotherapeutic solution of the problem and perhaps precipitate the suicide her doctors strove to prevent? Or should the analyst risk working analytically with Wynne for a trial period, in the hope of helping her initiate a permanent improvement? It is not pleasant for any analyst to start therapy under such a threat, with such a transference, but if this offered the only hope for the patient, then there would be no choice and the analyst must do so and risk his reputation. Therefore, it was decided to try analytic therapy. Wynne seemed capable of some positive relationship with the analyst, and it seemed she could be protected from the external precipitants, her parents. The risk of psychotic depression and of suicide is greatest when there are bad relations with much hostility to *both* parents. Her history did reveal some slight sympathetic feelings toward her father, at least occasionally. This was a slender positive transference to depend upon, but the analyst had already seen dangerous patients through to tolerable or even reasonably satisfying lives. He agreed to trust Wynne if she in turn agreed to trust him and have a trial of working out her problems. One favorable factor was her severe emotional suffering, which gave her a good therapeutic urge to relieve this pain by analytic progress. This, too, was not without risk because the frustrations of daily living can never be controlled. If some person or incident hits an emotional vulnerability before it is analyzed, the suffering might exceed the patient's limits and tempt her to seek immediate relief in suicide rather than in therapy. It should be remarked that all the few known available drugs had been tried with Wynne, but without success. It was thus agreed that if, for any reason, she felt worse or experienced increased suicidal impulses, she would phone her analyst at any hour of the day or night. Wynne did utilize this option, but only occasionally, and always in a considerate way. Whatever his doubts, the analyst had no choice but to trust her; without therapy, suicide was certain. With therapy, there was at least a chance. Balancing his reputation against her life, the analyst had no choice.

Needless to say, therapy was strenuous for both Wynne and her analyst. There was slow, rather sawtoothed progress, with occasional dangerous acting out. Her bitter hostility and fear toward her parents had not yet appeared in the transference. If only this would come into the open, she would be on her way to permanent improvement and some kind of life other than a locked ward of a mental hospital. Of course, her family was fully apprised of the risks, and a male cousin phoned Wynne's analyst, warning him of times that looked like danger points.

Wynne seemed to show slightly increased interest in others and in her life. She spoke with her analyst about visiting her teenage daughter who was in school in Wisconsin, and this visit she reported as a great success—one of the best times she and her daughter had ever had together. Now, Wynne said, she felt up to visiting the man in St. Louis whom she loved and who loved her, and whom she hoped to marry. The risks were discussed in case all did not go well and in case she felt rejected by him. It was agreed that if anything disturbing occurred, she would phone her analyst immediately from St. Louis no matter what the hour, day or night. Wynne felt sure it would go well. She had received a letter from her daughter expressing appreciation and love after the Wisconsin visit. Wynne said the family would be angry if they knew she was visiting the man in St. Louis, and begged her analyst not to tell them if they phoned. This might have been a ruse, because the analyst would never reveal the confidence of their therapeutic hours anyway, and to betray her would have demolished the therapy beyond repair. Her analyst certainly could not at that point betray her and still ask her to trust him.

She was to leave late Friday afternoon, but Monday morning she was found unconscious from an overdose. It came out later that she had just obtained a bottle of 100 tablets of a sedative from a pharmacy far across the city from her home. It was against the law to sell her so many, and her analyst never learned from whom she got the prescription or whether the trip to St. Louis was a planned ruse or a bona fide trip, or whether at the last moment the man rejected her and this was too much for Wynne. Nor could it be determined whether, suddenly having obtained the overdose, she could not resist taking it. Wynne was rushed to the hospital but had severe pneumonia from depression of her respiration by the drug and she died.

No doctor in any specialty fails to be upset if a patient dies. Nobody likes to be the butt of hostility. This was difficult for the analyst, who felt deeply the need to give Wynne the trial of therapy rather than recommitment to a mental hospital, which would sacrifice all chance of help and doom her to suicide. If recommitment froze her resolve to suicide, nothing afterward could have avoided it; once a person is fully determined on suicide there is no possible way to prevent it. However, one element in Wynne's case was even more tragic: she had gone to Wisconsin and poured out her love for her adolescent daughter, and then the girl in turn, whatever her own problems in reaction to her divorced parents, had responded with full measure of love. Having won all this love and devotion, and promising love in return, Wynne heartlessly robbed her child of it all by killing herself before her hostility toward her parents which had been redirected toward her daughter could be analyzed.

It seems that this was part of Wynne's psychotic personality. Behind the depression or covering it was a mask of reason, used to vent her irrational hostility upon herself and her daughter, and incidentally, probably following her emotional pattern, upon her parents and also her therapist. Even if irresistibly driven to suicide, if she had not been a psychotic personality, she could have found a method that would have seemed an accident or at least would not have hurt others, especially her daughter, so much. When Wynne was first seen, she was certainly not a typical psychotic depressive. At least superficially she was rational and active, and denied any physiological symptoms of depression. Although she was tense, rigid, strained, she showed nothing bizarre enough in her thinking to justify the label "schizophrenic." In those days, the concept and terminology to diagnose her as a psychotic personality with suicidal drives and depression were lacking. In retrospect, the suicidal impulses seemed to be part of the psychotic personality as well as of the depression—they were the psychotic acting out of her hostility, even upon her own innocent, trusting daughter. Wynne promised her daughter love and then rejected her, probably just as her parents had rejected Wynne. If only her hostility could have been analyzed, and thereby defused and somewhat reduced, she would not have hurt others and may have had at least a tolerable life.

Could the therapy have been handled in any different or better way if a diagnosis of "psychotic personality" were then known? Probably not—but the more clearly we perceive psychic reality, the more efficacious our therapy is sure to be. In terms of childhood pathodynamics as compared with overall regression, this case is clearly closer to John Orbison (Chapter 11) than to Irma (Chapter 9). In fact, the unresolved hostility to one or both parents is almost identical, except that John Orbison had considerable love from his mother and also some from his father. It is much harder to achieve a good therapeutic result through analyzing such hostility in a psychotic personality than in a neurotic one, but with persistence it can be done. In this case, it was properly attempted to prevent the patient's spending her life in a mental hospital, to save the patient's life, and spare her family the suffering she caused them by the way she lived and the way she died.

In review, Wynne does seem to fit the tentative criteria for psychotic personality: (1) regression or fixation at a level of serious withdrawal of feelings from human relations into narcissistic self-absorption; (2) repression or warping of reality sense; (3) psychotic elements diffused until they break out as suicide.

# 14
# EMOTIONAL ISOLATION: MACKLEY

Mackley, short and slender, but wiry and muscular, had always been a hard worker. He liked his younger brother, and for years the two of them had planned a bicycle trip, but it never materialized. Mackley fell in love with Marianne and they married when in their early twenties; he continued his studies while working hard to support them, while Marianne also held down a job and saved her earnings. After six years, they still had no children. Then, desperately eager to have offspring, they expended much time, money, and effort seeing various doctors. Marianne had her tubes blown out and then Mackley had an operation. At long and joyful last, after agonizing through all the visits to doctors and all the medical procedures, success crowned their sacrifice: Marianne gave birth to a healthy little girl. It was the happiest day of her life, to be exceeded only by the day when she returned home from the hospital with her beautiful baby daughter. However, Mackley, instead of being overjoyed, was depressed and hostile. He told Marianne that he had never really loved her but had lacked the nerve to tell her so before. When she asked how their child would develop properly without a father, Mackley said, "Oh, let the kid become a lesbian."

Mackley did finally agree to see an analyst. His childhood memories gave a clear indication of his pathodynamics. In all of these he was alone except in one memory which included a dog, but other human beings never figured in any of his memories or dreams. His history and dreams confirmed this sense of aloneness: from birth he had been close to no one, neither to his mother who was superficially gushy but emotionally remote, nor to his father who was rarely present and later obtained work in a distant city, nor to his siblings even though they looked up to him and respected him. Mackley told the analyst that he had met another girl who was the first person to whom he had ever felt close. It was so marvelous a feeling that he would not sacrifice it for wife or child. He wanted to change his "life-style."

"Do you think your own happiness and life-style are more important than the welfare of your wife and child?" he was asked. Mackley hesitated. His reason almost visibly rose to the fore, blocking out the selfishness and callousness with which he had intended sacrificing his wife and new baby, who were completely dependent upon him. His ego became its usual reasonable self, and for nearly a week Mackley was kindly and interested toward both his wife and his daughter. Then he again grew distant; he slept on the couch and left early each morning. Communication between Mackley and Marianne dwindled to the vanishing point, and a few nights he did not come home at all. One day he attacked Marianne verbally with obscenities, and with this she gave up on him and saw a lawyer. It was all too obvious that some compulsion of rejection and withdrawal was mushrooming within him against all resistance, reason, and controls.

Mackley wanted to be rid of his wife and of the child he had so desperately yearned and sacrificed for. He felt he would be happy at last with the "other woman." He said the woman did not want to marry him but only, like himself, to enjoy the closeness which her life also had lacked.

Marianne was seen by the analyst. Everything in her history, dreams, and earliest memories bespoke easy, good human relationships with those around her from birth onward. This seemed genuine and raised the question of why she had married Mackley. It appeared that he fit remarkably well into the role of Marianne's older brother, the central emotional figure of her entire childhood, on whose unconscious pattern it was that she had sought a husband. Mackley had no interest in treatment or in any attempt to save the marriage, but only said that the sooner Marianne was out of the relationship, the better it would be for her and their daughter. Mackley seemed to be a psychotic personality or a somewhat compensated psychotic of regressive schizophrenic type. Four weeks later, Marianne told her husband that he could have the divorce he had been pressing her for and which was to make him so happy. To her naive surprise, he casually thanked her but remained depressed and uncommunicative.

Mackley typifies a young man who seems completely rational, a hard worker who gets along in his job and seems to be a good husband. Then one bit of irrational behavior occurs, and an analytic interview reveals infantilism, regression, almost total lack of all human relations, self-centeredness, and callousness, in short, isolation and hostility of psychotic proportions. He is not a delusional psychotic, but he does not relate emotionally to any human being, and his rationality serves psychotic purposes; there is some distortion of his reality sense that is at least partly repressed. He seems to be a psychotic personality.

Six months later Mackley returned to his wife in a contrite, penitent mood, telling Marianne he had made a terrible mistake to leave, nothing had worked out with the other woman, and he was miserable. He wanted to be a father to his child, life was not worthwhile alone, would Marianne take him back, forget and forgive, and could they go on as before the unfortunate episode? Marianne thought of her own life, raising the baby all alone, trying to give it proper mothering, trying to support them both—it was a bleak and difficult prospect. Perhaps Mackley had learned something. Why not try it? Marianne ignored the whole past incident, suppressed her feelings about it, and tried openheartedly to live as they had lived before. Mackley lasted four weeks, his unhappiness only increased after his return, as did his irritability, and again he left. This time he also left his job and moved to another state for the apparently realistic reason that he had an opportunity for a job there. Now Marianne had the added threat of interstate legal complications if he discontinued paying the support for herself and the baby.

This pattern of behavior is far from rare in husbands, and probably also in wives. With distressing frequency the analyst hears the story of a husband who, with no warning and after a routine family day, often with tears, blurts out, "I hate so to hurt you all, but I am fed up with marriage, and I'm leaving." Sometimes the husband returns contritely in two days, sometimes in two weeks, sometimes in two years. Mackley returned in six months.

Generally such men return because the child in them is so dependent upon the wife, as it was on their mother. Then, once back, they cannot stand this dependence and, repeating the childhood pattern toward the mother, they leave again. These men cannot stand it because their mothers kept them overly dependent and dominated them into submissiveness, rejected them, or otherwise treated them in ways that generated hostile but ineffectual rebellion. Never big and strong enough in early childhood to rebel successfully against their own mothers, living their whole lives in conformity to such dictates, they now are motivated unconsciously to use this opportunity to act it out toward their wives—against the marital family instead of the parental family. They try it and usually they are miserable. They come back, but it doesn't work any more. Some who are very successful financially gravitate into the luxury singles' condominiums. To less financially secure men, this may sound like heaven—a luxurious apartment with every facility and service, gymnasium, swimming pool, the best restaurants, being competed for and sought after by the youngest, most beautiful girls. Here is everything to gratify the desires of man. Yet human happiness lies within—one can dwell in such a paradise, but be living in the hell of one's own psychotic personality.

Reviewing this case, we see that Mackley's emotional withdrawal (distance in human relations) is more than neurotic, and he seems to fit the criteria for diagnosing psychotic personality.

# 15
# MARITAL PROBLEM:
# MAHLON BOWE

Mahlon Bowe was an unusual man, and the courtship of his wife, Bess, sounded unusual from the start. Bess was a girl who "knew her own mind." When she met Mahlon, she felt that she could not stand him. However, he "hung around," he was never too close, never insistent, but never entirely absent. After almost two years of this flattering proximity, Bess began to find Mahlon fascinating. When asked why he pursued Bess, he replied that he was intrigued by her remoteness and her air of being "hard to get." And it took him two years. Bess and Mahlon married, but just as "age and disease do as they please," so also does biology and they had three daughters who grew to sturdy, healthy womanhood.

One element which may have influenced their misalliance was Mahlon's good looks. He was handsome, of middle height with an athletic build, curly blonde hair, and dark eyes. He had come into a sizable inheritance and increased it by his business sagacity. They lived in a northern suburb of Chicago and were both active in civic affairs.

Mahlon was so tense and difficult in his first interview with the analyst that notes were hard to take. Written after the visit, they showed the following:

PATIENT: I don't know why I've come to see you. Be sure you do not tell my wife I have come or that my mother helped arrange it. If my wife knew she would give my mother a bad time, and if she did that, I would punch my wife in the nose. For 10 or 15 years I have been increasingly dissatisfied with my wife; she is dominating, arrogant, and a fanatic. She knows everything and puts everyone straight on everything. I began to drink because of my wife, and I just want a quick, quiet divorce.

ANALYST: What about your wife and daughters and their position and welfare? Are they correct in saying you are quite alcoholic, and when under the influence you strike them physically, that you have other women, one in particular, but expect your wife to do everything you want?

P: I would be generous in any financial settlement. And I don't have bad fights with anyone—I never had one with Charlene, whom I intend to marry immediately after I get my divorce.

A: Can you tell me a few things about Charlene?

P: She is a lot younger than I, and we have been enjoying being together. I am 100 percent definite on wanting a divorce—I have two lead horses, my mother and my wife. Mother says return to my wife and hope for the best and give her and the children a lot of love. Well, I can see that Mother is right insofar as if I threaten my wife she only digs her heels in. I wish you would tell my wife of my decision to divorce when you see her and that I would agree to anything within reason financially.

A: What were your relations with your father and mother in early childhood?

P: Father was always working and hardly ever around. But I think he was nice when he was home. Mother was very close but was nice and not dominating like my wife, even when I was a child. I can get along with anyone except my wife. She is the only one I fight with.

A: Can you give me an example?

P: If I say "vanilla ice cream" my wife says "chocolate." And I am upset because my wife thinks I am sick mentally.

A: Why would she think anything like that? Have you done or said something to suggest it to her?

P: Well, I once said that I feared that if I lost my will, my control, I would do her violence. To put it simply, my wife irritates the hell out of me. The more she refuses me a divorce, the angrier I get.

[What has not been conveyed in this interview is the sense of being unable to feel a normal rapport with Mahlon, as one person to another, of being unable to discuss Mahlon's dynamics or even take an adequate history of his 0 to 6. He was strongly defended against revealing any feelings beyond his anger at his wife. He was reasonable enough, but something of a compulsive talker, while revealing little and not relating normally at all. Without a clear concept of the childhood pattern, the analyst was really working in the dark. It seemed important to follow Mahlon in dealing with his immediate pressures, in the hope that he would be capable of some positive transference and that it would soon be possible to get his childhood pattern and basic dynamics. At this point, the analyst had some fear that his wife's holding him in the closeness of the marriage might increase the danger of violence, and wondered if Bess and Mahlon should live separately for a time. However, there was a feeling of intangible unreality about Mahlon and everything he related, as though the analyst could not come to grips with tangible psychic reality or genuine feelings.]

Mahlon agreed to another session, to see if his marital problem could be better understood: "I spent Father's Day with my three daughters; I was so nice, and they said they so much wanted a home that I thought perhaps I should give in to them, desert Charlene, and return to my wife. I told Bess, my wife, that I would try it for 90 days and if it did not work out I wanted a divorce. But Bess fought with me 80 percent of the time and still said, "No divorce!" so I felt trapped and resentful. I don't think our marriage can be saved because we have been married for 25 years, and for the last ten of those I have been increasingly irritated with her. Our oldest daughter is 22 now. What I cannot stand is my wife's arrogance and domination and her certainty that she can never be wrong, that she knows more than anyone else, even in a specialized field. If you don't agree with her then you know nothing. If you enthuse over everything *she* wants, you can get along with her. If Bess says, 'Let's visit the So-and-So's,' I must reply, 'Wonderful, there is nothing I would like better.' It is the same when we decide to go to a show or anything else Bess wants—but if I say 'vanilla' she invariably replies 'chocolate.' If I want roast beef, she says we just must have lobster.

"Once I was going somewhere with our daughters and Bess said that she had to shop for some items. I had not seen her for two weeks and indicated that I wanted to accompany her, but she ordered me to go with the girls and we had a big fight because I wanted to go with her. My wife is hostile to my mother and that is something that is a constant irritant; I simply will not stand for it. Another thing I despise is my wife's spending. Last year I earned 50 thousand dollars and she spent it all! I can't get to my wife, I can't discuss things with her. But Bess tells her complaints against me to everyone.

"If you have another session with me *you* will need a psychiatrist! You will wish you were a bartender, so you could hear the stories but not have to give answers—you'll be so upset by me that you will wish you were in a different field.

"I really want a divorce. From childhood I learned that once you made a decision you should not wait. My wife should give me a divorce without delay; I have Charlene, this younger woman, because I cannot stand being alone. I can't do house things; I can't even make a bed."

[These last four associations at the end of this session were free enough but gave the impression of bordering on the irrational, although without definitely crossing the line.]

The sense of reality, especially of psychological reality, is a most precious and fragile capacity of the human mind. One of the greatest compliments one can pay another person is to call him a "realist." Any analyst worth his fee devotes his entire life to understanding emotional realities. Yet there is another quality superior even to reality, and that is "love" in the broad sense, or "goodness." How did all that Mahlon Bowe related look to the mind of his wife, Bess? According to her:

"Mahlon is not nice to me. He shows me no respect, he is not considerate. No sooner were we married than he began to think of me as stupid and himself as brilliant. All I want is just a little kindness and courtesy. He discusses all my faults or whatever he sees as a fault with other people and not with me. So how can I know what to do? I try to get along by staying out of his way. He tries to influence our daughters against me, to destroy their love of our home. A few guests were coming over and he said, 'Where do you want to serve the cocktails?' I said, 'Wherever you prefer,' and he replied, 'Mrs. God, you say—just give me the orders!'

"Mahlon wants undivided attention. Our oldest daughter asks me how I can stand his coldness and rudeness. She says I should not treat him as a patient, but that is the only way I can stand his hostility, by treating him as a sick person. He became worse about five years ago when he had problems in his business; he felt the business reverses were a defeat. He wants everyone to do just as *he* decides. Everyone must enthuse over what *he* wants. If Mahlon wants steak I don't dare prefer lobster, or his evening is ruined. He accuses me of extravagance and self-indulgence, but those qualities are his, not mine. He projects them onto me. Yesterday he ordered me to come home to discuss how our oldest daughter spends her allowance. But we give it to her to save or spend as she sees fit—and we should not interfere. From the beginning of our marriage he has tried to 'buy me off.' He offers me money, jewelry, anything to get what he wants. It is an indignity that I can't tolerate and that angers me."

It is not uncommon to see the exact complaints of husband about wife repeated by wife about husband. Usually one is indeed seeing his or her internal trait in the other.

At this point, Mahlon's dynamics had become slightly more clear, but a good detailed personal history (0 to 6) was needed. He seemed to have an excessive, probably pathologically strong attachment to his mother, which he hated in himself, and which kept him in a rage at his mother. This pattern was repressed and deflected toward his wife, Bess. In other cases where a husband perceived traits within himself as being in his wife, there were extremely strong dependent love needs to his mother and rage at her, directly transferred and repeated toward his wife. The unconscious rebellion and hostility were transferred to his wife, the "love" and identification to Charlene. He was heavily defended and resisted not only analyzing this rage but also any insight into its roots. He might be somewhat paranoid in his feelings of being abused by Bess, and she might be at least partially correct when she said Mahlon projected his own traits onto her, accusing her of what was in him. As the analyst saw them, Mahlon seemed subtly disturbed while his wife seemed down-to-earth and realistic. The overall picture was of a handsome, energetic, rational, capable businessman, unhappy in his marriage and able to afford a mistress— or even a divorce and remarriage. Yet there was inner disorder, possibly of a serious nature. Since Mahlon refused to go into his own dynamics with the analyst or even to see him again, nothing remained but for the analyst to be available to Bess as long as she benefited from his support and understanding, and got anything worthwhile from the contact. Support and insight were available, without any hint of advice or opinion regarding her behavior toward her husband, or her decision to try to hold the marriage together or grant him the divorce. This worked well.

Many years later, the rest of the story emerged when Bess contacted the analyst during a trip East from Chicago. Bess had never met Mahlon's mistress, Charlene, and said, "I never want to! He thinks she is so great and says he wants to marry her, but from all I have heard, she is an adventuress and I feel I should not only save our home for the sake of his reputation and our daughters' security and development, but also save Mahlon from her clutches. I may be only the jealous wife protecting the nest, but I think I am correct in this." She always gave the impression of being trustworthily realistic, while Mahlon seemed always to distort and defend.

Over the years their marital problem rocked along, somewhat less distressing to Bess because she no longer had to worry about deleterious effects on the girls who were now no longer so young and vulnerable. They turned out well with careers of their own and happy marriages.

Then one day Mahlon's name stood out in the obituaries. The problem had ended, as all problems do eventually. The wayward husband had died and solved the problem for Bess and her daughters.

Several years later Bess gave the analyst a follow-up: Mahlon's judgment in his successful business was being questioned by his associates; some of the confidence that he and others felt in himself was beginning to falter. Then also, he began having serious difficulties with Charlene. He would turn up late to see her, and she felt badly treated. Bess had evidently been right about Charlene's role as adventuress. It turned out that she was carrying on affairs with other men, for her own financial advantage. As Charlene's relationship with Mahlon became more hostile and disagreeable, she drifted away to become the mistress of a charming millionaire. Mahlon was understandably upset; he had a loyal, intelligent wife, three fine grown daughters, and a thriving business; he was only middle-aged, still healthy and handsome. He could have found another mistress readily, but his childhood pattern of dependent love needs toward his mother was too strong and rigid. His balance had been too precarious between mother, wife, and Charlene. It seemed that his attachment to the woman he could not have was stronger than the attachment to mother, wife, and daughters. The dependent element upon Charlene was too strong, as was the sexual element, free of the inhibitions toward his mother and her substitute, his wife.

His strongest desire was for the unattainable woman, and if one were to look at the situation only superficially, one might agree with Mahlon's insistence that Charlene was the one great love of his life and, paradoxically, that her role as an adventuress might even have contributed to this.

At any rate, Mahlon changed his will, announced that he was going on a hunting trip, and set off. While he was in the country, he shot himself. Whether or not his death was a suicide could not be determined positively.

His will as changed designated a large sum to a worthy charity, with the proviso that a certain percent of the interest be paid annually to Charlene. Bess was contesting this "on principle." It was indeed true that she had lived her life on high principles and it was consistent for her to fight this bequest now, even though it could cost her more in lawyers' fees than she would receive. That was not her point. Her point was to prevent Charlene from acquiring ill-gotten reward. Bess saw Charlene as "the other woman" who had seduced her husband and might have ruined the home life of Bess and her daughters. Therefore jealousy, hatred, and revenge might have lurked behind her principle—that would have been only human. However, the analyst, although he said nothing whatever, could see that there was a possibility that Charlene had really saved the marriage and saved Mahlon's sanity—he might have "cracked up" if he were too close to his wife, for his unconscious dynamics, following the childhood pattern toward his mother, could not tolerate that closeness. Like so many other husbands, he could not tolerate toward his wife the dependence, submissiveness, rebellion, and hostility that existed in his dynamics toward his mother. Mahlon's mistress might well have been an indispensable safety valve and, as such, merited the percentage which Mahlon's will allotted her. However, Bess had benefited from the analytic work she had done, and she would go on handling her own life in her own way, which had proved successful in all areas over the years.

Mahlon always had ample drive; his problem resulted not from the *overall* fixation at a very early age (like Irma, Chapter 9), but from the intensity of the trauma from his mother and the pathodynamics this caused.

Bess said that ten years after Mahlon first saw the analyst, he had seen another, and then subsequently a third. The last doctor strongly recommended hospitalization, which Mahlon refused. It was a few months later that the break came with Charlene. Then Mahlon changed his will and a few days later he was dead, probably by his own hand. His psychodynamic forces had always been in precarious balance. The hostility was barely controlled and it, along with dependence, rebellion, sex, and other forces, warped his sense of reality, giving it a paranoid coloring.

If one considers the strength of Mahlon's frustrated dependent love needs and hostility and possibly sex, Charlene's rejection of him in favor of her millionaire could well have precipitated a suicide. Nevertheless, even if his hostility was so intense that it might drive him to shoot himself, he still had the ego strength to change his will to leave the money for Charlene. Bess felt that changing the will was Mahlon's last blast of hostility against the world. She may well have been correct. Certainly it is consonant with Mahlon's dynamics toward his mother—the repressed conflict of his submissive dependent love needs with his rebellious hostility against her. How must she have felt to have her handsome, successful son commit suicide? His "last blast of hostility," as Bess expressed it, might have been against his mother and her substitute, his wife. And how must Mahlon's daughters have felt?

A review of Mahlon's life revealed a singularly attractive, successful businessman, realistic in the affairs of the world, with a superior wife and superior daughters. He had tensions in his marriage that were aggravated by his having a mistress, but there was no overt sign of psychosis in his daily life, and a suspicion arises that a serious disorder was concealed beneath his superficial appearance. Why would he be so defensive and unable to relate emotionally to the analyst, to tell him anything frankly about his 0 to 6? And why did he not relate closely to anyone? His disorder was severe, and he was afraid to face any fragment of it. His wife's strength and that of his daughters as they grew up enabled the marriage to survive. His own ego strength was sufficient to keep him oriented and capable in daily living, but he was holding in check not just neurotic reactions but psychotic ones. His fear of doing his wife bodily harm was real; when he finally did lose control of himself as he feared he would, he probably turned the hostility on himself and committed suicide. We need not ask what the outcome would have been if he got worse; his actions showed what would have occurred; conceivably then it would have been a paranoid psychosis or else assault or murder.

When Mahlon was first interviewed, the analyst sensed the poor prognosis because of the patient's resistance to rapport, to insight. The concept of psychotic personality would have been helpful.

*In general,* the prognosis for the psychodynamic treatment of the neurotic character is usually good, especially if there is considerable suffering. However, it remains to be learned whether the prognosis for the psychotic personality is good or not, because the individual's ego, superego controls, reason, and sense of reality have to remain in command while under severe pressure from his biological (id) impulses for a longer period of time, and because of possible periods in which therapy temporarily intensifies this pressure of the powerful, barely repressed emotional forces.

In the earlier days of psychoanalysis, if the patient did not progress well, someone would suggest (with tongue slightly in cheek) that it was because the patient was a latent schizophrenic. In these days of predominantly personality disorders, if the patient does not do well we must beware of falling back on the easy out of saying this is not a neurotic but a psychotic personality. That diagnosis may well be correct, as some of the vignettes in this book illustrate, but it would be a failure in conscientious responsibility to jump to this diagnosis as an excuse for failure, while we are studying the psychotic personality and ways to increase the effectiveness of therapy for it. For the present, we can only say that, from clinical evidence, psychotherapy of most psychotic personalities is extremely difficult, at times risky, and usually lengthy. In certain persons who have the perseverance, the results are very good and well worth the investment of time and money for a long period.

# 16
# LOIS DUNSTON

The Chicago Institute for Psychoanalysis is situated just a little north of the Loop and not far south of the "Gold Coast," where live the very rich. Since it seems that often the very rich and the very poor take the worst beatings in life, it is not surprising that a few denizens of the Gold Coast occasionally trickled into the Institute. One early spring morning a Mr. Dunston called:

MR. DUNSTON: The improvement of my wife, Lois, after seeing you for only two or three months this winter was simply incredible. She stopped drinking and became reasonable. But recently, maybe because she is more independent, she has become a tigress and is determined to divorce me. Her lawyer told her, "What you need is not a lawyer but a psychiatrist." But she refuses to see you again.

ANALYST: Do you know why she refuses?

MR. D: No.

A: Is she embarrassed because she broke off seeing me? There is no need for that. . .I would be glad to see her if she would come in. If she does not want to see me in particular, I'll be glad to suggest other analysts whom I consider tops for her, and whom I think she would like.

MR. D: I'll try to talk with her about it, but I don't think there is much chance.

A: Do you really think she became a tigress and wanted a divorce because she became more independent through seeing me? Or was it that money thing? You remember there was some change in the income tax ruling and she panicked for fear her income would be cut to only about one million a year. She reacted by an explosion of acting out—mostly firing people—firing her accountants, firing her gardener, firing her cleaning lady—all in order to save money, even by cleaning the floors herself; she fired me as her analyst and also you as her husband. I think you know that I tried to get her to come to see me only one more time, and she finally agreed but then phoned the day before the appointment to cancel. I wrote her but have not received a reply nor heard from her since then, six months ago.

MR. D: Yes, I remember. We are leaving in a few days for a vacation trip of two weeks.

A: There is nothing I can think of right now that might work. If I get an idea I'll phone you before your trip. If not, at the moment I see nothing to do for your wife but try to get her to visit me on your return, or else to visit Dr. A or Dr. L—in any event, call me on your return.

\* \* \* \*

Lois was intelligent, blonde, attractive, vital, slightly below average height, with steely blue eyes. She seemed tense, as though resisting some strong reaction to the analyst or to the visit. Asked what her main complaint was, she replied:

PATIENT: Everything! I am losing touch. I drink too much alcohol. My sister, five years younger than I, is also in trouble but she won't do anything about it. There was a terrible scene 10 or 12 years ago at the time of my divorce when my anxieties came out. I saw another psychiatrist then. To the world, I am functioning fine, but I know I am not. I can't figure out why I am here; the mystery of life and death; I feel other people know something I don't so maybe I am paranoid too.

ANALYST: What do you mean by "losing touch"?

P: I am functioning like a shadow, and am losing touch with reality. It's as though I am over here looking at me functioning over there. Could this be from drinking too much, causing maybe brain damage? Over the years I have been getting worse. My first husband treated me like a child. Then I met my second husband, who was also married at the time, but that was not the reason for divorcing the first husband—I would have left him anyway. Also, he used our daughter as a pawn to hold on to me. But that backfired and she turned against him. He talked against me but eventually my daughter said she loved me and would not listen to him. He then remarried a very nice girl but now she has left him also. The divorce was hard on me but I did it.

My second husband's name is Roger. He had three children and they clashed with my daughter because of different standards. But Roger is relaxed so it has worked out pretty well. I love him, but I don't trust him—financially or with other women, and this annoys him. . .that is, that I should be suspicious of him. There are some beautiful girls where he works and he takes some of them out for dinner, claiming it is all a business relationship. That may be so and in all innocence, but it preys on my mind, which maybe is sick on my part. My days are very active. . .I run the house and like swimming. Roger comes home and does not like dinner until eight o'clock and before dinner I am very let down and we have cocktails; I drink too much, more than he does.

A: Would you say how much?

P: About three 3-ounce jiggers. And now also to relax I have a few drinks at bedtime. Otherwise I toss around and I cannot stand that, not being able to go to sleep. The doctor I saw after my remarriage gave me some pills but they did no good at all. Do you think it could be the alcohol that is fogging my head, causing the pressure? I continue in a state over my little daughter. I am overprotective. I have help with her, a nurse, and she goes to school so that I am not really overwhelmed with her care, but I do things with her.

[The analyst felt this covered her complaints sufficiently for the first interview. To learn what was behind all this, he wanted to get to the childhood pattern while there was still time left in the interview because he thought she might be very disturbed and he would feel safer if he could get her main dynamics.]

A: What were the main features emotionally of your childhood from birth till age six or seven?

P: I remember living in the city before the family moved out to the suburbs. I remember happy things, not my parents fighting, but big parties. And my younger sister would come into my room and we would watch the parties from the top of the stairs. I had a nurse, and I was happy when it was her day off. I idolized my younger sister, Vicki, even though she was Father's favorite. Once I walked into Mother's room and saw Mother unlock a safe in the wall behind a picture where she kept valuable things. Mother was upset and forbid me to tell anyone whatever. I told my sister though, and then Vicki used it as a threat. She would say, "Give me whatever I want or else I'll tell Mother you told me about the safe." I had a friend whom I loved whose family was very different from mine, because their house was not nearly so big but their family was so happy. I think I must have been lonely, only I had the nurse but that's all I had. But then I became very lonely indeed after my sister and I were sent away to different boarding schools. My father was promoted in the company and had to travel a lot and was gone for long periods of time. One morning when I was at home Mother came into my bedroom and said she and Dad were going to divorce. I had no feelings of sadness, but on the way back to school I found myself crying.

I was a scrawny kid; I had terrible feelings of jealousy. Sister Vicki was pretty and Father enjoyed taking her places. When I came home again from boarding school it was to Mother's new house—Mother had remarried—but by then I hated to be with her. Then Mother got a divorce from this second husband and I worked occasionally. I had a heavy beau, but that sort of frittered away.

Soon after that, I met my first husband. We got married about a year later. I had feelings of jealousy with him too, but they disappeared when he treated me so badly and I no longer loved him; then it just didn't matter. It never occurred to me that I would ever divorce him; I knew there were difficulties, but I thought that once married I would never get a divorce, but that's how it worked out.

A: What came out of your treatment with the psychiatrist you saw after your divorce?

P: He got over to me that life was good and I should be happy. I have always had a good relationship with Father's second wife. Do you think it could be a chemical imbalance, making my problem?

A: I doubt it. I think we should go into the psychological parts first, but then I would certainly be in favor of your having all the biochemical tests that might reveal anything physical at all.

[In the second interview, a few days later, the analyst went from the general question to the more specific one: "Who was the most important person, for you, from birth until you were six or seven years old?"]

P:  I suppose it was my sister, Vicki. [Lois fell silent.]

A:  In what ways?

P:  Just that my sister was the only friend I had in the house, even though sometimes she was my enemy. I was closest to her even though there were servants and nurses. Certainly I could not get close to Mother and I do not remember Father in those days. I don't think when I was very small I had any particular relationship to him. I don't know why; I really don't remember Mother either. They were always out doing things, I think. I had no particular sadness, but I was horribly scared; one time it was because Father and Mother drove to New Orleans on a long vacation trip. Vicki's room was closer to mine than the nurse's, and I would go in there if I were scared. I guess there must have been a sibling relationship.

   I told you of the incident when my sister threatened to tell Mother about my telling her about the safe. . .she has told me since then that she used to hate me in those days.

   In the basement was a furnace and all sorts of power tools, and everyone was forbidden to go in there because it was so dangerous, and when she got older, Vicki would threaten to push me down there. . .that's all I can remember.

   I had a nurse, or rather a number of nurses, but I hated those nurses more than I liked them, except when I was about eight years old and I had one nurse I liked pretty well, but I disliked the idea that I needed a nurse. I think it was nice living in the city—I liked it, as I recall. I got on with the help other than my nurse pretty well. One of the girls used to take me to church.

[From the general question regarding the main features of Lois' childhood, the analyst got a picture of her being much deprived of love and closeness, and of some intimidation. The specific question as to the main persons in her childhood showed deprivation linked with the idea that Vicki was all she had, and even Vicki was hostile to her. The analyst went on to ask for first memories.]

P:  When I was about four, the night of a big party, I went into the closet and saw a button on the floor and I was terrified because I thought it was a bug. My second memory is when I was three, or possibly four, it was nap time. It was summer and terribly hot. I swallowed some kind of metal thing, I don't remember whether

I told anyone about it or not—probably not. My bed was placed along the wall and I scribbled on the wall all the time with a crayon and they tried to get me to stop. My third memory: when I was four years old I was swinging on a rope and the rope broke; I just got a little bump, nothing serious. Fourth memory: from the age of three to five I had some kind of rash and the doctors would come and the treatment was horribly painful. Summer vacations we spent on a farm and the family there had an adolescent son and I would follow him around. When he went to do some job in the barn or the workshop I would love to sit in there. Sixth memory: one time at that farm the dogs got after the sheep and I remember the family burying the torn-up sheep. Seventh memory: I was sick in bed and the nurse brought me some food. I didn't like it and I would hide it behind the laundry and they found it and I was punished. Eighth memory: my sister had some bad childhood disease and I got a shot to immunize me which was very painful. Ninth memory: I went to school and was caught in a lie and terribly humiliated. Tenth memory: when I was about four I went to a party and they gave me some candy and I was happy about that. Eleventh memory: when I was sick I had horrible fever dreams. I also have them occasionally now, too.

[Two common elements in all the dreams were the same as in the childhood memories: of being alone and of something bad happening to herself or someone else, i.e., hostility to self or others. The analyst said nothing at this point.]

A: Do you remember any dreams from your early childhood? Any repetitive ones?

P: Only this fever dream. It is a horrible feeling that I am tiny. . .it is just a feeling.

A: [Wondering whether being "tiny" could indicate a regressive sense of being a small child.] Did you dream last night?

P: I don't remember. My husband wakes me up all the time to get me out of these terrible dreams that I have. I weep and kick and moan, and they are so lifelike that in the dreams I am hoping they are only a dream. They are about horrendous, terrible things.

A: Can you give me an example?

P: I can't recall now. Well, I picture my husband with another woman. That kind of dream happens all the time, and I just ache inside. And then I usually try to hurt him back. I used to have this kind of dream about Father because he preferred my sister, Vicki. I just can't handle man's inhumanity to man anymore. I can't stand those pictures in the history books. . . .

I think the world is getting worse; I am scared constantly for the safety of my daughter. I think of her getting her head smashed in car doors or falling out of windows. I am now so anxious, to the point of being ridiculous. It certainly is not usual to think those grotesque things that I think. . .my daughter lying under car wheels, or in captivity and kidnappers doing things to her. . .I torture myself with these thoughts. I think of my dead mother, not in sadness but lying in her coffin. [Such dreams and conscious thoughts are usually caused by repressed hostility and guilt.]

A: Do you have friends today?

P: Yes, I have a lot of friends. . .good friends, and one lifelong friend. Six months ago I was very upset and asked Roger, my husband, to speak to Father and recommend someone for me to see to get help, but Father would not believe it. He said that I had a good relationship to him and he couldn't believe there was anything the matter with me. But his wife said that if I feel that I should have help, then I should. My husband and my daughter are always my main concern and I wish I were a little less of a homemaking type because almost everything I do is in connection with my husband.

[At this point the analyst began to discuss the main emotional themes of the material with Lois, to try to tie it together a little bit because it had not come out in a well-integrated form. He was a little suspicious about her having good, close relationships with anyone. They did not appear in her first memories or dreams, or in her spontaneous remarks.]

A: Your insecurity, loneliness, and frustration of your dependent love needs all during childhood may have increased your tendency to cling to your husband. . .is that right?

P: Yes. Sometimes I phone him at the office and I know that I shouldn't, and then I hate myself for doing it, especially since it only drives him away from me.

A: Let's talk about your repressed hostility.

P: This is very clear against my husband because of my jealousy.

A: And is it possible that some of this hostility is also turned against yourself in the form of beginning to drink too much and of hating yourself, and in the fantasies of horrible things happening to yourself and your daughter, and your stepchildren? Is it possible that you have been letting your anger, because of your feelings of deprivation and other feelings, drive you into alcoholism, and that this anger is causing your anxieties and nightmares? [It was in reaction to this interpretation that Lois cut down her drinking.] Also, have you not developed any good reaction to yourself because of not having been adequately loved and admired by your parents?

P: I can confirm that, too, because my weight is getting out of hand, my psyche, as I told you, is in an awful state, everything is awful, and then I have these fantasies of my daughter and stepchildren which are horrible. Like driving at 80 miles an hour into a telegraph pole. . .but what has the past to do with today?

A: Everyone has emotional patterns of thinking, feeling, and behaving, which have been formed in childhood mostly by our personal relations then; and if these patterns continue too strongly in a person's adult life, especially if they are disturbed patterns, then (as in your sufferings as a child) the individual tends to react at age 40 with emotional patterns that were realistic at age four. Therefore, the childhood pattern disturbs the present life. I do not know yet whether the childhood pattern of jealousy for your father's preference of your sister might enter into and intensify your current jealousy of your husband.

[All this Lois seemed to follow in a vague way, but the main dynamics had not yet been elicited with enough clarity to begin to be therapeutic. The reason seemed to lie in the large number of traumas she had lived through in childhood.]

* * * *

After about 12 sessions, Lois abruptly left treatment, refusing to talk things over with the analyst in even one last meeting. This was part of her sudden explosive acting out mentioned earlier, when she thought (falsely) that a few of her millions were threatened.

Here is a summary of Lois' dynamic diagnosis:

*Childhood:* Deprivation severe, main close person being sister who was not consistently accepting, often intimidating, and was the object of hostile jealousy because openly preferred by father. Difficulties with mother not elucidated. Distance from people, frustration of dependent love needs, deprivation, and jealousy cause intense hostility, mostly repressed, causing compulsive thoughts of injury and death to self and others.

*Current:* Feelings of deprivation with jealousy, especially to husband, leading to fight-flight—patient's hostility appearing overtly toward husband and in nightmares and fantasies of death to daughter and self, and unconsciously in destructiveness to family and self by alcoholism, and in other ways. Flight mostly into competitive swimming (healthy and normal) but also into alcohol plus withdrawal from feelings toward people.

An unusually wide gap between the early infantile level of her dynamics and the mature strength of her personality, i.e., a small infantile girl trying to behave as an exceptionally strong and mature woman. She is struggling to hold on to the relationships, maturity, and sense of reality she has and not "lose touch" and sink into a psychotic regression.

*Strengths:* By inheritance from and identification with both parents, (1) a stubborn will to survive, (2) physical health, (3) attractiveness betokening a wish to love and be loved despite hostility and masochism.

\* \* \* \*

Reviewing Lois' case, the analyst could see from the first interview that she was not a typical neurotic character who was acting out her childhood pattern of deprivation, frustration, jealousy, anger, hostility, and guilt. After the brief initial improvement, she seemed unable to continue to use the insight and transference as effectively as could properly be expected. Although it is not clearly demonstrated in the above report, her strong resistance to forming any transference attachment (consonant with the absence of any really good relationship in childhood) was obvious and typical of her withdrawal from people. She told the analyst that she drank excessively because of her suspicions of her husband's infidelity. The analyst pointed out that these suspicions (vigorously denied by her husband as groundless) were probably unfounded, but even if justified, why should she let this destroy *her*? With that, Lois cut down her drinking appreciably. She seemed entirely rational and realistic. As her father said, she ran her home well, enjoyed her swimming, gave exemplary parties, and was ostensibly a good mother to the children. There was no cause to suspect Lois of being anything but a rational, reasonable, sensible, down-to-earth person who had experienced bad luck in her two marriages and, understandably, like so many of her set, drank too much. Yet the analysis did not succeed in coming to grips with her main dynamics or establishing a "therapeutic alliance." She was capable of some insight but it was superficial and ineffective, and the transference was all defense against any feelings toward the analyst, positive or negative. He suspected that all the good friends she told about were also superficial relationships, and he wondered if she would have them if she did not have her wealth.

Analytic therapy is probably always "carried" by the transference, that is, by the patient slipping the analyst into the figure of some kindly imago (i.e., some good relationship of childhood), as Freud put it. However, Lois had no good, close relationship to anyone in her childhood to provide a model and pattern for a good trusting relationship to the analyst. Perhaps he erred by not dealing with this more explicitly at the outset, but that too has risks. Psychotherapy is extremely difficult if not impossible when a good transference relationship must be developed from nothing, without any basis for it in a good childhood relationship. Lois' relationships to her sister and nurses were not close enough and steady and supportive enough to "carry" a marriage, or even an initial transference, without which therapy is rarely if ever possible.

Lois' enthusiastic interest in her initial insight into her childhood dynamics evaporated along with the transference. She could think of nothing to say. For fear of stirring up more anxieties in Lois, who was already under much emotional pressure, the analyst hesitated to mention this lack of any good relationship, any good figure (imago) in childhood. He began to suspect that Lois was developing a possibly hostile transference to him, largely as a defense against too strongly dependent love needs which she felt would, as in her childhood, only be frustrated and cause her deeper rage to erupt. This suggested an inability to tolerate even that much closeness. Her two marriages showed that in these close relationships such a defensive pattern emerged, but before the analyst could discuss this with her, the slight threat to her income occurred and precipitated her unrealistic, irrational acting out. Under the guise of reason, despite her millions in capital and income, she would economize by firing her accountant and even her cleaning woman, and would scrub her own floors. In part, it was all a rationalization for withdrawing from human relations. The hostility directed to those she was bound closely to (i.e., to husband, self, and children) of course continued. If, diagnostically, the analyst were to consider what Lois would be likely to do if she got worse, the answer was distressingly clear: she would not be merely neurotic or alcoholic, but she would become psychotic and might indeed live out her dreams and fantasies of driving her children, husband, and herself at high speed into an obstacle, killing them all. In other words, she was not a neurotic character, but a psychotic personality. Behind her facade of reason she was using reasonableness for the irrational, psychotic ends of revenge on those close to her for the many abuses and deprivations suffered in her childhood, which is what everybody does, venting on others, for life, hostility for what was done to them in childhood. And of course, by firing everybody on the excuse of saving money, she was rejecting others as she had been rejected in childhood, and also reestablishing the traumatic isolation from human contacts which characterized her childhood.

With the possibility of another divorce and a legal battle, the psychotic elements which permeated her personality diffusely might coalesce and cause a psychotic break. However, after all the trauma Lois survived in childhood, she may well have developed adequate defenses of her sanity.

Here we must consider an important, somewhat technical point in the psychodynamics of the psychotic personality: it is possible that keeping all these dire emotional forces (needs for love, rivalry, jealousy, frustration, rage, revenge, escape, withdrawal, and so on) in a state of diffusion throughout the personality in all its thinking, feeling, behavior, and human relations will act as a *psychological defense* against their power. If they ever coalesced, might they not form an emotional force which, being unified and integrated like coherent light, would break through the ego's organization as psychosis?

If so, then an essential of the psychotic personality is that in it we witness the ego's *defense by diffusion* against a psychotic breakdown. It would be correct to say that the diffusion serves to defuse the explosive power which is present but not organized in the psychodynamics into a coherent psychotic emotional force.

By "losing touch," did Lois really mean a fear of losing touch with reality and being overwhelmed by frank psychosis? Is this the main anxiety in all psychotic personalities? Is it also the main anxiety in *all* personalities except the most fortunate, most harmonious ones who are able to relax under the pressure of volcanic emotional forces? If so, then we can sympathize with Lois' fear of analysis and her need to break off after only a few meetings. We can see that her fear of losing touch might well be fear of losing control, a fear of insanity. (She could not know, and the analyst did not have the opportunity to tell her, that the danger was much greater with these forces unconscious than with them conscious.) If these concepts had been worked out and available at the time she was seen, then the analyst would have understood sooner and more accurately what was going on within her and possibly have been better able to help her handle it as it emerged.

Meanwhile, nobody except her husband and her lawyer could see anything very much wrong behind her mask of reason. Her husband, in calling her "crazy," used the term loosely, but he may have suspected indistinctly what could be triggered at any moment to explode into psychosis, murder, or suicide. She seemed set on acting out her impulses and not analyzing them. If she refused to see any analyst or psychiatrist, what could the analyst tell her husband and how could he protect her and her children? Could he be sure if she did not return to treatment with anyone that his fears were unjustified and that those close to her were not in danger?

This case alone makes clear not only the difficulties of diagnosing quickly the psychotic personality as opposed to the neurotic but also the vital practical importance of doing so. If Lois was only a neurotic character, the prognosis with analytic treatment was excellent. The supportiveness of the transference, providing in the professional situation what she so lacked in childhood, would carry her through. However, if she was a psychotic personality, unable to form a substantial positive transference, and lacking the stability of ego and supergo to use analytic treatment, she might well sink into some form of behavior which would in some degree drag all those close to her down with her.

# SECTION III
# PSYCHOSOCIAL MEDICINE

*Fools, visionaries, sufferers from delusions, neurotics and lunatics have played great roles at all times in the history of mankind and not merely when the accident of birth had bequeathed them sovereignty. Usually they have wreaked havoc; but not always. Such persons have exercised far-reaching influence upon their own and later times, they have given impetus to important cultural movements and have made great discoveries. They have been able to accomplish such achievements on the one hand through the help of the intact portion of their personalities, that is to say in spite of their abnormalities; but on the other hand it is often precisely the pathological traits of their characters, the one-sidedness of their development, the abnormal strengthening of certain desires, the uncritical and unrestrained abandonment to a single aim, which give them the power to drag others after them and to overcome the resistance of the world.*

S. Freud and W. Bullitt, *Thomas Woodrow Wilson*

# 17
# PSYCHOSOCIAL MEDICINE*

Science often struggles with problems which seem bafflingly complex and produces answers which are intricate and unsatisfying until other data make the matter almost absurdly simple. On a broad scale, an example is the fantastic theories that prevailed concerning the causes of many diseases before the discovery of infectious microorganisms. Prejudices against new ways of thinking long prevented acceptance of the infectious nature of puerperal fever, even in the face of positive proof by Semmelweis.

Psychosomatic medicine arose chiefly from the applications of psychoanalytic insights to the study of emotional factors in various medical disorders. The growing understanding of motivation and emotion began to bring into science what had long been recognized as part of the art of medicine (Alexander and French, 1948). The early studies were chiefly clinical. Now they are becoming more experimental. This adds the scientific rigor of design and procedure, but medicine is still clinical, and clinical observation still has much to yield.

## POTENTIAL OF VETERINARY MEDICINE

Veterinary medicine should be a rich field for psychosomatic studies. It has been relatively neglected. Psychoanalysis developed through observation of human beings, chiefly of their free associations conveyed by speech, and psychoanalysis grew in cities. Yet wherever and however homo sapiens lives, he is still a mammal, inescapably a species of the animal kingdom.

For these and other reasons, psychosomatic medicine still has much to learn from the direct, clinical observation of animals. Indeed,

*Material in this chapter is reprinted by permission of the publisher from Psychosocial medicine and observation of animals, by Leon J. Saul, *Psychosomatic Medicine* 24(1):58-61. Copyright 1962 by Elsevier North Holland, Inc.

veterinarians have a great deal of knowledge about motivation, neuroses, psychoses, and psychosomatic conditions in animals. From veterinarians, from farm life, from living with pets, one can readily become acquainted with the occurrence in animals of anorexia, depression, neurotic "personalities," criminal types, perversions, and the like, all intelligible in terms of their early history or as reactions to current stresses. Obvious are demands for love, primitive sibling rivalry, and a quality of giving and a camaraderie all too rare among humans who are unique in the extent to which they carry out organized cruelty and murder of others of their own species.

True, we cannot study the detailed intrapsychic processes of animals through their free associations and dreams, but much can still be learned from their more free behavior. It is not easy to observe and interpret the day-to-day behavior of humans, but the other animals, being less inhibited, devious, and hypocritical, have less use for masks. Hence, what in human beings must be inferred from words, our animal friends express frankly in behavior. The growing interest in animal ethology is encouraging, but its literature will not be reviewed here. We propose only to show that clinical observations of animals who live with us as pets can be valid and illuminating, making one think wholesomely and twice when reading certain intricate formulations pertaining to human behavior.

This has been succinctly expressed by Stanley Cobb (1958):

Many psychologists and psychiatrists who deal with human beings become engulfed in the complexity of their material and never become acquainted with the simple and important facts of "natural history." Training in the simple biology of barnyard and forest is a great educational advantage. The fact that many leading psychiatrists are urban products, knowing little of these biological fundamentals, has led to much misunderstanding of what an instinct really is, and to too much vague use of such terms as "instinctual."

## OBSERVATIONS OF ANIMAL BEHAVIOR

A very simple observation of dogs yields much that seems instructive on the subject of heterosexuality and homosexuality. When a female boxer, Bonda, was advanced in years, the family acquired a half-collie, half-German shepherd puppy, also a female, named Angy. Bonda was a good mother to Angy, and the puppy would hang on her and play with her. Very soon, Angy was large enough to push Bonda aside when one of the family was present, in an effort to get all the petting herself. Angy became the dominant animal, literally the top dog, for when she pushed Bonda aside, she frequently mounted her, behaving precisely like a male in copulation. The hostile aggression stimulated active homosexual behavior in the dominant female.

Three years later, from Angy's mother but by a different German shepherd father, came Shep. Bonda mothered him and, as he grew up, he too forced her away and demanded for himself all the petting from the humans. This brought him into conflict with Angy, who by then had been spayed. As he became strong enough to dominate, he would try to mount Angy. One day when Shep was about eight months old, he encountered a large, powerful male dog. The big stranger tried to mount Shep, who sat down like a female and came to his master for protection. Clearly, male mounting can express domination, regardless of the sex of the dog. Wolves, as a sign of submission, are reported by Konrad Lorenz to expose their necks to the victor, and monkeys "present" their hind ends in submission and appeasement, a frankly homosexual gesture when signifying submissiveness by a male toward a more dominant male.

A form of behavior characteristic of dogs when stroked or patted is to roll over on their backs, spreading the hind legs as though inviting a sexual advance. This craving for loving attention from the all-powerful human master or mistress comes to expression in a supine, passive, receptive, feminine position of invitation, whether it be a male or female dog.

If this is a general animal mechanism which exists in humans, it may illumine some instinctual mechanisms of homosexuality in love-starved and submissive men and women. Freud observed that animals and children understand each other and that they are similar in their dependence and submissiveness toward the all-powerful adult parents. Masculine sexuality seems to be one form of expression of domination and drive (power over another is a strong aphrodisiac), and feminine sexuality an expression of submissiveness and desire to receive attention and love. When the drive and domination are strong toward another animal, they lead to male sexual behavior in the female as well as in the male; and when submissiveness and need for love prevail, they lead to female sexual behavior in the male as well as in the female, the submissiveness frequently being offered as a bribe for the love and attention.

Another observation will illustrate something more subtle, namely "personality" characteristics. That animals have their individualities and unique personalities is known to all who are capable of empathy— or even simple sympathy—with them, and we have already alluded to the occurrence of various emotional disorders in animals. K. Lorenz tells us that we can form no idea of the personalities of many of the animals in zoos because so many of them have become psychotic. No doubt human prejudices, preconceptions, and supreme egotism have led to looking down upon animals rather than to understanding them. Now that man threatens to exterminate his own species and even to render the earth uninhabitable, perhaps he may realize that he can learn something from animals about the treatment of one's own kind.

Returning to our example, Shep had always been extremely demanding of attention, shamelessly pushing himself between Angy and anyone seeking to bestow a pat upon her. In fact, frequently he would so attack her and push her aside that this squabbling prevented any patting of either. On the other hand, Shep was extremely shy, easily frightened by anything unusual, even in members of the household, and obviously afraid of strangers. If guests entered the house, this fear might gradually lessen so that he would accept much petting from them. From the age of three weeks, when he was separated from his mother, he transferred his attachment to Angy and remained inordinately dependent upon her. Angy knew her own mind—she never showed indecision—about entering or leaving the house, chasing a car or a rabbit, or anything else. But Shep was entirely indecisive about almost everything, only following Angy. If a door was opened for him, he stood there, perhaps making a gesture of entering, but making no decision until Angy came along. Then, if she entered, he did; if she did not, he did not.

## SPECTRUM OF EMOTIONAL DISORDERS

In reading some of the tortuous clinical arguments that struggle to explain the psychology of some forms of human behavior and some symptoms, one wonders if the writers are well grounded in zoology and if they mean to attribute intricate human patterns to animals. Bonda was classically depressed for three months after the last puppy of her litter was killed by an automobile. Depression may be a biological re-action seen throughout the animal kingdom. Catatonia is seen in mam-mals and as far down the evolutionary scale as reptiles, as deJong (1945) has shown. Much that we struggle to solve by free associations *alone* becomes intelligible if we shift our focus from the human psyche, expressed in the office through speech, to the overt behavior of our animal cousins. Though inferior to us intellectually, we can learn much from them about the emotions, including the nature of maturing and maturity, for animals react without disguise.

All emotional disorders can be arranged on a scale or spectrum, from the most silent and internal to the most overt, acted-out ones. The psychosomatic symptoms, if one uses this term for physiological dis-turbances of largely emotional origin, are the most *internal*. Essential hypertension, insofar as it is a result of emotional tension, is very silent and internal. Not even the person himself is aware of it. This grades through neuroses, psychoses, perversions, and addictions to the various disorders which involve direct acting out as criminoid and criminal behavior or other aberrant behavior.

A fine start has been made in psychosomatic medicine, but what threatens mankind is the psychopathology of individuals, organized and coming to expression in *social pathology,* especially in cruelty and violence. Medicine, especially dynamic psychiatry, is now urgently needed in "the larger political and social life of our time" (Virchow, 1958). The urgent need now is for *psychosomatic* medicine to expand to or be supplemented by *psychosocial* medicine. Here we should not disdain to learn from animals (which are "lower" only in intellect). We should study not only their physiology and biochemistry, but also the psychology of their emotional life, especially family living and natural maturing. Most of all, if the human race is to survive, we must learn about mature behavior within a species—love and hate—and how to increase love at the expense of hostility.

Moreover, it is now urgent to think in terms of *prevention*, not only of psychosomatic disorders in which emotional tensions have chiefly *internal* effects, but of psychosocial disorders in which these tensions, especially hostility at the expense of love, are acted out on other humans.

It seems that the direct acting out of hostility as overt violence must be understood at several levels. The deepest is the dynamics of the individual's 0 to 6 (i.e., how he was treated from conception to age about six or seven) which caused excessive arousal of his fight-flight reaction. It is noteworthy that such persons are reported as caring nothing for their own lives. They want to escape from life. This vital element in their thinking is usually overlooked because it is overshadowed by the fight part—the deed. On the surface we see the immediate socioeconomic and political state of the individual who acts out, his personal environment, his nation, and the world at large. The tendencies to kill and to escape are strong in his mind, but probably are only acted out in attempted murder if the socioeconomic and political forces encourage them or at least provide him with an effective rationalization for his actions. There are many other levels which need to be understood to explain fully this behavior. Rather than professing ignorance of the motives behind assassination attempts, our leaders have a duty to their country to learn what the whole complex of causes at all levels are, and to tell the rest of us.

Genius, it is said, is but a step from the madhouse. The future of humanity and its very survival depend upon how it handles its social and economic problems. Will the most intelligent beings on this planet destroy themselves by overpopulation, eventuating in atomic war, and go the way of the dinosaur? Our hope now lies in our understanding of the human mind and its place in the motivations of masses of people. Death from *psychosocial* problems is now more threatening than symptoms and death from *psychosomatic* problems. Most people crave authority and leadership, a return to what they had from their parents when young. The recent movement toward studying psychohistory is promising. We must at least mention this and the psychosocial field.

* * * *

All the parts of the body operate by their own internal, interrelated mechanisms. The motivations and emotions *affect* their functioning but *do not primarily cause or determine it.* Society (the body politic and all human organizations), however, is composed of individual human beings just as the body, although composed of various parts, operates as a unit. Therefore, the behavior of societies is actually caused and even determined by the motivations and reactions of the *individuals* who constitute it. It is unlikely that the social sciences will become truly scientific and formulate the basic principles on which any society operates without taking cognizance of the psychodynamics of the individual human beings who compose society. In all likelihood, the social sciences—which are psychological rather than physical—must be based on psychodynamics, i.e., scientific knowledge of human nature.

It is not now clear just how to use our knowledge of psychodynamics. Here are a few possible preliminary approaches:

1. A basic principle of psychodynamics is that the child we once were lives on in all of us. Depending upon how he was treated by his parents and others, this child may have been frightened and angry, and may grow up to be overtly or latently neurotic, psychotic, perverted, or criminal. A statistical, sociological question then arises: How many persons with each kind of disorder are at large in the population, and how do these persons affect the behavior of society as a whole? Groups form through the tendency to follow a leader and identify with other members of the group. The details of these identifications need to be examined: the enormous need in most people for an authority figure; the connection of this need with the child's need for his parents; the origins of this need in the child's dependence and submissiveness toward parents and others; how treatment of the child affects this need; how the psychology of the individual affects the adult society.

2. The history of the development of government is one of progression through slavery, feudalism, and all forms of dictatorship to democracy, in which every adult is expected to take some responsibility for his society's well-being. Then we may ask: Is this historical development of democracy connected with the maturing of the dependent, submissive *child* into a more independent, mature *adult* who is responsible for spouse, children, and society? Is this like the connection of ontogeny (the development of the individual) with phylogeny (the evolution of the species)?

3. To what kind of authority figure does a society entrust itself, and why? Germany, under severe stress, turned (or yielded) to Hitler. Was this a form of regression? The English stood alone in the blitz. Was their fortitude connected to the way each individual was raised as a child?

4. Why has the worldwide crime rate risen so dramatically? Is this a response to the immediate pressures of life, or can it be traced to the disruption of family life in the generations during World War II and

thereafter? Are we unconsciously raising neurotics, psychotics, perverts, and criminals in our homes by the way we treat our children? What are the connections with abortion and equal rights for women before the law? Does the right to life have much validity if the infant is raised to be neurotic, psychotic, or criminal—would it be better (as the Greeks said) for such a child not to have been born?

5. Individuals with similar psychodynamics are attracted to one another. With the catalyst of a leader, these persons form groups and organizations. If this is universally true, can anything be done to inhibit evil, criminal, antihuman organizations and to foster benevolent groups which will benefit suffering humanity, foster a better life, and help to save society from annihilating the entire human race?

Perhaps the above questions are simplistic, but they may stimulate us to ask more significant questions. They are meant only to *indicate* the importance for the social sciences of psychodynamics, of understanding the interplay of the emotional forces of motivations and reaction in the adult, and how they were shaped during earliest childhood into patterns of feeling, thinking, and behavior which continue throughout one's life. All play their part in shaping the individual's society and the collective behavior, conscious or unconscious. The study of how to apply our new understanding of psychodynamics to our great social and economic problems challenges the upcoming generation of social scientists.

Reading parts of C.G. Jung, one gets a clear impression of a person who handles his life rationally and normally, while nevertheless repressing tendencies to overt psychosis which are strong enough to cause anxiety and which profoundly influence his thought and work. As a single brief example (Jung, 1965):

In order to grasp the fantasies which were stirring in me "Underground," I knew that I had to let myself plummet down into them, as it were. I felt not only violent resistance to this but a distinct fear. For I was afraid of losing command of myself and becoming a prey to the fantasies—and as a psychiatrist I realized only too well what that meant. After profound hesitation, however, I saw that there was no other way out. I had to take the chance, had to try to gain power over them; for I realized that if I did not do so, I ran the risk of their gaining power over me.

As one reads this autobiography of Jung, the impression strengthens of psychotic or semi-psychotic thinking, of his own unconscious fantasies dictating his observations and interpretations rather than perceptions which are realistic and relatively objective, so that he reads his own fantasies into the observational data and reaches his interpretations through these personal fantasies.

We must be happy for him, as a fellow human being and fellow psychologist, that under severe enough emotional pressure to threaten psychosis he could live a long, personally satisfactory and productive life. We can be stimulated by his intellectual brilliance and erudition, but assuredly we cannot feel confidence in him as a scientist or in his results. For in him the mysticism and superstition which always oppose the grasp of reality basic to strictly scientific observation, study, and formulation have opposed, distorted, and contaminated the scientific efforts of his own mind.

From this autobiography it seems clear that Jung clung to reality and science as best he could to save himself from psychosis, but his personal, emotionally generated fantasies influenced and to a large extent even dictated his conclusions. As a result, Jung was more a mystic than a scientist. It may be that his popularity was determined by the wide segment of the population which could not tolerate the truly scientific study of the human mind and emotional life that burst upon the world so suddenly and in so complete a form in the work of Freud. Such people could only accept the new science of psychoanalysis in a form diluted and distorted by the mysticism and superstition generated by fantasies formed by the infantile emotional forces, which externally, throughout human history, have opposed the progress of humanity's grasp of reality as scientific knowledge.

Perhaps an example must be included: Jung has a dream, one he selects because he is impressed by it. He looks into the past for a similar theme or character. Of course he finds it because it has been known since Chaucer (if not much earlier) that only a few plots exist in all the works of history, mythology, and creative literature. The great creative writers of fiction can only tell the old stories in different and hopefully more intriguing ways.

All informed thinkers of Jung's era were acquainted with Darwin's work. Jung apparently thought that incidents or ideas entered the racial unconscious in only a few hundred years, thereby misunderstanding the time spans of evolutionary theory. His reasoning is therefore the fallacious *post hoc, ergo propter hoc;* i.e., since his or the patient's dreams come after the incident, character, or myth, they are assumed to arise *because* of it. There is no rigorous proof of any of this.

## REFERENCES

Alexander, F. and French, T. (1948): *Studies in Psychosomatic Medicine.* New York: Ronald Press.
Cobb, S. (1958): *Foundations of Neuropsychiatry.* 6th ed. Baltimore: Williams and Wilkins.
DeJong, H. (1945): *Experimental Catatonia.* Baltimore: Williams and Wilkins.
Jung, C. (1965): *Memories, Dreams and Reflections.* New York: Vintage Books.
Virchow, R. (1958): *Disease, Life, & Man: Selected Essays.* Standford University Press.

# 18
# CULTS*

*"Then where is your way of religion?" she demanded.*
*"In bread and in water," he replied, "in sleeping and in walking, in cleaning my house and making my garden, in feeding the lost children I find and take under my roof, in coming to teach your son, in sitting by those who are ill, and in helping those who must die, that they may die in peace."*

Pearl Buck, *Pavilion of Women*

## INTRODUCTION

Some warping of the grasp of reality is one of the most important characteristics of the psychotic personality. This distortion is not always obvious, however. It is often masked by a superficially correct sense. Perception of reality is not full-blown in the newborn infant, but develops over a lengthy period of time. Indeed, analysts generally have concluded that even immediate physical reality is not perceived at birth: the infant believes the breast to be part of himself until repeated separations make him notice that it is a different object. Psychological realities are enormously more difficult to comprehend than the physical. Most people know this: "When I was a child, I spoke like a child, I thought like a child, I reasoned like a child: when I became a man I gave up childish ways" (1 Cor. 13:11). That is why it takes a lifetime to become a good analyst or accurate observer of human life and motivations.

Humans have the ability to fantasy vividly, even to hallucinate. It is thought that infants, when they want the breast but do not have it, hallucinate it. Whether or not this is true, it is much easier for adults as well as children to imagine a desired satisfaction that to labor to obtain

---

*This chapter is by Silas L. Warner, M.D.

it in reality. In life we all act largely to avoid pain and obtain pleasure, i.e., the "pleasure principle" as distinct from the "reality principle." You enjoy your climb up a mountain better if unencumbered by sweaters and blankets, but your reality sense tells you that you will freeze during the night if you do not have them. The longer-range eventual pleasure is greater through the comprehension of reality. Here fantasy, such as the imagination of icy winds on the mountain top at night, helps you achieve the greater pleasure of the whole climb, rather than settling for the immediate, brief satisfaction of an unburdened start. This kind of fantasy helps you to grasp reality.

In childhood, the firm grasp of reality is not fully developed: then we are protected less by our own understanding of reality and our adaptation to it than we are by our parents or other adults responsible for us. Therefore, if a danger or difficulty arises, we are apt to wish and fantasy that the parent would come to solve the problem for us, rescuing us. This fantasy of help is a natural part of the psychology of the child. The child's parent, by contrast, as a mature adult, must try to grasp the reality of danger and act realistically to solve it, rescuing the child. This too may take imagination, but that kind of fantasy is in the service of handling the reality.

If a primitive man is frightened by lightning or wild beasts, he may deal with reality by seeking shelter or devising weapons—or he may do nothing to protect himself in reality but only wish for help and, in the absence of good parents, fantasy spirits and gods coming to his assistance. With man's propensity for identification and projection, he may fantasy the dangers as evil spirits and pray for good spirits to fight and destroy them. This spares him the effort and energy of protecting himself and follows the psychological pattern of his childhood when his parents were fully responsible for him.

It seems that this is one main source of the ancient conflict between superstition, mysticism, and science. Superstition is the quick, easy way of the child for immediate relief of fear through fantasy. Science is the long, arduous, mature, permanently effective way of understanding reality and solving its problems and dangers. God helps those who help themselves—not to take selfishly for themselves like children, but to try as relatively independent adults to solve their own problems and dangers by understanding them.

It is difficult for an adolescent to face making his way in the world of more experienced and often advantaged adults. Youth's vanity is wounded by ignorance of life compared to experienced adults and by insecurity compared to those who are established. Youth's income is uncertain and therefore so is shelter, food, clothing, and entertainment. There is also apt to be insecurity about acceptance by the opposite sex and about love, marriage, and family. All these problems and tasks confront the immature youth (and the many adults who are still children or adolescents emotionally). It is natural for young people facing these problems and dangers to feel anxious and to meet their anxieties with the childhood wishes and fantasies of help from parents. If the parents will not or cannot help, or if the youth cannot accept help when offered by his parents, and if a cult steps in, the youth (or immature adult) may yield to his fantasies and accept the cult's support. However, if the mature part of the youth prevails, his thrust toward life powers the effort and responsibility for self which carries on to success and satisfaction; the reality principle of maturity overcomes the immediate gratification of the pleasure principle of childhood fantasies; the youth becomes ever stronger in the real world instead of escaping the world's challenges, responsibilities, and required efforts by yielding to regression in some form.

We see a remarkable parallel between the child's and the adolescent's search for personal values and the long process which mankind has gone through in evolving a culture. This would be another analogue of the biological concept of ontogeny repeating phylogeny. Both start with early infantile levels of thinking in which omnipotence, grandiosity, and attempts at magical wish fulfillment predominate and compensate for the reality of weakness of body and mind, helplessness, and ignorance. Later thinking features symbolism and animism, but still has not achieved the level of the reality principle. Certain ancient and primitive religions are an outgrowth of these early levels of pre-reality thinking, as are many of the modern-day cults. Those of today's youth who seem unable to mature beyond this primitive pre-reality thinking become prime candidates for cult membership.

Modern cults are largely composed of individuals who are unable to accept reality as it is known to science and accepted by the cultural majority. The original cult leaders are individuals who themselves believe and preach an early stage of reality, guided by the pleasure principle. Magical thinking, intimating that they are especially entitled to the best in life, usually with great sacrifice, is offered them by supernatural forces, and they in turn offer this to their followers. Many cult followers are emotionally at the same primitive level as their leaders, with the same lack of the reality principle. Some cult followers are emotionally needy and exploitable and so can be easily persuaded or coerced into becoming followers by the use of brainwashing techniques. This latter group may be victimized into an ongoing group-like psychosis from which they cannot escape. They seem to represent a spectrum: at one end is the individual who shows a primary psychotic personality which fits in with, and becomes part of, a cult whose belief system is based on psychotic thinking. These followers institutionalize their own psychotic personalities by joining a cult which is on a similar level of reality testing. At the other end of the spectrum is the individual who is a secondary or cloned cult member and who did not originally have a psychotic personality. This needy individual who was "psychologically kidnapped" into cult membership seems to have lacked the necessary defenses to withstand the onslaught of propaganda and psychological persuasion, and cannot resist the offering of a utopian community. An example of this would be the People's Temple members who were "massacred" at the insistence of their leader, Reverend Jones, in Jonestown, Guyana, in 1978.

Can a cult lose the special features which make it a cult and gradually become a legitimate and respected religion? One such example of this phenomenon is the Mormon church. To explain why this change took place over the past 150 years, we can draw certain parallels to our concept of the psychotic personality. The early leaders of the Mormon church showed a pre-reality principle view of the world as a closed system. This cultist thinking led to outside persecution which forced the early Mormons to move to a safe place to survive; closely bound together by this thinking and by the effects of persecution, they were fortunate to find the Salt Lake City area in Utah in which to start their new lives. They gradually allowed the outside world to affect their beliefs and life-styles, becoming a successful political body which professed to being law-abiding citizens of the United States. Managing to stay together on a religious level, yet changing enough in their own beliefs and practices to satisfy the requirements of being United States citizens, the Mormons advanced into living by the reality principle. There is a parallel here to those individuals with psychotic personality characteristics who are able to modify their thinking and behavior in accordance with the reality principle and become relatively normal individuals. This is seen most often in adolescents who have psychotic personalities that are not totally fixed. Such fortunate individuals experience corrective emotional experiences in psychodynamic therapy or in the outside world, which result in their being relatively normal and realistic in their thinking.

To survive, a cult must successfully provide answers for its members in certain areas. (1) It must offer a basic orientation or outlook toward the outside world. Is the world seen as an accepting place or is it a threatening place? (2) Who is the ultimate authority for any questions or decisions? Usually the cult leader becomes this ultimate authority even though he may claim his own source to be from the supernatural or may claim to have a "direct pipeline to God." (3) The cult must provide in detail the structure by which its members live their everyday lives.

To answer these three needs, the cult develops a belief system characterized by "closed-mindedness," a dogma which at all costs must be protected from outside criticism. This leads to the cult standing alone, isolating itself from the outside world which is seen as threatening and destructive, and cult members are encouraged to develop a paranoid attitude toward the world. There is, of course, a kernel of truth, as there usually is to all forms of paranoia: some individuals in the outside world *do* feel antagonistic toward the cult.

When cult members are indoctrinated into the dogmatic cult belief system, they usually are convinced that those on the outside who question their views are malicious, malevolent, and guided by the devil. This closed-mindedness leads to an institutionalized dogmatism with total intolerance to any position or belief other than the cult's. The secret society's isolation and its claim to being guided by supernatural forces provide the glue by which cult members are held together.

### INDIVIDUAL MOTIVATION FOR JOINING A CULT

Many who join cults have previously shown some emotional instability with intense emotional needs that have not been met. Most have tried other life-styles but have failed to find the proper blend of structure, discipline, idealism, and narcissistic gratification. They seem to need something which transcends reality and their own sense of ineptness: their lowly self-concept is immediately enhanced as they become a part of the cult's charismatic movement. At first, the cult seems to answer all their needs, and promises much more. After showing initial interest, most recruits are swept into the cult which promptly provides them with complete caring and total acceptance. It is during this initial recruitment and indoctrination stage that the recruits find themselves led into believing the grandiose delusions which underly the cult's reason for existence; from being emotionally needy and unstable, they are brainwashed into becoming devout cult members who no longer are able to think rationally and critically for themselves, and hence, seen as individuals, they show signs of "psychotic personality."

Once fully indoctrinated, they follow the cult's group thinking; their internal problems are externalized and they accept the cult's fantasied concept of reality; they lose their individuality and uniqueness, blending into a powerful group which professes alone to know the truth and "heroically" protects this truth against a hostile outer world which is seen as bad and wrong. This "wicked" outer world includes parents, lawyers, teachers, physicians, psychologists, and former friends—all of whom are seen as trying to get them out of the cult in any possible way, and all of whom also want to destroy the cult. Undoubtedly there is some truth in this perception. However, this element of truth does not negate the paranoid delusional beliefs, it only provides the usual kernel of reality found in all paranoia. Moreover, these outside authority figures—parents, teachers, physicians, and others—are humans who live by democratically established laws which prevent them from using violence. Since the First Amendment to the United States Constitution promises its citizens freedom to practice the religion of their choice, the cult can simply label itself a "religion" to guarantee itself protection against prosecution.

The various cults must appeal to certain unconscious needs in those who have been recruited successfully. Usually a cult is perceived as a new family by a prospective member, and there is inevitably a comparison between the recruit's original family and the new family. Several possibilities then present themselves:

1. The recruit was part of an original nuclear family which met his needs, especially dependency. Part of him never wanted to separate from this original family, but another part wanted to escape or else was forced out by circumstances beyond his control or his family's, and he was left with longings for another family. Society offers some

family-like institutions such as college, graduate school, or the military as a temporary answer to these dependent needs after high school. Educational institutions limit the time of enrollment, but the military allows reenlistments up to 30 years. Traditional, long-established religions encourage membership for an entire lifetime. Oftentimes individuals who are emotionally unstable and have tried temporary family substitutes lose their eligibility to enter academic institutions or the legitimate church family and also cannot accept or be accepted by the military services. Thus such individuals are especially susceptible to what the cults offer, and they join what they feel (consciously or unconsciously) to be a better family. Their lives are so well structured by the cult's requirements that their dependent needs are met, but at the individuality-shattering price of complete obedience and sacrificed sense of reality.

2. Another factor motivating "grown-up children" toward cult membership is often resentment, for whatever reasons, toward their original family. What better way to pay back their parents than to join a cult to which their parents are vigorously opposed and then tell them what a wonderful life the cult offers? Their long hours of handing out publications or selling crafts in public places often represent behavior very different from that shown at home and rub more salt into the rejected parents' wounds. Again the children are swept along by peer pressure and other inducements until they feel they have no choice but to become highly obedient and self-disciplined.

3. The resentment toward the original family usually stems from many errors of omission or commission by the parents during childhood that make the young adult feel neglected and even rejected, inferior, or in other ways mistreated. When the cult members tell such a person that they want him, will pay attention to him, will provide him with a permanent and important role within the cult, it can become irresistible for him to join.

4. Some young adults are attracted to a cult because of its seemingly unselfish and idealistic way of life. In most cults, personal possessions are kept to a minimum, everything of value is turned over to "the hierarchy." Usually at the top is an all-powerful leader to whom the members must swear total allegiance, a leader who claims to be a messiah, deriving his wisdom and power from God, giving the cult members a set of rules and beliefs by which to live. These "doctrines"

or "truths" promulgated by the leader are divine, absolute, and never to be questioned. Some cults promise to improve society or the world, but inevitably these efforts also are guarantees of the cult's survival and usually enormously profitable financially for its leaders.

To insure its survival, the cult has to continually recruit new members, successfully indoctrinate these recruits into the cult's way of life, and raise funds by which to live and pay tribute to the messiah-leader. All the energy of its members ultimately goes into the cult's survival, so "surviving in a hostile world" becomes an additional cause or ideal by which the cult members live. If the cult can survive, growing larger, richer, and more powerful, it can promise to benefit society. The cult offers its members to society as role models in the hope of bringing more recruits into the cult. A cult such as the Unification Church ("Moonies") has acquired assets numbering many millions of dollars and owns various businesses including its own newspaper. It has even been accused of using its wealth and power to influence the United States government.

What is the difference between those youths today who become interested in and try out a cult, then reject it, as opposed to those who stay with the cult? There must be a fit between the inner needs of the prospective recruit and what the cult has to offer. To complicate this, the recruit is often deceived about the cult's identity early in the recruiting.

For example, a young man, a college senior whom we will call "M", rejected a cult. "M" took off the second semester of his sophomore year to hitchhike across the country. He got to Berkeley, visited a friend, and on leaving, ran into two men who invited him to dinner. He thought they were "loonies" and ignored them, but when he was unable to obtain a ride he located them and accepted their hospitality. He ended up on a large farm 100 miles north of San Francisco, and only much later did he learn that it was owned and run by the Unification Church (the "Moonies"). The following is from an interview with "M" which appeared in *The Phoenix*, the Swarthmore college newspaper, in October 1979:

M: The days were pretty full [on the farm]. We woke up or "jumped up" very early in the morning. "Jumping up" was simply the act of standing straight up out of your sleeping bag as soon as you were the slightest bit awake. There was work; while I was there, I helped build a flight of steps and a bridge across a stream. There were meals—the food was always good—and we played volleyball, and during the games we would chant, "We love you." That was really weird. They also had lectures several times a week, in which they preached love, generosity, and understanding. There was also a time each day during which you were supposed to be alone—a meditation period. We would go to sleep very late, and the next day would be pretty much the same.

INTERVIEWER: What struck you most about the camp?

M: The unbelievable amount of happiness. Everybody was happy 24 hours a day, and I mean everybody. It was just fantastic, being so happy all the time.

INTERVIEWER: Was there anything you didn't like?

M: Not really at first; I didn't even mind the almost total lack of privacy too much. But there was one thing that kind of unsettled me. One of the things we did at the camp was sing. We would stand in a circle holding hands and sing, and after dinner each person would get up and sing a song. This one time I sang a Tom Lehrer song "The Old Dope Peddler" and got booed because the song expressed negativity. They were totally against negativity of any kind—a belief I didn't agree with at all. Another time we were putting up these posters, and one showed a dark jungle; they refused to put it up because it didn't show a sunny field with flowers and grass. They were really adamant about that. Everything had to be sunny and cheerful all the time.

INTERVIEWER: Were there any rules which you had to follow?

M: There was no smoking or drinking. We weren't allowed to wear shoes indoors, I never did figure that one out. They also wanted us to cut our hair really short, but I never did.

INTERVIEWER: How long we you at the camp?

M: I was at the first camp for five days. After that they asked me if I wanted to go to another camp, and I said okay. This second camp was an old converted Girl Scout camp.

INTERVIEWER: Was there any difference between the two camps?

M: The second camp was on a higher educational level than the first. There were more lectures. Whereas the lectures of the first camp fit in pretty much with my philosophies, I didn't agree with these later ones at all. They would give the same lecture maybe three times in a row and the instructors tried to tell us some pretty bizarre things. For instance, they gave their theory of spiritual growth; that as the physical body grows by means of food, light, and water, generosity and good deeds give growth to the spiritual body. Each good deed brings the soul closer to God's love. They also believe that everything was put in the universe for the benefit of men, and that Christ failed his mission as Messiah because he let us kill him. This last was one of their many weird interpretations of the Bible, which they used exlusively. They also believe that Russia is the Antichrist, and they are very opposed to communism. To them, the foundation of substance is America, and it's "us against them."

INTERVIEWER: How did you discover that the camp was run by "Moonies"?

M: About a week after I arrived, this guy was leaving for Detroit, and he said that he was glad there was a Unification Church located there. It took me a while to connect the Unification Church with the "Moonies." The people at the camp always referred to the Unification Church; "Moonies" or the Rev. Moon were never mentioned.

INTERVIEWER: How many people were at the camp, and what were they like?

M: The number of people varied between 60 and 120. Most of them were really nice; like I've said, we were always happy. Many of them were travelers like myself who didn't take the camp too seriously; they had a lot of good stories. The people who were really into the religious thing were all sort of washed out, all the same.

INTERVIEWER: Was there any kind of physical discipline?

M: There was none of this "locking people up in small rooms" kind of thing, if that's what you mean, and the only kind of "brainwashing" was the result of one's sudden confrontation with full happiness. There was no torture of anything. No one *wanted* to leave. And that's the best thing they've got going for them, the most crucial thing.

INTERVIEWER: Why did you leave the camp?

M: I became really depressed and unhappy when I was transferred to the second camp. The lectures got more and more ridiculous, and

I just wasn't happy anymore. Also, I had had a "spiritual brother" assigned to me at the first camp who answered any questions I had and would try to convince me to believe the lectures. When I was transferred to the second camp he left, and I got another spiritual brother whom I didn't like too much. Mainly, though, the happiness just wore off. If I had stayed happy that second week, who knows?

From the above it seems that "M" is a fairly typical, bright college student of the late seventies. Taking off a semester from college is the usual way for a student to widen his horizons, hoping to sharpen the focus on his identity. His accepting a ride from strangers and showing a strong curiosity about life on this farm are not at all unusual; the "unbelievable amount of happiness" that he observed appealed to his idealistic side. He could even tolerate the lack of privacy. What he could not appreciate was the "Moonies" singlemindedness in only recognizing "good" and their complete inability to tolerate anything negative: they lacked even a sense of humor about his singing a Tom Lehrer song. "M" was unwilling to close his mind to *reality*, which is why he was incapable of joining their ranks. He does sound a note of caution by wondering if, had he had stayed for the second week, he would have "converted" to their narrow point of view. The brainwashing or psychological coercion might have taken hold of his mind and tempted him to become one of them. We believe that he had sufficient maturity and grasp of reality to have resisted this temptation and maintained the integrity of his individuality.

Another young man joined a religious cult because it answered so many of his emotional needs: Ben was in his late teens when he went into a very rigid and Orthodox yeshiva, much against his parents' wishes. Whether or not he will ever choose to leave this fanatical, rightwing, fundamentalist Judaic group, only time will tell. Ben's parents are both open-minded, free-thinking, Reform Jews with successful professional careers. His father is a college professor of philosophy who has written extensively on all aspects of philosophy and religion, and his mother is a public health nurse, also well-known in her community. Ben's older sister suffered organic brain damage at birth and has attended special schools all her life; she has a "short fuse," and Ben vividly recalls her frequent blowups at home and how grating it was on his nerves to witness his parents trying to "domesticate" her. He suffered from not getting all the time and attention that his sister required, but he profited from being the favored, bright, good child, in contrast to his sister.

Ben was a delight to his parents and teachers until his adolescence. It was then that his parents' inability to get along with each other surfaced and resulted in their separating when he was 12 years of age. It was agreed that he and his sister would live with their mother during the week and visit their father over the weekend. Both parents had emotionally invested themselves in their children, but especially in Ben. The mother found him to be bright, charming, and amusing, and always took genuine joy in singing his praises. His father felt the same way and especially enjoyed Ben's getting older, which made increasingly possible "deep intellectual discussions." Each parent wanted to be favored over the other in Ben's eyes so Ben learned to please both and could skillfully manipulate either to get his way. His parents both agreed that Ben was very special but each had vastly different ways of dealing with him: the father was more indulgent, giving Ben whatever he wished. The father had been too close to his own tyrannical mother and strongly believed that early efforts should be made to psychologically free Ben from his mother's emotional orbit. In subtle ways he tried to undermine the mother's authority with Ben. The mother believed that the father was "too wishy-washy" with Ben, and so she tried to put more structure into his life. She felt that Ben's father "lacked a backbone" and got this message across to Ben. Thus Ben felt it necessary to please and protect each parent. Each parent gradually became involved with a paramour. The mother was very discreet and never had her new boyfriend spend the night with her when Ben was home, but the father felt this was deceitful and he openly had his girlfriend stay in his bedroom when Ben was there. Ben finally complained about this and, with his mother's backing, insisted that his father stop this practice. The father had rather ambivalent feelings toward this woman and decided he would not fight Ben's ultimatum, so he abruptly stopped seeing her. Ben must have felt that he had his father "back in line" and was again his father's favorite: to celebrate their reestablished unity they went to Israel together, where his father proudly lectured to Ben about the wonderful heritage of Judaism with its glorious history. Ben found himself wondering why neither parent was active in a synagogue yet both were proud of being Jews. Ben asked his parents if he could attend a Jewish school and they happily complied, sending him to one which emphasized good secular scholarship and freethinking but only secondarily taught Jewish history and religion.

Gradually Ben became more depressed from the constant tug of war between his parents and their efforts to align him to their particular side; nothing seemed to help his inner pain which stemmed from being the favorite and having to choose between his parents. He also resented their inconsistencies and learned to clam up or lie rather than face their confrontations. By the age of 15 he had decided on attending the strictest, most right-wing yeshiva boarding school he could find, so he ran away from his parents in the summer and stayed with a rabbi from this yeshiva, who told him that his duty to Judaism transcended his duty to his parents and that he needed to live at the yeshiva to pursue his studies full time. His parents were shocked, tried to reason with him, and attempted to legally block his entering the yeshiva, but to no avail.

Ben seemed happier than ever as he spouted the "party line" and obeyed the rigid rules required at the yeshiva. All his inner needs seemed to be answered: he no longer had to deal with his parents; he had an all-consuming religious interest and way of life that kept him constantly challenged and busy. He had "externalized" his problem: all he had to do was study, pray, and exercise and he would prosper as an outstanding scholar. He was not required to make any adolescent sexual adjustment and could temporarily postpone any social interaction with the opposite sex. He was taught that Darwin's theory of evolution was false and he could "prove" that the Old Testament's version of the creation of the world was "scientifically valid"; his mind was cleared of doubt and uncertainty and he no longer experienced ambivalent feelings; he became well trained in the disciplined but narrow teachings of extreme right-wing Judaism. He was polite and respectful, but in a mechanical fashion.

Here again we see an example of a "cloned" psychotic personality. To put to rest the emotional turmoil of complex, conflictful interrelationships with both parents, Ben entered a codified, strict religious movement which closed his mind to the realities of the world as most people know it. We do not know if Ben will stay with this cult or not. However, for the next few years he does seem destined to remain a voluntary prisoner with a group that appears from the outside to be wearing blinders.

John is an example of a young man whose inner needs led him into a cult but whose psychopathology was too severe to be resolved by it or even for it to allow him to remain. John was first seen at age 17. He sought psychiatric help because of emotional instability, painful preoccupation with his bodily functions, and confusion about his identity and goals. He seemed in danger of decompensating into a schizophrenic reaction.

John was the second of three sons born to very liberal and idealistic middle-class Jewish parents. He was given maximum freedom within the home "to find his own path." He tried to conform at school and was a good student but could not make close friends. John dropped out of school in his sophomore year and tried to set up his own "alternative education" with his parents' consent: he studied Eastern religions, started experimenting with drugs, and spent long hours painting in his "studio." A gradual withdrawal took place which his parents interpreted as a natural part of "discovering himself." As his thinking became fragmented, his parents became concerned and sought psychiatric help. John oscillated in his thinking from grandiosity to a feeling of total failure and self-loathing; he wondered if he was not being controlled by some outside force. At times he blamed his parents for being indecisive and letting him do anything he wanted, but at other times he would praise them for showing confidence in him and trusting his judgment. After a month of outpatient psychotherapy with antipsychotic medication, he abruptly left the United States for Europe.

He returned to the United States two years later and was immediately placed in a psychiatric hospital. By then John was overtly schizophrenic with totally fragmented, grandiose thinking centering around his health, bizarre religiosity, and guilt with self-destructive thoughts. The interim history was pieced together. It gradually revealed that he had wandered through Europe and headed for the Middle East looking for a transcendent religious cause. His personal hygiene and nutrition were poor, and he was soon reduced to malnutrition and rags. Then "miraculously" while in Holland he had the "highest experience of his life." He met with a member of the Children of God (Rudin, 1980) and was immediately converted to their "family of love," and indoctrinated to believe that God is love and that if he loved himself he could be saved. He later was told that his parents were the enemy, the United States was evil ("America the whore") and its system doomed. He was also exposed to strong anti-Semitism, including hatred toward Israel and all Jews. John learned the cult's history and was told that the Children of God's leader, David Brandt Berg, a former Baptist minister, closed most of the communes in the United States and moved to Europe because (Berg said) the United States was "doomed." These communes were called "colonies" and included 6 to 12 members who were led by a "shepherd." Children of God had to read and memorize Bible passages for 12 hours a day and were told that God would strike them dead if they returned to the evil world.

About a month before John's return to the United States his parents were called from a general hospital in Rome and told that he was in intensive care, emaciated from malnutrition and delirious with a fever. They flew over and, as soon as he was physically recovered, brought him back. It remains a mystery how and why he ended up in the Rome hospital. He was put in a psychiatric hospital in the United States and gradually stabilized emotionally, mentally, and physically. Then two representatives from the Children of God contacted him in the hospital and persuaded him to rejoin a local colony. Because his parents agreed to this, he was signed out of the hospital against medical advice, although he was still delusional and self-destructive, albeit less fragmented in his thinking. He spent a month with the cult and was taken by them to another city to be away from his parents. While en route, he savagely tried to pluck out his eye: he had apparently "seen something bad" and felt the need to inflict self-punishment. He was rehospitalized in a general hospital where he came close to losing the vision in his badly injured eye. Then his parents intervened and tried to bring him home, but he was whisked away to another colony. Six months later he was placed in a state psychiatric hospital with a "florid psychosis of a schizophrenic type."

John has subsequently been living in a halfway house, eking out a marginal existence in a sheltered workshop, rarely visiting his parents, and expressing some interest in returning to the cult but lacking the initiative to follow this idea through. The cult members apparently have given up on him as a "sickie" and no longer pursue him. He could best be described as a "burnt-out schizophrenic" who tragically had his "revenge" on his parents and paid very dearly for it (i.e., his hostilities took masochistic form).

Are most of the members of modern religious cults psychotic personalities? What about Tom, a Hare Krishna (Rudin, 1980, pp. 45-54) devotee who solicits weary travelers in an airport? He constantly smiles, chants, and wears an Indian robe. All hair on his head has been shaved off except for a top braid or knot, known as a *shika,* which will allow the Hindu god, Lord Krishna, to pull Tom into heaven at the appropriate time.

Tom is a 25-year-old member of the International Society for Krishna Consciousness (ISKCON) who is estranged from his middle-class family because he believes they do not understand his fanatic devotion to the Hare Krishnas. They remember him as a promising and bright young man, valedictorian of his high school class, subsequently admitted to a prestigious college which he never attended. Instead, Tom went through a period of "finding himself," trying out "alternative life-styles," and using psychedelic drugs excessively. Then after two years of "searching for an identity," Tom "impulsively" joined the Hare Krishnas. Now his every minute is tightly scheduled. He sleeps on the hard floor of a Hare Krishna temple, gets up every morning at 3:30 A.M., and puts in four hours of chanting and meditation before the strenuous work of the day. He eats twice a day, the diet mainly consisting of vegetables, rice, fruit, and milk. Various chants are repeated hundreds of times daily praising Krishna, their god of the poor. Tom is one of the 12,000 full-time Hare Krishna members living in 40 different temples in the United States. His religious duty is to solicit book sales in public places. The Hare Krishna Publishing Trust publishes a magazine *Back to Godhead,* as well as many books written by His Divine Grace A.C. Bhaktivedanta Swami Prabhupada, who in 1966 founded ISKCON in the United States. Tom can earn up to $100 a day from this soliciting.

ISKCON discourages rational thought: all members live an austere, hard-working existence and regularly study Sanskrit and Hindu scripture. They are descended from the 4,000-year-old Hindu religion of India. Hindus basically follow the thought that "since the physical world is temporal, all our worldly desires are doomed to frustration and this frustration is the cause of all human suffering. Real peace can therefore be found only in the control of desire, by turning the mind to the one enduring, everlasting reality—God" (Time, Inc., 1957). Yet how does a religious movement advocating control of desire, peace, purity, and total dedication survive in a Western competitive society? They are obviously forced to compete, and as a result the idealistic Hare Krishna philosophy has had instances of "breakdown in the marketplace." For example, they have been accused of "hard-sell" or deceptive solicitations, and charged with falsely claiming to be raising money for other charities and also with strong-arm tactics (including brass knuckles). They have been known to have firearms (Conway and Siegelman, 1978) on their Krishna farms and to have smuggled drugs to raise money. Their leaders deplore such activities and blame them on ex-drug addicts who became members and are "bad apples."

Imagine how Tom's parents feel as they read this "bad publicity" or see other Hare Krishnas happily and fanatically soliciting travelers. Is this the life they worked so long and hard for Tom to enjoy? He used to talk about being a lawyer, a scientist, or a scholar, and all his teachers said he had the aptitude for it. Where did they go wrong? Should they have insisted that Tom follow their own Lutheran religion about which he seemed so lukewarm?

Individuals like Tom show a pseudoindependence during their adolescence which covers up their more basic need for nurturance and a secure dependency. They experience the cult's charismatic leader as "enlightened" and are happy to slavishly follow his directions—such is the power of the need in the human mind for an authority figure to be dependent upon and submissive to. This leads to a voluntary loss of their own individuality. Instead, they incorporate their leader's concept of the world with his rules about how to conduct their everyday lives, and feel strengthened by being given absolute answers; they are willing to give up their doubts and intellectual curiosity, in fact their maturity, for the security of group membership in the cult.

## CHARACTERISTICS OF MODERN CULTS

There are currently about 3,000 cult groups in the United States with their actual membership estimated at about six million. A cult can be roughly defined as a religious group which significantly differs in belief and practice from the average, normal religions in a culture. Most cults go through a natural evolution, starting as a radical or bizarre fringe group following a self-appointed "messiah" leader. Typically, this leader has himself survived some severe, personal discomfort during adolescence, and subsequently experiences an altered state of consciousness such as a vision or hallucination which authenticates his uniqueness and proves to him that he has been chosen to lead a special spiritual mission. His own doubts, pain, and anxiety are miraculously erased by this "transcendental calling," and he feels compelled to share his vision and beliefs with others who then become his followers or disciples. His new belief system is "ego-syntonic," (i.e., accepted by the rest of his personality), and allows him to externalize his previous intrapsychic problems. These inner problems often resulted in his having felt chronically insecure, bad, or angry, and he is now able to project these feelings onto those in the outside world. He comes to feel secure, good, and loving, and he offers himself and his enlightenment to those in the outside world so they will not suffer as he once did. He accumulates followers who promote his mission by "spreading the word" about the remarkable events and ways of thinking which gave him health and happiness, and he gladly accepts the role of messiah with all its uniqueness and responsibilities, and usually huge financial income. Whether the cult survives or not, then, depends on the inspiration and timeliness of the messiah's message, as well as on the charismatic personality and organizational skills of the leader and his disciples, and on his abilities to make and manage money.

### Christianity

Cults that fail or sputter along with a marginal existence are the rule. Of the many ancient religious cults and sects, only a very few have survived and prospered. A good example of extreme success is Christianity. Jesus Christ was considered a remarkably inspirational, altruistic, if not masochistic, Jew during his life-time of 33 years (Hart, 1978, pp. 47-51). He was but one of many other sect leaders of that time, offering a special message. That his sect turned into a highly successful religion is a tribute not only to his short but exemplary and inspirational life, but also to the devotion and organizational skill of his disciples. It was Paul especially who not only spearheaded the organization of Christian theology but also worked extraordinarily hard to proselytize the people of the central Mediterranean area (Hart, 1978). Paul was tireless in proclaiming and framing the gospel; it is possible that without his energy and religious fervor Christianity might have died out. If one objectively analyzes the message that Jesus' life gives us, it is clear that he was primarily a spiritual and ethical leader. Central to his philosophy was the "Golden Rule," an already accepted precept of Judaism and also of the Chinese philosopher Confucius. Jesus' message differed from most other established religions in his emphasis on forgiveness and love ("Love your neighbor" and "Turn the other cheek"). Most Christians give lip service to these ideas and honor them as "ideal," but feel unable to live up to them.

### Buddhism

Another highly successful religious leader was Gautama Buddha (563-483 B.C.), a prince, the son of a king in northeast India. At 16 he married his cousin and lived unhappily in the royal palace, preoccupied with the deprivation and need in which most Indian people lived and, therefore, unable to enjoy his own luxurious life. Immediately after the birth of his first child when he was 29, he left the palace, his family, and all his possessions to go in search of truth. In his travels he studied with scholars and holy men, and tried living an extremely ascetic life, including severe fasts and self-mortification. He concluded that tormenting his body muddled his brain, so he resumed normal meals and discarded asceticism. Sitting under a giant fig tree at age 35, he had a flash of insight and became convinced that he had the solution to understanding life. This turned him into a Buddha, or "enlightened person," and for the following 45 years he traveled all over northern India preaching his new philosophy. This philosophy is summarized in what Buddhists call the "Four Noble Truths": (1) human life is intrinsically unhappy; (2) the cause of this unhappiness is human selfishness and desire; (3) individual selfishness and desire can be brought to an end when all desires and cravings have been eliminated (nirvana); (4) the method of escape from selfishness and desire is what is known as the "Eightfold Path"—right views, right thought, right speech, right action, right livelihood, right effort, right mindfulness, and right meditation (Hart, 1978, pp. 52-56).

### Mohammedanism

Mohammed (A.D. 570-632), like Jesus, was of humble birth. He not only founded and promoted one of the world's great religions (Islam), but also became a successful and effective political leader (Hart, 1978, pp. 33-40). He was orphaned at age six and raised illiterate in modest surroundings in Mecca, giving no special indication of being a remarkable person until he was 40. His finances were made secure when, at age 25, he married a wealthy widow. He was exposed to the few Christians and Jews living in Mecca and became aware of their worshipping a single, omnipotent God and having a Bible encompassing their faith. By age 40, he was convinced that this one God (Allah) spoke directly to him and had picked him to tell others what constituted true faith, so he vigorously shared his true faith with others, gained converts, and brought the Koran into existence. The local authorities in Mecca viewed him as a dangerous nuisance, and at age 52 he fled 200 miles to Medina in fear for his safety. He rapidly acquired many converts there, and became an acknowledged religious and political leader. A war was being fought between Medina and Mecca which ended in A.D. 630 with Medina the victor. Mohammed celebrated by returning to Mecca both as a conqueror and as a religious leader. Up to this point, most Arabs believed in many gods and were considered pagans. In the last two and a half years of his life, before his death in A.D. 632, Mohammed became the ruler of all southern Arabia and converted most Arabs to his new Islamic religion which ruled as a theocracy. After his death the small Arab armies, unified by Mohammed, set out as an invading army and conquered most of Mesopotamia, Syria, Palestine, and Egypt, ultimately conquering the known world from North Africa to the Atlantic Ocean and, finally, most of Spain.

Mohammed played the key role in proselytizing the new faith and establishing the religious practices of Islam. Moreover, he is the author of the Moslem holy scriptures, the Koran, a collection of certain insights that he believed had been divinely revealed to him by Allah.

Reviewing the world's great religions, one cannot but wonder what role in their success is played by the enormous and ubiquitous human needs for authority figures to be dependent upon and submissive to.

### The Mormon Church

Today's Mormon church is a good example of a fringe cult group which was persecuted in the nineteenth century but survived, evolving into a highly respectable, thriving, modern religion (Martin, 1977, pp. 147-148).

Joseph Smith, Jr. ("The Prophet"), born in 1805, lived in New York State, the son of a mystic father who spent most of his time digging for buried treasure. The father was soon joined by his son, both hoping to locate Captain Kidd's plunder. They used divining rods, and young Joseph possessed a "peep stone" which was said to guide him to the special areas in the earth in which treasures were most likely to be found.

In 1830, while praying in the woods, young Joseph was allegedly the recipient of a marvelous vision in which God the Father and God the Son materialized and spoke to him. He was told that the Christian church and world at large were faltering and needed restoration, and that he had been chosen to accomplish this task. In 1823, the angel Moroni appeared at his bedside and reemphasized to Joseph his mission and its importance. In 1827, Smith, guided by his visions, discovered on top of a hill a stone box (or crypt) containing golden plates which were inscribed with unfamiliar writing. He also found "two transparent stones" which allowed him to "translate the Reformed Egyptian" into English with the help of a former school teacher, Oliver Cowdrey, and was also aided in his translation by some miraculous "spectacles" left by the angel Moroni and known as the "urim and thummim." (It should be noted that leading Egyptologists and philologists all agree that they know nothing of the apparently nonexistent language "Reformed Egyptian.") This translation resulted in the Book of Mormon which the Latter-Day Saints believe to be the genuine Word of God and equal to the Christian Bible.

Smith then had another vision in which John the Baptist appeared and ordained Smith and Cowdrey into the Aaronic priesthood. In a further vision, Peter, James, and John appeared, conferring on the two men the priesthood of Melchizedek and presenting them with the holy apostolic keys. In 1830 Joseph Smith founded the Mormon church in Fayette, New York, and had as charter members six of his followers.

The Book of Mormon is over 600 pages long and traces the ancient records of two great tribes or races, the Jareds and a remnant of the house of Israel, who formerly inhabited America (Rosten, 1975). The remnant tribe was supposed to have left Palestine in 600 B.C. and migrated to North America where it built up a civilization but was ultimately destroyed by warfare between its two largest tribes, the Nephites and Lamanites, in about A.D. 421. Moroni was the last historian of the Lamanites and is said to have deposited the records in the stone box which Smith later found. Smith believed the American Indians were all that was left of the Lamanites. The golden plates and sacred stones were returned when a messenger called for them so they were never inspected by any impartial experts. Supposedly, 11 other persons besides Prophet Smith testified to having seen the plates.

The Mormons grew so rapidly that their neighbors, who had known the Smith family for years, rose in opposition and claimed that his new religion was a sham and a hoax. Smith was said to have "conjured up revelations" instructing him to move to Ohio, then to Missouri, and finally, to Nauvoo, Illinois. It was there that persecution by hostile neighbors led to the death of Joseph Smith. The Mormons' practice of polygamy was "exposed" by an anti-Morman publication known as *The Nauvoo Expositor*. When the headquarters for this publication was destroyed the Mormons were suspected, and Joseph Smith and his brother Hyrum were put in jail to await trial. On June 27, 1844, a mob stormed the jail and murdered Joseph and Hyrum, and of course this assured martyrdom for Prophet Smith. Brigham Young, then 43 years old, took over the Mormon leadership.

In 1847 Young led the Mormons west to the valley of Great Salt Lake. On first seeing the area he exclaimed, "This is the place," and Salt Lake City was established as the home of the Mormons. The Mormons felt "a spiritual deed" claim to possession of this area, especially when, in June of 1848, their crops were saved from the destruction of locusts by a large army of sea gulls.

Brigham Young was courageous but subject to "fits of ruthlessness." Because he was determined to control Utah at any cost, he ordered Bishop John D. Lee to annihilate a wagon train of 150 helpless immigrants in 1857. Bishop Lee performed this heinous act and 20 years later was tried, convicted, and executed by the U.S. government for his crime. When Brigham Young died in 1877, 17 widows and 47 children survived him. In 1890, polygamy (adopted to increase strength through numbers) was abolished by federal law as against public policy. The Mormons believe in honoring and sustaining the law, and have complied with this 1890 law ever since.

Today the main branch of the Mormon church numbers in excess of 3.3 million members all over the world. Each year they average 80,000 conversions, and the birthrate of its members is significantly higher than the national average.  The church is well organized by dedicated people to teach sound moral traits, pursue education, help each other and disadvantaged people, and keep the minds and bodies of its members strong and pure. Every part of a Mormon's life is structured and planned from cradle to grave. Mormon historians have revised their history to make it romantic, miraculous, and respectable.  Critics brand the Mormons "a non-Christian cult system," labeling it "a polytheistic nightmare of garbled doctrines draped with the garment of Christian terminology" (Turner, 1966).  They point to the real source of the Book of Mormon as being an expansion upon the writing of one Solomon Spaulding, a retired minister who was known to have written a number of "romances" with biblical backgrounds similar to the Book of Mormon.  Such critics add that "it was Joseph Smith who declared theological war on Christianity when he ascribed to God the statement that branded all Christian sects as 'all wrong,' their deeds as 'abominations,' and all Christians as 'corrupt—having a form of godliness, but denying the power thereof.'" Critics also say that the sincerity of the Mormons' faith and their positive actions do not alter the very questionable foundations of their church (Turner, 1966).

The Mormons' version of ancient civilizations on the American continent has no scholarly support outside of their own sources: anthropologists specializing in genetics point out that Mediterranean races from whom the Jews and Semites came bear little or no resemblance to American Indians.  A careful study of the Book of Mormon shows it to contain at least 25,000 words from the King James Version of the Bible.  Some of the plagiarisms include verbatim quotations of some length.  One Mormon answer to this is that when Christ appeared on the American continent after His resurrection and preached to the Nephites he quite naturally used the same language as recorded in the Bible.

Despite the lack of authenticity of its early history, the Mormon church remains a powerful force for good in the modern world. Its members have been highly successful in all fields, and there are proportionately more Mormons contained in *Who's Who in America* than are found representing any other major religion. Mormons give more money, unpaid work, and other contributions to their causes than any other major religion, and have more than 18,000 active missionaries in the field today. They encourage their young people to dedicate two years of their lives to missionary work on a self-supporting basis; they take care of their own people and consider it sinful for a Mormon to receive welfare funds from a governmental source. In no other religious group in the United States are the home and family more important than with the Church of Jesus Christ of Latter-Day Saints (Mormons).

The Mormon church has thus succeeded in progressing from a typical closed-minded cult to a highly respectable religion. The change was made when it accepted outside reality: this meant abiding by the laws of the United States and not hiding and isolating its activities. Mormons now travel everywhere, and are a strong force for good and progress. They totally accept outside "reality."

\* \* \* \*

Cults of today attract the same alienated youth who became the flower children-hippie-love feast converts of the mid-1960s and angry antiwar radicals of the late 1960s. The form of their protest has changed, but its essential ingredients have remained the same: alienated youth, hostile to their parents, narcissistically preoccupied with their own needs, who claim a new idealism that transcended the "failings" of their elders. During the hippie-flower children era there was a return to the "natural" way, a distrust of science and technology, and a morality in which love and simplicity would overcome all that was bad and wrong in our society. It was Rousseau's "noble savage" returning in the twentieth century. Communes sprang up featuring egalitarian sharing of everything, including food, money, resources, thoughts, and sex. It was group living, supposedly without leaders, bound together by eternal love. Only a few of these idealistic communes have survived the two decades, and this failure has been attributed to a basic human need for leadership plus the emotional instability of many of the commune members (to say nothing of the maturity required for the responsibility, effort, and hard work necessary to earn a livelihood).

Two other factors seem to have changed the nature of these groups: one was that, in the past, they only looked inside themselves for strength, creativity, and wisdom. This inner wisdom could be released by meditation, Eastern religions, and certain drugs. Using psychedelic drugs became a shortcut for getting in touch with inner truths, experiences, and wisdom. College and high school students throughout the sixties used and abused such drugs, and it was only a matter of time before they sought more self-discipline from an outside source by putting themselves under the authority of a mystic, guru, or messiah. This led to the popularizing of cult movements whose seemingly omnipotent or divine leaders were worshipped and closely followed. The alienated youth's narcissism was satisfied by his image of himself as a member of an elitist cult.

The other important factor was external: the war in Vietnam. This served as a rallying cry for alienated youth to unite in righteous indignation against the establishment and its military-industrial complex. The "wicked" American exploiters had to be fought using their own tactics. The "Yippies" who emerged in 1969 soon were advocating "violence to fight violence." Burning draft cards, leaving the country so as not to be drafted, and even bombing any part of the military-industrial complex seemed justified in this new crusade, but when the war ended, the more violent and radical of these alienated persons lost their primary cause. Other causes such as protesting against nuclear power, the draft, and poverty remained as targets, but the protesters lacked organization and zest. This vacuum invited cults to surface and attract the alienated youth who were barely limping along. A complete package, the new cult, which totally regulated their lives in all areas, appeared to answer all their needs.

We have found no satisfactory sociological answer to the questions of whether and why more of these hostile-withdrawn (fight-flight) youth existed in the sixties and seventies than in other decades. Perhaps world conditions affected child rearing, especially during the critical 0 to 6 years. Crime has continued to increase since then, and this too must be the result in part of traumatic experiences of children throughout the world.

Johnson (1977, pp. 28-29)* sums this up:

Actually, the similarities between the low-feasts of 1967, the pitched battles of 1969 and the sidewalk chantings of 1974 far outweigh the differences. There is a common thread of desperation and self-

From "A Temple of Last Resorts: Youth and Shared Narcissism," by A. Johnson, *The Narcissistic Condition* edited by M. Nelson. Copyright 1977, Human Sciences Press.

preoccupation running through all these movements, leading ultimately to a total rejection of the adult world and the effort to find a permanent substitute for it, or avoid it altogether by a regressive, narcissistic retreat from the world. The regressive withdrawal from the real world into one's own mind and the over-compensation for this infantile weakness by vanity and egotism (narcissism) and the rage because of it characterized the stoned flower-children and the radical bomb-throwers as well as the pacified religious devotees. Witness:

The total self-absorption of both drug use and meditation.

The grandiosity implicit in the belief that by bombing a branch bank in California one can halt a war in Asia waged by the largest government on earth.

The belief that by arcane measures like the practice of astrology and witchcraft one can be so powerful as to predict the future or control the forces of nature.

The childish effort to aggrandize the self through an unrealistic choice of one's supposed previous incarnations.

Last, but hardly least, the shared retreat into a new world of one's own making, occupied only by the chosen few of one's peers.

All this could as well have been written as a description of the psychotic personality.

* * * *

The Unification Church (or "Moonies"), discussed earlier, is one of the wealthiest, best organized, and largest of the new cults (Rudin, 1980). Its founder, Reverend Sun Myung Moon, was raised as a Presbyterian in Korea, became a wealthy industrialist, and then turned evangelist. He makes no public claim to be the Messiah, but nonetheless within the church is referred to as such. He does claim to be a divine being sent to earth to breed an "ideal race" which would finish the work of Jesus Christ. His church was founded in Korea in 1954 and officially is known as the Holy Spirit Association for the Unification of World Christianity. It owns munitions factories in Korea as well as other factories manufacturing ginseng tea, titanium, pharmaceuticals, and air rifles, and recently entered the fishing business off the United States coastal waters. Reverend Moon's United States residence is in a large retreat in Tarrytown, New York. The church's national headquarters is in Manhattan in what was formerly the New Yorker Hotel. His followers, popularly known as "Moonies," spend long hours in public places such as airports, busy city streets, or college campuses selling flowers, candles, or incense to raise funds for their cult and its avowed purpose of "unifying the human family."

Reverend Moon's philosophy combines some aspects of Christianity with Asian sun-god worship, along with a dualism which pits an Absolute God against Absolute Evil (maybe an appeal to the duality of child versus parent); he views humans as divine creatures who have fallen following Eve's sin of having sexual intercourse with a serpent. To atone for this original sin, the Unification Church initially sponsored ritualized sexual relations to cleanse its followers. Since Reverend Moon was believed to be a pure man, having sex with him purified his female followers, but this was later changed to his selecting the two partners for a marriage which would guarantee the purity of each of the partners. Such a marriage creates a God-centered family in which church members are brothers and sisters, and Moon and his present wife (his third) are worshipped as "true parents." Jesus Christ is viewed as having "failed" in his mission because he never married and therefore had no sinless children. Because Jesus "failed," Moon's book of *"Divine Principle"* transcends the authority of the Christian Bible.

The Unification Church has a training manual known as *Master Speaks* which describes its recruitment techniques of "scientifically coercive persuasion" or "psychological coercion." It employs front groups on college campuses posing as philosophical-religious discussion groups, such as the Collegiate Association for the Research of Principle (CARP). Such a group will invite interested students to join its members for a meal featuring a lecture and discussion on topics such as morality or values in a troubled world; the regular participants are all "Moonies" who are recruitment experts. They size up the needs of the prospective recruit, offering him subtle "ego stroking" by showing great interest in him, and then invite him to a weekend retreat where good food, warm companionship, and acceptance are mixed with written and spoken confessions of a cathartic nature. The confessions of the recruit's inner thoughts are later used by the "Moonies" to apply pressure and persuade him to join the family. The lecturers emphasize the dualistic nature of the world and leave no doubt that one must align oneself with the forces of absolute good against the selfish, sinful, corrupt secular world. The retreat gathers momentum with long, continuous sessions of intense lecturing with no questions allowed, interspersed with group singing and strenuous physical exercise such as a volleyball game. The recruit's mind is focused on the moral message, his own sins, and the supportive, caring people offering him salvation, and this intense riveting of attention on their message is in contrast to a total lack of any other viewpoint being expressed. The emotional impact of being immersed in a warm, accepting togetherness with totally dedicated and loving people creates the basic conditions for brainwashing. Later it becomes clear that the front group are "Moonies" and the new recruit is now easily indoctrinated into the Unification Church. More meetings and programs are held, and ultimately the new recruit cuts all his ties with the outside world and joins the "family."

Charges of deception in its recruiting have been filed against the Unification Church. After the recruit has joined the "Moonie" family he is warned against contact with his parents, friends, and outside authorities, warned that he can be threatened or harassed if he responds to outside people who might kidnap him and try to "deprogram" him. He is told it is better that he considers suicide rather than defect from the "Moonie" family. Unification Church members are not to "have any consciousness of existence—(but) just serve" (Rudin, 1980). A recent psychological study was made of 20 Unification Church members (Galanter et al., 1979). Church members filled out a questionnaire with scales in the following three categories: (1) neurotic distress scale at four different time periods in their church affiliation, (2) religiosity scale measuring the intensity of their religious commitment, and (3) general well-being scale during different periods. The 20 members were generally unmarried, white males with an average age of 25 years who had been Unification Church members for an average of three years. Before age 15 they had all considered themselves members of their parents' religions, and most had previously experienced a commitment to an Eastern religious sect or to a Christian fundamentalist sect. Of course statistics based on less than 100 are of little if any validity, but we present the following as of some interest. More than 50 percent had begun college and 25 percent had finished college; almost 40 percent believed they had suffered from serious emtional problems in the past, and almost one-third had sought professional help for their problems. About 25 percent admitted to serious drug problems in the past. Conversion resulted from a series of church-run workshops (run from 8 A.M. to 11 P.M.). Typically, it would be a one-day workshop followed by a two-day workshop and then a seven-day workshop. The average convert experienced emotional distress prior to joining; joining the church provided relief from neurotic distress, and continued membership appeared to stabilize those with neurotic distress. This seems to fit William James' comment that "[religious] conversion is in its essence a normal adolescent phenomenon, incidental to the passage from the child's small universe to the wider intellectual and spiritual life of maturity" (1902). He did not see, however, the great task of adolescence, the separation from the parents in the move into psychological independence. These subjects did not report brainwashing or physical or mental abuse.

Wilma provides us with an actual case history of a "Moonie." When she was 26 years old, Wilma joined the "Moonies" and her parents finally "disowned" her. They felt they were exhausted by all her problems and that it was not fair to her younger sister and two brothers for them to spend any more time or money trying to help her. She had had "every opportunity to succeed"; her parents had already deprived her younger siblings of too much time and money in order to provide Wilma with special attention. They knew they would get no cooperation from the "Moonies" in bringing her back home, and they hoped the strict discipline of being a "Moonie" might help Wilma get some semblance of the self-discipline which had been so conspicuously missing in her for the past ten years.

Wilma was born on her mother's twenty-fourth birthday and was given her mother's name. Her mother had been gifted with extraordinarily good looks and was headed for a Hollywood career when she met her husband-to-be, a successful movie producer with a vigorous personality who was ten years older than Wilma's mother. It was love at first sight, a whirlwind romance, with marriage a year later. Within another year Wilma was born, followed shortly thereafter by another daughter and then twin sons, all within four years. Wilma was beautiful from birth and always the center of attention. Her mother, having given up her screen career to be a housewife and mother, seemed happy but often wondered how far her career might have taken her. She lived vicariously through her husband's work and silently longed to be more in the spotlight; she hoped that Wilma might herself satisfy some of these needs for her. She allowed Wilma to have a minor career as a child actress despite the warnings from her husband that such public exposure was sure to harm her. Wilma was soon aware of her own beauty and charisma, and developed some prima donna characteristics, expecting to be indulged by everybody. She could be quite unpleasant if she was not given what she wanted. She was quick to cry and have temper tantrums. She went to an exclusive private school which allowed her to take time off for her acting. She treated her younger siblings poorly, often demanding that they do favors for her, and did not get along well with her peers because she felt superior to them and they resented her. When she wanted to, she could be very charming, and some of her teachers received this favorable treatment. She was bright but never studied very hard and depended mainly on her charm to get along academically. There was a crisis in the sixth grade when her teacher refused to pass her, so her parents sent her to another school which she entered in the seventh grade. The term "spoiled brat" was sometimes used in describing her. She had a stormy early adolescence with drug use and abuse, sexual promiscuity, and chronic academic underachieving. She was sent to four different local schools, succeeding at none, and at 15 was sent to a fashionable eastern boarding school, where she barely survived the year and was asked not to return.

She was then, at 16, sent to an open psychiatric hospital which had its own school where she spent two stormy years. She was diagnosed as having a severe adjustment reaction of adolescence with sociopathic trends. She ran away three different times from the hospital, continued her sexual promiscuity and use of "speed," LSD, and heroin. She would have a few weeks of relatively normal behavior in the hospital and then "take off," leaving abruptly, finding underworld-type characters, and leading a self-destructive existence. She was finally successful in passing a high school equivalency test. Attempts at intensive psychotherapy were only partially successful: it was clear that Wilma felt criticized and rejected by her father, who always seemed more interested in his career than his family. He was only minimally cooperative in family therapy. Wilma's mother was guiltridden by feeling personally responsible for having indulged her too much. She could not break this indulging, and so Wilma still exploited her periodically, but mainly told her what a wonderful mother she was. Wilma gained some insight into how her hostility toward her father and her ambivalence toward her mother led to acting out. She lacked a clear identity and tried to achieve a better defined self-concept by playing roles. Although she did not have a true multiple personality, she easily slid into acting "as if" she had certain personality qualities (probably good dynamics for an actor): in the hospital she was usually the "attractive good girl," but when she "took off" she became a slutty street girl. She was gradually able to clearly identify these two sides and to modify the extremes of behavior in both roles.

Psychological testing at age 18 showed Wilma to have a narcissistic personality disorder with schizoid, passive-aggressive, and paranoid trends. There were no signs of delusional thinking, but it was felt that under severe stress her tendency to project might make it difficult for her to adhere to reality.

Wilma decided, after her discharge was "approved," that she would continue outpatient psychotherapy and live with a girl she had known in the hospital. She got a job selling popcorn in a movie theatre but was barely able to support herself, and complained of being bored and depressed at times. Through her roomate she met a man of about 40 who fascinated her. He was of a totally different background and race, and seemed to have had some Mafia connections. Within a month of her discharge from the hospital she was living with him, was back on drugs, and had discontinued her psychotherapy. Her parents were not able to prevail on her to end this relationship, which lasted for about two years. From the few bits of information they could obtain, he was a Charles Manson type who had about six young and attractive girls as his "harem." He supplied them with heroin and turned them into prostitutes.

Somehow Wilma, with the help of one of her customers, was able to break away from this life; she regained her health and sanity living with the man who helped her to escape, a long-distance truck driver who apparently treated her well but was away much of the time. Wilma had minimal contact with her parents during this period, as she felt she had to prove herself to them before returning. She became pregnant and had a son by her paramour, which made her very happy, but her truck driver was already married to a woman who was permanently in a mental hospital, and he had been told he could not divorce her.

For the first time in a long while Wilma felt some self-respect and genuine happiness.

Then her son was killed at age three by a drunken driver. Wilma felt shattered and suicidal, and put herself into a state psychiatric hospital where her mood slowly improved; she was discharged to a halfway house, to lead a banal existence, receiving public assistance and doing some baby-sitting. She felt she could not trust any male, so she turned down all requests for a date and wondered if she were homosexual. She did have a roommate who was illicitly using Valium and Quaalude, and soon Wilma was back on drugs again. It was then that she met a young woman who told her about the "Moonies." She attended their recruitment meetings, and felt an inner calm and joy for the first time since her son was killed. She was only too happy to believe what they believed and to follow their rules and discipline in order to have their companionship and safety from her own masochistic trends that doomed her to self-destruction without outside help. Perhaps for the kind of psychotic personality which Wilma exhibited, the "Moonies" offered more than the outside world.

There are some new developments within the "Moonies," or more correctly, the Unification Church, which indicate it is trying to improve its image and become a more respectable religious group (Nichols, 1980). Mr. Mose Durst, the new president of the Unification Church of America, is a 40-year-old former college English professor who was raised as an Orthodox Jew in Brooklyn. In May 1980, he resigned from his job of teaching college students English in Oakland, California, to lead a nationwide "moral revolution." He married a Korean woman missionary from the Unification Church nine years ago and has succeeded in having 38 Unification Church members enroll in the country's best divinity schools, including Harvard, Yale, and Fordham. The Unification Church now has its own newspaper *The Newsworld* (in New York City); the New York City Symphony Orchestra is under the church's direction. Durst is described as bright, well-spoken, honest, and convincing. The Reverend Sun Myung Moon suffers from a poor public image and will apparently remain in the background in low profile.

It is to be hoped that this change in direction is similar to what occurred in the Mormon church. It undoubtedly represents a better understanding by the Unification Church leaders of current realities in the United States; their attempt to make internal changes will help them to gain acceptance as a respectable and "legitimate" church instead of a "cult."

Alexander Deutsch, an American psychiatrist (1975), has closely followed a self-appointed American guru, known as Baba, and his cult since 1972. Deutsch was able to interview Baba and 14 of his devotees. Almost without exception, the followers gave histories of poor relationships with their parents and chronic unhappiness. Eleven of the 14 had extensive previous experience with hallucinogens which seemingly led them into exploring Eastern religions; they all had psychotic or psychotic-like symptoms in their histories, either induced or aggravated by psychedelic drugs; they all had a mystical experience on becoming followers of Baba. This experience was akin to a union with the divine, or a feeling of fusing with an absolute cosmic power. Their unhappiness melted away as they developed a strong attachment to Baba, whom they saw as all-wise and all-loving. They had all been very conflicted by their angry demands for love and attention from which they had always felt blocked, and apparently their fantasies built Baba into what they wanted. In these fantasies they got what they craved but were denied by reality.

Baba himself is a former insurance salesman. At 18 he had experienced a brief episode of mutism and paralysis (which he interpreted as "mystical"), and at 21 his father killed his mother and then himself. Baba married and had two children, but divorced his wife five years later. He then traveled widely, freely used psychedelic drugs, and had one psychiatric hospitalization.

He saw a documentary film about a Hindu religious leader and was deeply affected; he felt himself spinning through space, beyond the stars, heading toward two large eyes (these often are very early memories of the parents' eyes). He felt compelled to visit with the Hindu religious leader Sai Baba in India in his ashram. After two years there he returned to New York City wearing Hindu garb. His wife refused to join him but he found a new follower, Sid, who was to become his closest disciple.

Baba and Sid devised a sign language and temporarily gave up speech. Baba welcomed those passing by in Central Park as family members, speaking to them for hours about seeking knowledge and loving God, pointing out that sex, wealth, and power are "traps" to be avoided.

The family members chanted together and joined in silent meditation. They perceived Baba as being very close to God, saw him as having found his own way into the divine realm of God, and through him felt a unity with God and the cosmos. The devotees' yearnings for unconditional love were magically solved by joining Baba's family.

In a follow-up report on Baba and his cult (Deutsch, 1980), Deutsch records how Baba became increasingly bizarre, cruel, and destructive. Baba and 30 of his followers purchased a bus in 1973, left Central Park, and traveled to a mountaintop in a northeastern state. There, on "the hills," they established an agricultural commune. During the next two years the cult's family membership came to over 100 followers, but after this growth period Baba's megalomania increased alarmingly and many of his followers left him. He then bought himself a Jacuzzi bath even though there was no electricity for it in the commune, and became increasingly irritable and physically and verbally assaultive to his followers. He broke one follower's eardrum, and subjected his female followers to public and private sexual exploitation. He commanded his followers not to have sexual relations among themselves; his speeches and tirades became incomprehensible and frightening to his followers; his mental status deteriorated into bizarre grimacing, fragmented language, and finally, complete withdrawal. He decided that the devil was within his heart and had infested the entire commune and had to be exorcized, but his frenzied attempts at exorcism failed and he accordingly dismissed all his remaining followers, dissolving the cult.

Of the 14 followers of Baba that Deutsch originally interviewed, six remained loyal to their leader up to the end. They excused his increasing bizarreness and cruelty and his deteriorating mental status as being due to "a divine madness" or as "teaching us all a lesson." What is striking about the six followers who remained loyal is the tenacity of their original belief in the god-like qualities of Baba: this blind belief literally closed their eyes to the reality of his psychosis and sadistic behavior. It was only when Baba told his followers that he no longer wanted them that they could free themselves from him. They had built up a satisfactory religious belief system based on Baba's preaching and example, and they could not bear to abandon it until they had no other choice. During their days of being active family members, they would appear to have psychotic personalities; together, the group was voluntarily part of a group psychosis.

Contrast Baba to Reverend James Jones and his more than 900 People's Temple followers in Jamestown, Guyana. Jones dissolved his group by a mass suicide (Conway and Siegelman, 1978, pp. 227-247). He was originally a fundamentalist Christian, Holy-Roller-type minister who appealed to many middle-western whites in the Bible belt. He became increasingly aware of how strong an influence his words and personality could have on people. Jones developed political ideas and turned toward communism, comparing himself to Mao Tse-tung before his long march through China, hoping to build a socialist utopian community under the protective cloak of fundamentalist Christianity. He thought Christianity was the ideal by which to build a Marxist social group in the United States, and in 1956 he founded the People's Temple in Indianapolis. In 1965 he moved with 100 followers to Redwood Valley, California. His followers were racially mixed. They believed in shared labor and equitable distribution of wealth. The great majority of Temple members were underprivileged blacks, but there were also fundamentalist Christian whites and middle-class white intellectuals.

It soon became clear that life was far from utopian within the People's Temple: Jones wielded his power with increasing force as he demanded that his followers totally commit themselves to his cause, break off all ties with the outside world, and liquidate all their outside assets to fill up the Temple's coffers. In August 1977, Jones leased 27,000 acres of land from the Guyanese government for the establishment of an "agricultural mission." He moved his People's Temple there with more than 1,000 followers. They were virtual prisoners in the steamy, hot jungle, where they were ordered to grow crops and build a compound, but the crops would not grow and the followers barely survived on imported rice. Jones felt his grip loosening; he reportedly became emotionally unstable and paranoid in his thinking. A few people defected and told the outside world about the severe deprivations suffered and the physical abuses inflicted on Temple members, and this finally prompted Congressman Leo Ryan of California to begin an investigation of Jones and the People's Temple. Evidence accumulated that not only was there cruelty and abuse going on in Johnestown, but there existed a large cache of arms.

Reverend Jones seems to have undergone a gradual personality change during his last few years. He was no longer the optimistic, devout Christian who spoke of seeking a social utopia. He now began to attack everything around him as bad and wrong. He is reported to have denied God, to have cursed God, to have called Mary a whore while throwing his Holy Bible across the church. He soon predicted earthquakes, holocausts, and even a race war between blacks and whites; he demanded that the marriages and families among his followers be broken up; he declared sex evil and forbidden, but indulged in it promiscuously with his female followers. He threatened the lives of potential defectors, and there were reports that some defectors had been severely injured.

His megalomania increased to the point that he claimed to be God, and at other times the reincarnation of Christ or Lenin. He developed a "suicide drill" to test his followers' loyalty, ordering them to drink some special "wine." After they complied, they were told it was poisonous and they would die within an hour. When the hour was over, Jones admitted it was a lie and that he was testing them. The camp in Jonestown was run increasingly like a concentration camp with special tortures developed to punish members charged with infractions of Jones' rules. Jones warned his followers that they had to prepare for attacks from CIA guerillas or the U.S. Army, predicting that since the commune was soon to be attacked and destroyed, they had to prepare for a "mass suicide for the glory of socialism." Representative Leo Ryan, some media members, and representatives of the concerned relatives' group finally embarked for Guyana in November 1978. While at the airstrip, Ryan and three newsmen were shot, killed at point-blank range by four members of the People's Temple, and at about this same time, Jones ordered the mass suicide. A bathtub was filled with fruit juice and large amounts of cyanide, tranquilizers, and painkillers. Babies were killed first by shooting syringes filled with the lethal juice down their throats; then the others formed a line, drank a cupful of poison, and lay down in rows with their faces down. The final stage before death was that of convulsions; within five hours, 912 people were dead. The final death was that of James Jones, who killed himself by putting a bullet through his head.

His followers had lost the ability to think for themselves because they were brainwashed and isolated from all outside contacts. They claimed to have joined Jones originally to answer an inner need to live in a utopia of socialism with an all-wise and caring leader in whom they developed total trust. In reality, they must have had very strong passive-dependent needs which led them to look for an all-powerful leader, as a very young child needs a caring, protecting, providing parent. Those who remained with Jones regressed to such an emotional infantile level and believed they were being cared for by an all-powerful parental leader. His illusion of an ideal community became their shared belief. They may have been aware of his hostility, paranoia, and cruelty, but they were helpless victims of it—they had been so taken in by his promises that they regressed emotionally and could no longer act independently. A few of his followers successfully defected before the move to Guyana, but they lived in terror of retaliation from Jones. His true followers believed that they had achieved their childhood desires of being taken care of by an all-knowing father figure and tried to live out their lives within this happy delusion.

One can legitimately ask the question whether this was a "group psychosis." It differs from group psychosis as reported in the past, and may more closely resemble a severe group *hysteria* in which there are symptoms in a group due to fear and suggestibility. These "collective psychoses" appeared in the Middle Ages in such a psychic epidemic as St. Vitus' dance or tarantism (Arieti, 1959). There have been reported (and are even reported today) in Italy cases of lycanthropy in which individuals believe they are transformed into animals, especially wolves. They take on the animal's characteristics and often are punished for this behavior.

## SUMMARY AND CONCLUSIONS

Let us try to correlate our data about cults with our concept of the psychotic personality. The following is a brief summary of tentative criteria for diagnosis of the psychotic personality.

### Tentative Criteria for Diagnosis of Psychotic Personality

The psychotic personality involves fixation or regression of part, not all, of the personality (all would be psychosis) to a level of

1. serious *withdrawal* from human relations (i.e., repressed deficiency of object interest and relations)
2. into heightened *narcissism* in the form of absorption with self and self-interests (possibly like Freud's amoebae with pseudopods withdrawn into self)

3. somewhat repressed *warping of the sense of reality*
4. the psychotic elements *diffuse* throughout the personality or ego, and not apparent as psychotic symptoms but repressed behind a mask of sanity

It seems clear that by becoming a bona fide member of a modern cult one has to have had previously all of these personality characteristics of a psychotic personality or else one has to acquire at least temporarily such characteristics, probably because they have been latent.

1. *Withdrawal:* Cult membership automatically points toward deep conflict with most of the rest of the world. Human relationships are virtually nonexistent with non-cult members. It is only when a cult member has been an integral part of the cult for many years that he is even trusted to have any contact with the outside world because of the fear that he might defect or be "kidnapped," and even when the cult member is trusted enough to be allowed to have such contact, it is very perfunctory and businesslike. In this sense, cults are much like the Communist states which have allowed their people little or no contact with the outside world. We have also pointed out that it is only when the isolation of the cult starts to open up and allow interaction with the outside world that the cult has a chance to normalize by making some internal changes.

Massive withdrawal from all outside human relations is a cult characteristic. However, one can ask if the human relations within the cult do not make up for the total absence of human relations with the outside world. Certainly there is a strong attachment found among cult members, although this attachment is forced on the members by their circumstances and could be likened to the attachment of a group of individuals forced to live together and interact because they are all caught in some common disaster, such as a fire, earthquake, or war. One difference is that in the cult, there is a similarity of needs and beliefs, a mutual attachment by identification. Such similarities do not guarantee sufficient identification for compatibility, so there must often be a forced attachment among individuals with very different backgrounds. Entering into a cult has to be different from an individual's previous experience; it must be experienced as a rather severe withdrawal from everything and everybody with which an individual was previously familiar into a more or less common psychosis. As happens with any sensory deprivation, withdrawal from familiar people and things causes a marked narrowing of interest and awareness, and brings out self-centeredness, which leads us to the second point.

2. *Narcissism:* There must come out in cult members a heightened narcissism with an accompanying self-absorption. This tendency may have existed prior to joining the cult as was seen in some of our sample cases, but the cult's total isolation must invite or necessitate a marked increase in narcissism. If the new member was lacking in pride and self-esteem prior to joining the cult, developing these qualities is emphasized and pushed by the cult. In fact, it is generally very difficult for an outsider to have a "normal" conversation with a cult member: the typical member is so preoccupied with the cult and what it stands for that he is unable or unwilling to talk about anything else. Psychologically, his own identity and the cult fuse, so that when he is talking about the cult he is talking about himself and vice versa.

3. *Repressed warping of the sense of reality:* The cult member's sense of reality is constricted or warped by his isolation from the outside world and his indifference to the rest of the world. The only important subject to him is the cult, and although he is aware of many aspects of the outside world, he does not value any part of it. Parents are shocked by how their children, on joining a cult, no longer care to know about the rest of the family. Because the cult is so possessive of and protective toward its members, it strongly discourages communication with and interest in the member's family and friends; even if a close family relative dies, the cult may try to withhold such news or not let the member attend the funeral.

The cult's belief system, which is dogmatic and closed, must be adhered to by the cult member even though it may be patently irrational and inconsistent. Because it is largely an emotionally based system of beliefs, and not reality, cult leaders claim that it doesn't require scientific proof but can be accepted on faith. Much of the dogma circulated by the messianic cult leader has to be considered bizarre, infantile, and unable to stand up to careful scrutiny—there must be some degree of psychosis in common. An example of this warping of reality would be the experience described earlier of the college student who lived with a group of "Moonies" for a short while, finally leaving because "the lectures got more and more ridiculous and I just wasn't happy anymore." What he was hearing just did not correspond to the reality which he knew and had always accepted. Some cult members who have defected report a growing sense of unreality within the cult which results in an ever-increasing question in their minds that can be paraphrased as, "What am I doing in this strange place with these unrealistic people?"

4. *Psychotic elements diffuse throughout the personality:* There also seem to be psychotic elements contained in the personalities of typical cult members which do not show overtly as such. This is another way of saying that a cult member can sound and look pretty normal as long as he can stay away from the topic of the cult, but it is virtually impossible for him to do so, and everything he says has to be colored by his cult's belief system. The "mask of sanity" is his previously learned adaptive technique that allows him to appear normal, but as soon as one questions his values or what he thinks to be significant in the world, one is deluged by his spouting forth the cult's "party line." To the other person this monologue praising the cult has very little meaning or mutuality; one soon gets the feeling of talking to a person who partly lives in an unreal world of illusion and delusion.

Examining the four tentative criteria for a psychotic personality point by point, one is impressed by how closely they correspond to the personality constellation of a typical cult member.

In summary, we see the psychotic personalities fitting well into some cults which provide them with what they need.* This is beneficial for some, giving them a place and role in society. However, the price is very high, namely, regression of the total personality with failure to mature; also, some who could mature into normal independence and realism through therapy never get the chance because of being separated from their parents. By far the better solution to problems with parents is to *resolve* them (at least in the child's mind), not to escape them. If a cult provides what the recruit needs to save his sanity and life, it is helpful—but if it uses any sort of pressure (e.g., brainwashing, peer pressure, etc.) to force regression from a sense of reality and

---

*We also see the operation of a fundamental law of social living, namely, the attraction into organizations of individuals with like psychodynamics. Country clubs attract persons of similar makup. The Nazi party attracted those who identified with each other (as Hitler said, "The kind of men we want will flock to us from all over Europe"). This same attraction into organizations holds true for all kinds of identifications, which in turn are based on some similarity in the psychodynamics of the individuals.

independence, then it shatters the normal growth to maturity in a young person, which is the worst crime or evil that exists. To deny a young person the opportunity to mature emotionally and mentally by pressuring or luring him into regression from such maturity is as close to soul-murder as exists in reality. To distort a human being's sense of reality and of independence is to destroy what is most human about him or her. For the most specifically human capacity that distinguishes mankind from all other animals is exactly this: the precious sense of reality; only humans have the capacity for science and its comprehension of nature.

## REFERENCES

Arieti, S., ed. (1959): *American Handbook of Psychiatry.* New York: Basic Books, p. 552.

Conway, F. and Siegelman, J. (1978): *Snapping.* New York: Dell.

Deutsch, A. (1980): Tenacity of attachment to a cult leader: a psychiatric perspective, *Am. J. Psychiatry* 137(12):1569-1573.

\_\_\_\_ (1975): Observations on a sidewalk ashram, *Arch. Gen. Psychiatry* 35:166-175.

Galanter, M., Rabkin, R., Rabkin, J., and Deutsch, A. (1979): The "Moonies": a psychological study of conversion and membership in a contemporary religious sect, *J. Am. Psychiatric Assn.* 136(2):165-170.

Hart, M. (1978): *The 100, a Ranking of the Most Influential Persons in History.* New York: A & W Visual Library.

James, W. (1902): *Varieties of Religious Experience.* New York: The Modern Library, Random House, p. 196.

Johnson, A. (1977): A temple of last resorts: youth and shared narcissism, in *The Narcissistic Condition,* ed. by M. Nelson. New York: Human Sciences Press.

Martin, W. (1977): *The Kingdom of the Cults.* Minneapolis: Bethany Fellowship, Inc., p. 147-198.

Nichols, R. (1980): A son of Brooklyn rises to replace exotic moon, *The Philadelphia Inquirer,* November 29, 1980.

Rosten, L., ed. (1975): *Religions of America.* New York: Simon and Schuster.

Rudin, J. and Rudin M. (1980): *Prison or Paradise, the New Religious Cults.* Philadelphia: Fortress Press.

Time, Inc. (1957): *The World's Great Religions.* New York.

Turner, W. (1966): *The Mormon Establishment.* Boston: Houghton Mifflin.

# 19
# DESTRUCTIVE TYPE: HITLER*

## PROBLEMS IN DIAGNOSTIC LABELING

Adolf Hitler's personality left an indelible imprint (or "heelprint") on the entire world. Psychohistorians are still uncertain as to the precise psychodynamic factors which gave rise to this destructive personality. Hitler was labeled a "lunatic," "madman," "paranoid," "hysteric," or "psychopathic personality." There were even allegations that he had syphilis and that his impulsiveness, irrationality, and hostile destructiveness were the result of the treponema eating away at his brain. Another viewpoint pictures Hitler as sexually perverted, explaining his political actions as manifestations of an infantile sexual fixation which led to his acting out sadomasochistic compulsions.

In the last decade there has been a more scholarly approach to the study of Hitler and his personality, but unfortunately, clinical data available on his early childhood do not supply us with sufficient information to reconstruct with confidence and accuracy his childhood experiences and childhood emotional pattern. Available information about the emotional interaction within his family does, however, provide us with reasonably confident conclusions about these early influences on his personality structure. Further details about his early years and the personalities of his mother and father may never be forthcoming.

Hitler's written and spoken words are available in abundance, as are records of much of his actions and behavior. One must be especially careful in analyzing Hitler's use of language. Any interpretation of his words should be handled almost like a dream interpretation in which the apparent meaning should be grasped fully, but systematic effort is required to decipher the hidden meaning. Hitler's true motivations

---

*This chapter by Silas L. Warner, M.D.

were doubtless best revealed through his behavior.* His public and political actions are a matter of record, but for his more private behavior we have to rely on the recorded accounts of those who worked for him and knew him intimately. Fortunately, many such accounts are available, enabling us to piece together a fairly consistent picture of Hitler's postadolescent personality (see Resource Material at end of chapter).

## HITLER AS A CASE HISTORY

Hitler's life experiences ultimately converged to form what might appropriately be called a "psychotic personality." Hitler's father, Alois, was a minor Austrian official whose third wife was Adolf's mother. Alois was born illegitimately under his mother's name, Schicklgruber. He worked his way up from peasant origins to become a shoemaker's apprentice and then a minor government employee. There is speculation as to the identity of Alois' father and whether he was Jewish. Because of his illegitimate birth and perhaps because of his governmental position, Alois took the precaution in 1876 of changing his name from Schicklgruber to Hiedler (Hitler), his supposed father's name. Alois first married a woman 14 years his senior. They had no children, and were legally separated after seven years of marriage. A few years later she died. Alois then married his "maidservant," a girl 24 years younger who had already born him a son and who was seven months pregnant when they married. She gave birth to a daughter but soon after contracted tuberculosis and was sent to the country to recuperate.

A new servant girl, Klara Polzl, who was Alois Hitler's niece, was hired to care for the two young children and became Alois' new mistress. Klara was 23 years younger than Alois and called him "uncle." When his second wife died, Alois married Klara and within three years she had born him three children, all of whom died in infancy. In 1889, four years after their marriage, she gave birth to Adolf. It seems probable that, having already lost three infants, she was especially cautious and overprotective of him, but we cannot be sure of this. It is equally

---

*As Freud (1900) put it: "For all practical purposes in judging human character, a man's actions and conscious expressions of thought are in most cases sufficient. Actions, above all, deserve to be placed in the front rank." ("Interpretation of dreams," *S.E.* 4)

likely that she was living in poverty, worn out, and resentful of another child. From what was customary in late nineteenth century Austria, Adolf was probably breast-fed, and since Klara did not become pregnant again until Adolf was five years old, he may have been breast-fed until the age of three or four because prolonged breast-feeding was believed to keep mothers from becoming pregnant. A photograph of Adolf as an infant shows him to be a slightly obese and happy-looking child, but he was known to have been sickly as an infant. Alois worked a regular day and usually stopped by the local tavern for a few beers after work, so Adolf in childhood was usually asleep when his father returned home. Between Adolf's fifth and sixth years, the family was separated when Alois was transferred to a new duty post several miles away. Thus a close emotional attachment may have developed between Adolf and his mother, while a more ambivalent and detached relationship existed between Adolf and his father. Although Adolf first respected and feared his father's authority, in adolescence he rebelled against it. What is not clear is whether Alois was a brutal tyrant or a benevolent despot, but in any case, he was the final authority and ruled the home when he was there. Hitler's mother has been described as a hardworking, clean, mass-attending hausfrau who obediently submitted to her husband's will. She gave birth to another son, Edward, when Adolf was almost six. Edward died at age six, and a sister Paula, who survived until 1960, was born when Adolf was seven years old.

Adolf was lively, popular, and a good student in elementary school, where he developed an interest in reading American Wild West stories and military accounts of the Franco-Prussian War. He attended a Catholic elementary school run by the Benedictine order, and aspired to join their order and to achieve the highest position of abbot. In general, his deportment was good, except for his being caught smoking at age nine. Gradually as Hitler entered adolescence he showed signs of moodiness, irritability, and withdrawal. At school, he only applied himself to those subjects that interested him—history and drawing—while barely passing the others. His father urged him to follow in the paternal footsteps and become a government official but Adolf refused, steadfastly insisting on becoming an artist. He finally sabotaged his chance to obtain the necessary educational background for a governmental position by deliberately flunking out of school. Alois died when Hitler was 14, and then Adolf was given the chance to attend a trade school, but he frittered away the opportunity and spent a year at home, doing only what he enjoyed most: reading, sketching, and dressing up like a dandy, while his mother and older sister provided him with a comfortable living. His one close childhood friend, Kubizek, was his constant companion, and the two young men moved to Vienna, where Adolf was to prepare himself for art school. Although he was confident of gaining admission he was turned down with the suggestion that he confine his artistic work to architectural design. Hitler returned home at 17, a failure. Then his mother was diagnosed as having breast cancer. Her physician Dr. Bloch, a Jew, had a reputation for being dedicated to the care of his patients. Dr. Bloch recommended, and Hitler approved of, the subsequent treatment which involved surgical removal of the cancerous breast, followed by applications of iodine-saturated compresses to the area. Klara died shortly after the iodine treatments began, when Adolf was 18. Most authorities agree that Adolf remained friendly with Dr. Bloch, but there is a theory which links Hitler's subsequent anti-Semitism to the idea that Dr. Bloch was responsible for his mother's death.

When Hitler returned to Vienna for four years after his mother's death, he led a carefree, bohemian life, eking out a hand-to-mouth existence painting and selling postcards and living in "flophouses," all the while refining his oratorical skills by gathering other destitute men around him to lecture them on popular topics. Finally tiring of this aimless existence, he visited his older half-brother in Liverpool, England, and then moved to Munich, a truly "German" city, where he painted postcards until the outbreak of World War I in 1914, at which time he enlisted in the German army.

The order and discipline within the German army suited Hitler well. He served with distinction for four years as a dispatch runner and was awarded two Iron Crosses, obtaining the rank of corporal. As a result of exposure to poisonous British gas, he suffered a transient blindness and was sent to an army hospital, where through a "revelation" he decided on politics for his career. He was bitterly disappointed in Germany's unconditional surrender in 1918, especially since it had appeared to him that the German army was well on its way to a resounding military triumph. Looking for people to blame for Germany's defeat, he seized upon the Jews and the Bolsheviks as coconspirators in a plot to betray the Germans by "stabbing them in the back." Hitler used these two scapegoats in his takeover of a small splinter political party (the "Nazis"). Because he could orchestrate his audiences' responses by skillful manipulation of their emotions (particularly their emotions in common), his party grew from obscurity into a powerful political force, and in 1923 the Nazis unsuccessfully attempted a takeover in Munich during which Hitler was arrested and jailed for one year. This temporarily derailed his fast-moving express, but he used the time profitably as many jailed political leaders have done, to organize his thoughts, write *Mein Kampf*, and work out his future political strategy. He decided to move slowly and work within the established system. In a series of brilliant moves, through conniving, manipulating, and building up a dedicated following with the use of violence, Hitler intimidated all other parties and finally succeeded in 1933 in becoming Chancellor of Germany. Within a few years he had taken complete control of the German government and its already awesome military strength, moving into former German territory under the guise of returning Germans to their fatherland. This led to war with England and France, in response to Hitler's invasion of Poland in 1939; Hitler conquered France and almost defeated England. Then he broke the non-aggression pact with Russia and launched a surprise invasion. He almost succeeded in conquering the whole of Europe. Finally, the tide of war turned against him; Hitler's judgment became increasingly impulsive and desperate, his personal behavior became erratic and totally destructive to all around him, whether friend or foe, and just before and after the Allied invasion he definitely distorted reality. Although he was in Berlin, far from the Normandy front, he fired Rommel and Kesselring, taking personal direction of the armies. Soon two of his armies were encircled by Bradley, Patton, and Montgomery, but Hitler believed in the myth of his own infallibility and found a scapegoat in Kluge. Rommel wanted his Panzer divisions at the beaches; had Hitler not forbidden this, the entire invasion might have failed.

Hitler wouldn't take "no" for an answer. He was so completely out of touch with reality that in reply to Kluge's signal he sent another. . .the Hitler myth wasn't working any more. . .as the Fuehrer cannot be wrong, he laid the blame on Kluge. For von Kluge it was the end. He wrote a letter to Hitler which we found after the war. In it he told Hitler the true facts [of the Allied advances in France] and declared that the grand and daring operational concept ordered by him [Hitler] was impractical to exercise, a moderation of expression worthy of his officer corps background. On the night of August the eighteenth the Field-Marshal who had dared to question the Fuehrer's orders set off for Germany. He never arrived; he committed suicide on the way. (Winterbotham, 1974)*

Winston Churchill (1951) writes that:

[Hitler's] two hundred divisions on the Eastern Front could not hope to withstand the Russian flood when it was again released. . . . Now was the time for him to decide how to regroup his forces, where they should withdraw and where hold. But instead his orders were for them to stand and fight it out. . . . The German armies were thus condemned to be broken on all three fronts.

By way of contrast to the distortions of Hitler's reality sense caused by his hostility, vanity, and even megalomania, we read further in Churchill (1951) of Stalin's inexorable realism:

He said he feared that, though the three Great Powers were allies today, and would none of them commit any act of aggression, in ten years or less the three leaders would disappear and a new generation would come into power which had not experienced the war and would forget what we had gone through. "All of us," he declared, "want to secure peace for at least 50 years. The greatest danger is conflict among ourselves, because if we remain united the German menace is not very important. Therefore we must now think how to secure our unity in the future, and how to guarantee that the three Great Powers (possibly China and France) will maintain a united front. Some system must be elaborated to prevent conflict between the main Great Powers."

It was in part this realism of Stalin's that made him more formidable than Hitler when his armies swept into Europe heedless of the Allies who failed to heed Churchill's warning.

---

*From *The Ultra Secret* by F. W. Winterbotham. Copyright 1974. Reprinted with permission of Harper and Row.

In 1945, a few hours after he had married his paramour, Eva Braun, Hitler killed himself and his new bride. By this time his enemies, the Allies, had destroyed Germany's vaunted military power, dashing away his grandiose daydreams of conquering the world.

## HITLER'S PHYSICAL CHARACTERISTICS

Hitler was almost five feet nine inches tall, weighed 150 pounds, had short legs, narrow shoulders, a sunken chest, flabby hips, and a "mincing," Charlie Chaplin walk. His fingers were long and tapering; his nostrils were wide, giving him a prominent nose, which was partially hidden by his bushy mustache; his skin was white, shiny, and hairless. His teeth were brownish yellow with numerous fillings and bridges. His eyes, his most impressive feature, were light blue, contrasting with his dark brown, nearly black, hair. He could focus his eyes on people in a spellbinding, unforgettable way, and practiced piercing glances in the mirror.

Hitler's most significant physical aberration was finally confirmed when the Soviet doctors performed an autopsy on his charred body, and noted a missing testicle; apparently all his life Hitler had been disturbed by the undescended or missing testicle. While we can only speculate on the psychological significance, it seemed to have undermined his sense of masculinity and virility, especially when coupled with his previously noted rather effeminate physical characteristics. His preoccupation with stallions, bulls, and wolves, and his regular consumption of an extract made from bulls' testicles were probably all attempts to compensate for his feeling a lack of virility and relative sexual impotence. Of the six women with whom he sustained relationships, five committed suicide; all of these women were much younger than Hitler, just as his own mother was much younger than his father. He seems to have had a madonna-prostitute split in his perception of women: those who became closest to him were idealized and pure, while all others were impure, dangerous, and sexually exciting. It is possible that Hitler may have feared his own latent homosexuality and tried to compensate by heterosexual sadomasochistic fantasies and perversions.

## HITLER'S PERSONALITY

What can be said of Hitler's personality to help us understand his insatiable quest for power and grandiosity which ended in his *total destruction* of himself, as well as the destruction of his wife, his colleagues, his nation, and probably close to 50 million others? For the first 30 of his 56 years he seemed totally unremarkable: he lost both of his parents by age 18, had dropped out of school, and was leading a desultory and ineffective bohemian life. His first taste of success was when he performed with honor and devotion as a German soldier from 1914 to 1918. From 1919 to 1923, Hitler first showed his charismatic organizing power in creating the Nazi party. After his release in 1924 from one year in jail, his Nazi party was just one of several parties competing for dominance in Germany; yet in the next nine years Hitler's Machiavellian genius blossomed, and using astute timing, brilliant judgment, and violence, he steered the Nazis into undisputed control of Germany. Hitler alone was at the helm, the uncontested boss, *Der Fuehrer.*

Hitler's personality was marked by contrasting extremes: he could be cowardly or brave. In World War I, he won the Iron Cross and was fearless and loyal in carrying out his duties; he had a morbid fear of germs, water, moonlight, and horses; he could cold-bloodedly order the death or destruction of hundreds of people and yet worry lest lobsters being cooked suffer pain, which is intelligible if humans, but never animals, had made him suffer in his childhood; he could make himself and others believe he was totally trustworthy and his "word was sacred," yet he could precipitously reverse himself, break treaties, or order formerly loyal followers executed; he could be a hard-headed realist or take off into a world of fantasy and base important decisions on personal myths; he could be cold-blooded and detached, yet his speeches were full of passion and could lead his audiences to view him as warm, caring, strong, and brave, or threatening and intimidating.

Perhaps he was already entering that state of fantasy which must have become his defence mechanism against his journey to Valhalla.

[Hitler] sent his now famous signal to Rommel saying that "there could be no other course but that of holding out to the last man and that for the German troops there was only the choice, victory or death." Alamein was the first real German defeat of the war and also the first of this type of signal to come from Hitler.

Ultra [Allied reading of the German code] . . .showed how completely unrealistic the whole command structure in the west had become. . .through Ultra came the cry of a desperate man: "Why do you not do as I have ordered, why do you not answer?" (Winterbotham, 1974)*

## HITLER'S PROJECTIONS OR EXTERNALIZATIONS

It was Hitler's genius—or psychopathology—that successfully converted his own private neurosis into public policy. This was facilitated by the dovetailing of many of his political aspirations with those of the German people, who had historically wished for a strong, powerful leader to restore them to their "rightful place" as a world power, one who would undo the national shame suffered from their defeat in World War I, followed by the humiliating shackles of the Treaty of Versailles. Hitler felt these same nationalistic strivings; his "macho" and sadism were in part masculine protest to deny insecurity in his masculinity. He became the right leader at the right time for Germany, almost as though his followers had unconsciously selected him. His personal neurosis centered about his family romance and oedipal triangle, in which he and his mother were closely bound together against the father, the hated and feared enemy. We can surmise but not prove that reuniting Germany became symbolically the same as Hitler being reunited with his mother. To accomplish this, the hated enemy (father) had to be destroyed. Jews, Communists, and finally, the Allies, were designated as the enemies. As he came to power, Hitler identified his dying mother with Germany dying; his strong German nationalism was a projection of his own infantile narcissism by which he restored his own and his mother's fused omnipotence by identifying with and saving Germany (his mother). Germany (traditionally the "fatherland," but for Hitler "motherland") is seen as threatened from both within and without, and the Jews were held responsible for the sexual assault and degradation of the pure Germans, just as unconsciously he saw his father sexually assaulting and degrading his mother. Thus the pure German people (the mother) represent all that is good and virtuous, and the Jew (like his father) represents all that is evil and immoral. This shows the splitting and projection of Hitler's earliest "objects"—his mother and father—into polar opposites, the one all good and the other all bad. Hitler expands this splitting tendency by projecting these

*From *The Ultra Secret* by F. W. Winterbotham. Copyright 1974. Reprinted with permission of Harper and Row.

feelings onto many others. Austria, for example, his place of birth, was split into the good people (Germans) and the bad people (Jews, Slavs, etc.)

To further explain Hitler's hatred of Jews, there is evidence that he thought he may have had a Jewish grandfather; his father's mother was said to have worked for a Jewish family as a domestic. The Jewish head of the family is supposed to have sexually forced himself onto Hitler's grandmother, who then gave birth to Hitler's father, Alois. During his life, Hitler tried to both investigate and verify the question of his biological grandfather being Jewish, and ultimately he destroyed all the information he had unearthed. Whether true or not, it is not as important as Hitler's masculine protest and preoccupation with his ancestry and how this fed into his virulent anti-Semitism.

Another possible contribution to his anti-Semitism was the undisputed fact that Dr. Bloch, a Jewish physician, treated his mother at the time of her death. Although Hitler was apparently friendly with Dr. Bloch, expressing his gratitude for the care his mother received, he seems to have later done a psychological about-face and viewed Dr. Bloch as the Jewish "murderer" of his mother.

* * * *

Was Hitler a psychotic personality, and if so, what made him one? It seems inaccurate to describe him as overtly "psychotic." Hitler knew what he was doing, was in good contact with reality, and could easily have passed an expert's mental status examination to establish his sanity. Yet in spite of this, he held certain convictions, responses to his early life experiences, which were inhuman and sick. He really believed that Jews were vermin or scum, not humans, who had "contaminated" the "pure" German race and who, not being human, could be exterminated. This was not just a dislike or prejudice, but a total conviction and compulsion to wipe out an entire race. While we can speculate and even partially recognize Hitler's reasons for this conclusion, it remains an inhuman, savage, and crazy idea. It is typical of a withdrawal of human feelings for other persons. He was an excessively narcissistic, self-centered individual who, it seems, had no close feelings for anyone, who was sincerely unable to put his trust in anyone, with the result that everyone was potentially his enemy; he could be so convincing in his influence of his followers, because most of them had makeups like his own, that he could get them to kill those he labeled "enemies." As he said, "The kind of men we want will flock to us from all over Europe." Many successful dictators have slaughtered rivals or enemies in their climb to power, but only very few have come close to killing the 50 million humans for whose extinction Hitler was responsible. He actively sought World War II because he saw it as a means to gain his own personal ends. Hitler's genius was in persuading his followers that Germany's (his own) prestige and glory could be regained if they obeyed his will: he externalized his internal childhood psychopathology by making the political scene in Germany the stage on which he could realize his own irrational childhood emotional needs and goals while convincing his followers of the validity of his ideas. It was his organizational genius that made Germany the tool for him to achieve his own sadistic, destructive, and grandiose ambitions. He obviously had a special talent in applying group psychology to the German people by his oratorical and dramatic skills, but of course he represented exactly what so many of the people wanted. His oratory aroused the feelings they already had, including all the frustration, hate, and readiness to violence. His will catalyzed and justified their own motivations.

Hitler exemplifies the use of reason, talent, and skills in a rational way to accomplish *irrational* goals. His narcissism (mostly as egotism with belief in his own infallibility) and his sadistic hostility (as hate and destructiveness to both friend and foe, i.e., ordering Rommel, long his favorite general, to commit suicide) were raised to pathological intensity. He may have had periods of irrationality (as when the Allies crossed the Rhine and the Russians were closing in) but was never actually psychotic. Also, he was not a simple criminal in the usual sense of the word, but he did use reason for irrationally intensified egotism and sadistic destructiveness, and therefore was not simply psychotic, criminal, or neurotic. It seems correct to call him a psychotic personality.

What is known of him personally leaves little doubt that he was fixated emotionally at an early enough infantile level to be seriously withdrawn from human relations, which allowed him to see people as something other than human and to murder with impunity; to be almost totally narcissistic, absorbed only in gratifying his own feelings (which, when they coincided with those of his followers, gave him great charisma and power); to hide by repression the distortions, often subtle, of his sense of reality; and to avoid by diffuseness any overt psychosis while failing to hide the impression of being somehow a madman. Probably he acted out the usual psychodynamics of the individual who takes displeased revenge on other humans for what they (one or both parents) have done to him in early childhood. His revenge was on so vast a scale as to reveal this irrational element, this madness. His true goals were personal revenge for his childhood suffering and not the restoration of Germany to socioeconomic health and happiness. That is why his leadership by sadistic hostility doomed that great nation to defeat and partition. Hitler seems to fit well the criteria for psychotic personality.

Whatever the sources of Hitler's limitless and uninhibited hostility vented as rage and hate, it fell on Jews, gypsies, other minorities, and the weak and sick. Their powerlessness was an aphrodisiac which stimulated his sadism, which he could then vent on anyone or any number who were trapped within his power. We do not know if this stimulated his sexual feelings. The hostility was probably also connected with his own feelings of weakness and inferiority which caused him to hate in others what he hated in himself.

## REFERENCES

Churchill, W. (1951): *The Second World War: Closing The Ring.* Boston: Houghton Mifflin, p. 612.
Winterbotham, F.W. (1974): *The Ultra Secret.* New York: Dell Publishing Co.


## RESOURCE MATERIAL

Binion, R. (1973): Hitler's concept of Lebensraum; the psychological basis, *History of Childhood Quarterly* 1(2): Fall.
_____ (1975): Hitler looks east, *History of Childhood Quarterly* 3(1): Summer.
Fest, J.C. (1973): *Hitler.* New York: Vintage Books.
Fromm, E. (1973): *The Anatomy of Human Destructiveness.* New York: Holt, Rinehart, Winston, pp. 369-423.
Hitler, A. (1971): *Mein Kampf,* translated by R. Manheim. Boston: Houghton Mifflin.
Koenigsberg, R. (1975): *Hitler's Ideology. A Study in Psychoanalytic Sociology.* New York: The Library of Social Science.
Langer, W.C. (1972): *The Mind of Adolf Hitler.* New York: Basic Books.

Maser, W. (1971): *Hitler, Legend, Myth and Reality.* New York: Harper Torchbooks.

Payne, R. (1973): *The Life and Death of Adolf Hitler.* New York: Praeger.

Sherlin, H. (1976): Hitler as the bound delegate of his mother, *History of Childhood Quarterly* 3(4): Spring, pp. 463-508.

Smith B. (1967): *Adolf Hitler, His Family, Childhood and Youth.* Stanford, CA: The Hoover Institution on War, Revolution and Peace, Stanford University.

Waite, R.G.L. (1977): *The Psychopathic God, Adolf Hitler.* New York: Basic Books.

# 20
# CONSTRUCTIVE TYPE: MARY BAKER EDDY*

What American woman with little formal education, three times married, mother of a son raised by another woman, founded a major new religion, wrote her own interpretation of the Bible, claimed to have cured hopelessly sick people, created a large body of devoted followers, several new churches, and a great newspaper, and at the time of her death had amassed a personal estate of two million dollars? This remarkable woman was Mary Baker Eddy, "discoverer" of Christian Science and founder of the Christian Science religion.

Two facts immediately stand out in examining Mrs. Eddy's life and work: (1) she is the only woman to have founded a major religion, and (2) until she was over 40, there was little or no suggestion of her future greatness. Reconstructing her early life is difficult because of the paucity of hard facts. When she finally wrote her own autobiographical retrospections, she was in her seventies. Her memory seems to have retained mainly those experiences which best fitted in with her growing fame and success, filtering out less favorable items. People who knew her as a child or young woman and recorded their impressions too often seem to have slanted their views in accordance with their own strong feelings for or against her.

Let us begin with a skeleton outline of her life containing mainly undisputed data. She was born Mary Morse Baker in 1821 at Bow, New Hampshire, near Concord, and was the youngest of six children. Her father, Mark Baker, owned a 500-acre farm but left the farming to others, assuming the role locally of country squire and lay lawyer. He was said to be stern and austere with Calvinist religious convictions, a man who insisted on daily Bible readings for his family. Mary's mother, Abigail Ambrose Baker, appears to have been a housewife and loving mother. The combined attention of five devoted older siblings and

---

*This chapter by Silas L. Warner, M.D.

both parents seems to have created in Mary a sense of being special. In her autobiography (1891) she says that at age eight she *heard a voice* calling out her name repeatedly. Only her mother was nearby. Her mother denied calling her and finally read her the Bible story of Samual. She advised Mary to reply to the voice as Samuel had: "Speak, Lord, for thy servant heareth." Mary replied the next time she heard her name called, but received no instructions from the voice and in fact never again heard her name called. This anecdote begs the question as to whether it was a childhood fantasy or something Mrs. Eddy later created when she wrote her autobiography. Being an inveterate Bible reader throughout her life, she was undoubtedly very familiar with the story of Samuel and could unconsciously have indulged later in some retrospective falsification, or even at age eight, having read the story of Samuel, subsequently imagined hearing a voice.

It is also recorded that after her mother read to Mary from the Bible that Daniel prayed three times a day, Mary made a special point of praying seven times each day. Mrs. Eddy recalled in later years that her earliest ambition in life was to write a book. Her father, who often seemed in opposition to Mary, was said to be so alarmed by her hearing a "voice" that he consulted a physician, who gave orders to take away her books because "her brain" was "too big for her body." The physician also suggested that Mary not be forced to attend school regularly and not receive medicine.

Because Mary was always frail and delicate as a child and in frequent ill health, she was given special care and protection. She would experience seizure-like states which the family physician Dr. Loddy judged to be of a hysterical nature, often precipitated by anger or "bad temper." She was constantly "depressed or excited by the turbulence of school life," so her school attendance was irregular. Mary's education at home was supervised by her parents and her siblings. She regularly read the Bible and Lindley Murray's grammar, and later, with her favorite brother Albert's help, she learned Hebrew, Greek, and Latin.

Her education was expanded further to include natural philosophy, logic, and moral science. She irregularly attended a Professor Sanborn's private school and was said to excel in rhetoric. Her religious education was strongly influenced by her father's and her Congregationalist minister's insistence on the validity of the Calvinistic dogma of predestination, hell fire, and eternal damnation. She began to discuss theology with her father, and by age 12 she "professed religion" but could not accept predestination. When Mary was 15, the family moved from Bow to Tilton and Mary joined the Tilton Congregational Church. It was during this period that she formulated her own concept of a loving God, rejecting the then-prevalent Calvinistic concept of a punitive God. Her sisters and mother passively supported her position when she came out in open disagreement with her father over predestination.

Two significant events occurred late in her teens: one was a violent argument with her father over their different religious views, with neither one willing to yield to the other. Apparently exhausted from this distressing situation, Mary took ill and went to bed with a fever. When the family doctor was consulted he spotted the real problem immediately, urged Mary's father not to try to convert her to his Calvinistic views, and asked her mother to provide Mary with more tender, loving care. Then Mary put herself into fervent prayer to her own loving God and her fever broke. She arose feeling a "soft glow of ineffable joy" and records that moment as one when "the horrible decree of predestination—as John Calvin rightly called his own tenet—forever lost its power over me."

The second traumatic event of her early years was the death of her beloved brother Albert when Mary was just 20. This left its pall of sorrow on the whole family, but was felt especially strongly by Mary because of their close relationship.

At age 22 she married 32-year-old Major George Washington Glover, much to her family's delight. Glover was a friend of her older brother Samuel, with whom he had learned the building trade in Boston. In fact, Samuel had previously married Major Glover's sister Eliza when Mary was ten years old, and it was at their wedding that Mary first met her husband-to-be. After a joyous wedding on December 10, 1843, the newlyweds sailed from Boston to Charleston, South Carolina, where George Glover lived and conducted his construction business. In June of 1844, while in Wilmington, North Carolina, on a business trip, George Glover contracted yellow fever and was dead nine days later. Widowed and pregnant, Mary returned to her parents' home in Tilton in August 1844. Very little of Major Glover's estate could be liquidated into funds for Mary, but she did arrange to free all of the slaves with no recompense, and on September 11, 1844 (almost nine months to the day after their marriage) a son was born to Mary. He was named

George Washington Glover II after his father. The new infant was born strong and healthy, but his mother's frail health failed and she could not care for the baby. A woman lived nearby who had recently given birth to twins, one of whom had died in infancy; she agreed to wet-nurse young George while Mary recovered. The exact nature of her postpartum illness is not clear, but it is known that she had to remain in bed, weak and despondent, while both her parents and a nurse tended her. On November 22, 1849, Mary's mother, whose health had been gradually deteriorating, died, leaving Mary without husband, mother, or son, and totally dependent on her father. When, less than a year after his first wife's death, her father married a well-to-do widow, Mary moved in with her sister Abigail and family. Abigail had a son a little younger than Mary's, and apparently she feared her own son would be hurt by lively little George, so George remained with his foster family about 40 miles away.

Mary continued to live with her rather dominating sister Abigail Tilton until 1853, experiencing constant poor health, a painful lower back, spinal weakness, nervousness, occasional seizures, and prostration from sheer exhaustion. However, she kept up with her reading, especially the Bible, constantly prayed, and occasionally wrote letters to the local newspaper. Mary had some suitors who might have been interested in marrying her, but she discouraged all of them until she met a handsome, well-traveled dentist Dr. Daniel Patterson. She saw in him the potential for helping her regain her health, enabling her to reunite with young George, and so they were married on June 21, 1853 (Mary was then 32). Dr. Patterson had to carry his sick, frail bride downstairs from her bedroom for the ceremony. Another reason for their marriage may have been Dr. Patterson's lively interest in home-opathy, which appealed to Mary. This medical theory holds that small doses of the same ingredient thought to cause a disease should be given to the patient as a cure (*similia similibus curantur*).

Their marriage did not prosper. Dr. Patterson turned out to be a ladies' man who enjoyed staking out new territories for his dental and personal conquests. He wore a high hat and silk gloves, and always spoke in an ostentatious manner. Mary did get him to move into a neighboring town nearer her son George, but the visits between George and Mary were never very satisfying, and Dr. Patterson evidently felt these visits created too much emotional stress for his wife. According to Mary, he and Abigail then conspired in a "plot" to have George and his foster family moved to the Middle West in 1856. Mary's life was discouraging, with her constant poor health and a husband chronically in debt. She was usually worried and sick, and neither her husband's homeopathic techniques nor his hollow promises were much help; at one point she had to borrow money from Abigail to pay off Dr. Patterson's debts.

When the Civil War broke out, Dr. Patterson went to Washington to enlist as a dentist, and in 1862 he found himself a bystander at the Battle of Bull Run. Too close to a line held by the Confederates, he was captured and kept in Libby Prison for two years.

Ironically, also in 1862, Mary's son George, then 17, ran away from his foster parents in Minnesota, enlisted in the Union army, and was later wounded. Although he did correspond with his mother, they did not see each other until many years later when George was 34 years old.

Dr. Patterson had heard of a Dr. Phineas P. Quimby of Portland, Maine, who spoke of miraculous cures without medication. While Dr. Patterson was in prison, Mary found the handbill advertising Dr. Quimby's cures and wrote to him pleading that he come to see her, but he replied that it would be necessary for her to travel to Portland. Mary put aside small amounts from Abigail's allowance and finally saved enough for the trip to Portland.

On October 10, 1862 she arrived there so weak that she had to be helped into Dr. Quimby's office. She was extremely hopeful of being cured and was not disappointed: Dr. Quimby sat down beside her, stared into her eyes, and convinced her that she was being held in bondage by others, that "her animal spirit was reflecting its grief upon her body and calling it spinal disease." He then wet his hands, placed them on her head, and assured her that he was imparting healthy electricity into her system. She felt immediate relief and with subsequent treatments regained a sense of well-being, optimism, and greatly improved health. Within a week she was able to climb the 182 stairs of the city hall. Mary became an ardent disciple of Quimby, remaining in Portland for three weeks while being treated and studying his methods. She even wrote letters praising him to the Portland newspaper. Indeed, Mary was inspired with missionary zeal to understand his principles and pass on to others his healing gospel.

Mary went to live with Abigail Tilton later in 1862, much improved and full of praise for Dr. Quimby with whom she kept up a regular correspondence, and when her previous spells recurred she wrote to him requesting "absent treatments." She wrote that his "angel visits" had improved her, but that he should make another visit in his "omnipresence."

In the spring of 1864, Mary returned to Portland to confer with Dr. Quimby. She not only spent much time talking with him, but got to know two other patients well, both of whom she later visited. It was obvious that Mary was preoccupied with Dr. Quimby's healing technique and theory, and she even made a copy of Quimby's writings called *Questions and Answers*. Without being aware of it, she was "borrowing" some of his ideas to combine them with her own, drawing on her strong background knowledge of Christianity. In the autumn of 1864 she rejoined Dr. Patterson in Swampscott, Massachusetts. He remained unchanged in his erratic dental practice and philandering.

The year 1866 was to be a very important one for Mary: on February 3 she fell on an ice patch in front of her home. Dr. Cushing was called to see her and, according to Mary's account, found her to be in critical condition with a concussion and possible spinal dislocation. She also was said to have undergone "prolonged unconsciousness and spasmodic seizures." An eighth of a grain of morphine was administered to her "as a palliative," but according to her own account it was entirely through prayer and the cleansing of her mind of sickness that she recovered from this "serious" condition, and this "self-cure" seems to have given her the final impuetus to start the Christian Science movement.

In 1866 Dr. Phineas Quimby died of a stomach tumor. His son George had been his secretary, and many of Quimby's thoughts, theories, and "cures" were recorded. When Christian Science evolved as a curative process, numerous similarities were found between Dr. Quimby's theories and Mrs. Eddy's writings.

Then Dr. Patterson chose 1866 as the time to "elope" with the wife of a wealthy patient. He soon returned and asked Mary for forgiveness, but she had suffered too much and would not forgive him, although she did forgive his paramour. After Mary separated from Dr. Patterson in the summer of 1866, she was never again to live with him, and he gradually succumbed to his own vices. In 1873, after 20 years of marriage, she received a divorce from Dr. Patterson.

During the late 1860s Mary boarded with several different families, continuing to guard her health and to explore Christian means of preserving it. She developed a small group of followers; her first two "students," Sarah Bagley and Richard Kennedy, were trained by 1870. She completed her first book, *The Science of Man,* and conducted her first classes in Christian Science in the summer of 1870. Initially her healing showed obvious similarities to "mesmerism," but in 1872 she decreed there would be no laying on of hands or physical contact in Christian Science. Richard Kennedy balked at this, defected from her ranks, and pursued his own version of mental healing which included a laying on of hands (connected unconsciously with parents handling and fondly patting their babies?). Mary continued her teaching and finished *Science and Health* in 1875. By then she had eight students, each of whom paid her ten dollars a week. One of her students was Asa Gilbert Eddy, a sweet and gentle bachelor whose health was frail at best. Mary found him to be a loyal and devoted follower, decidedly unlike other "hostile" students who had defected from her ranks and who subsequently "harassed" her, and Asa was given ever-increasing responsibility as a practitioner and teacher. He and Mary were married on January 1, 1877 (when she was 55). By then she was spending most of her time writing and teaching, while her husband and close followers practiced Christian healing. In the previous decade she had been an active practitioner and had recorded all her "cures" so that her students were very familiar with her "miracles."

Because she strongly believed in "animal magnetism," she felt that she constantly had to protect herself against its adverse effect, and thought the students who had defected could cause her intense discomfort by focusing their animal magnetism upon her. Her own loyal students would protect her, staying near and praying away the animal magnetism. Evil "waves" could be transmitted by enemies, and aimed at Mary and her followers. She suspected animal magnetism whenever she felt physically ill or "drugged." Richard Kennedy, her former student, was thought to be her enemy and active in directing his evil animal magetism toward her.

In August 1879, the Church of Christ, Scientist, was chartered, and in 1881 the Massachusetts Metaphysical College was founded to instruct students in Christian Science. Asa Eddy died in June 1882, scarcely five years after the marriage. Mary was convinced that he had suffered from arsenical poisoning mesmerically transmitted from her enemies. Dr. Rufus Noyes, a medical doctor, had seen Asa prior to his death and diagnosed him as having an organic heart condition. This was confirmed by a medical autopsy by Dr. Noyes listing a physically diseased heart valve as cause of death. Mary had a director of the Massachusetts Metaphysical College, a Dr. Eastman, examine Asa's heart and he noted an abnormal amount of "metaphysical arsenic" to be present. It should be said that Dr. Eastman was sent to prison for five years in 1893.

Mary continued to expand her Christian Scientist movement by leaps and bounds, and before the Massachusetts Metaphysical College closed in 1889 it had trained 4,000 students. It closed because its principal teacher (Mary) went into semiretirement, moving from her Brookline home to Concord, New Hampshire, 70 miles from Boston. Revised editions of her key to the scriptures appeared, known as *Science and Health*. In addition, new property and buildings were purchased, including the original site of "the Mother Church" erected in 1894 in Boston; in 1883, a bimonthly newspaper was begun, known as *The Journal of Christian Science*. The ruling religious hierarchy was reorganized with Mary as titular head holding absolute power. Local churches sprang up all over the United States and, later, throughout the world.

By 1791 Mary was 70 years old, comfortably ensconced in her new home in Concord, New Hampshire. She became less active in the everyday running of the Christian Science empire but always had the final word in any important policy issue. An interesting sidelight was when a young physician Dr. E.J. Foster joined her ranks, studied Christian Science under Mary, and won her trust and admiration. She legally adopted him as her son. Her own son corresponded irregularly with her from Minnesota. He had been married and was raising his own children, and must have hoped to profit materially from his mother's accumulation of worldly goods. He had a cordial but unprofitable visit with his mother in 1888.

Mary Baker Eddy wrote and revised seven main editions of the Christian Science textbook *Science and Health with Key to the Scriptures*. The first main edition was published in 1875, and the last between 1902 and 1910. Each main edition had a chapter on animal magnetism, with the final main edition of 1910 containing the culmination of the changes in Mrs. Eddy's thinking on the subject. She entitled this final chapter "Aminal Magnetism Unmasked," thereby proudly announcing the victory of her divine metaphysics over animal magnetism. Mrs. Eddy postulated an absolute truth revealed through divine metaphysics or God's spiritual laws; her ultimate solution pitted divine mind against mortal matter. She "discovered" seven synonyms for God and elaborated on them in the Christian Science textbook, so that Christian Scientists could "enlarge their consciousness" by "being in harmony" with these seven synonyms for God: mind, spirit, soul, principle, life, truth, and love. She felt that man's true image is learned from knowing the true image of God, while animal magnetism, evil, and disease were the products of man's own faulty thinking and would disappear or be transcended by achieving a consciousness of God, with his plan for love and perfection. Human thought erroneously creates a duality between good and evil. Divine metaphysics reveals God's way, which is a one-value consciousness ("monistic") and has only a positive standard of values. Mrs. Eddy went one step further from divine metaphysics to the "science of being." "Spiritual laws" were discovered which revealed the logic of God's plan and a "science of spirit." She presented spiritual laws with their own orders and rules, all part of the "divine system."

In reality, to determine what constitutes a science, specific criteria are required. Generally speaking, observations are first made from which generalizations are drawn and then these in turn are tested, all steps being critically tested by others. Mrs. Eddy placed Christian Science in a special category that did not require validation or duplication: traditional scientific proof uses man-made criteria, whereas divine metaphysics was inspirationally revealed to her and put her in touch with absolute truth, or God's plan. Thus Christian Science is not subject to the usual scientific scrutiny. Its healing power could not be questioned because a failure only shows that the individual had not been totally cleansed of mortal beliefs and was still functioning at the false level of believing in, and being vulnerable to, evil and disease. Only when a person is in total harmony with God's plan can he live in the real world of divine perfection and thereby transcend evil and disease. Thus the failures come from an incomplete belief, from not working hard enough at getting into harmony with God's plan and discovering the spiritual laws by which we should live.

Let us examine how Mrs. Eddy's Christian Science helped her to solve her own life problems. One very painful area to her was that of death. Relatively early in her life she lost her favorite brother, mother, first husband, and father. These blows were softened by her conviction that death is a mortal illusion and that in God's real world people do not die. It also helped in facing her own death to think of herself as "passing on" to God's own world, the Kingdom of Heaven, where she would be reunited with those she loved.

During her earlier years she was plagued with chronically bad health, some of which probably had psychosomatic elements; she improved her health by studying the Bible and uncovering spiritual laws. Obviously, helping others and founding Christian Science resulted in her receiving great praise and fame, which was likely very gratifying.

She always wanted to believe that humans were good and lovable, not born bad and sinful, and she argued this point with her father, yet she may have feared that perhaps she was wrong and would be punished for her heresy. She tenaciously persisted in promoting her view that man was essentially innocent and good, and she even developed a method by which man could fully realize his own perfection. This gave her the ultimate victory over her father and those other mortals who stood in her way. She externalized her inner problems by creating a vehicle (her religion) by which she could win the total love and approval she so desperately needed in her own childhood, and also gave to others this same opportunity for salvation if they became good Christian Scientists.

Anybody who comes in contact with Christian Scientists knows how unselfish, caring, and highly principled most of them are; their lives are living testimony of the high level of their beliefs. Too often physicians focus only on horror stories, such as those of a Christian Scientist unnecessarily dying of appendicitis, but we should balance this with the good done by Christian Scientists. There are many medical conditions in which specific treatment does not result in cures, so that these patients have to learn to live with their condition. Christian Science provides a helpful "mind-frame" for some patients; some of the newer developments in psychosomatic medicine indicate how important a positive mental attitude is in any illness.

Why, then, should Mrs. Eddy be included in a treatise on the psychotic personality? Because of the positive, loving, constructive outcome of her dynamics. There is ample evidence that she suffered from paranoid delusions during her lifetime. Partly because of Christian Science's success she did have some enemies, but it was in the area of how these enemies expressed their feelings toward her that she strayed from reality. There is certainly no known way by which Kennedy or others could focus their animal magnetism upon her, making her physically suffer. It is conceivable that her own recognition of individuals who might have negative thoughts about her so disturbed Mary that she developed physical symptoms. It has been observed that in certain primitive societies the very anticipation of a punishment, "the evil eye," or ostracism can cause pain and disturbance, and even possibly result in the death of a previously apparently healthy person.

As she grew older and age took its toll on her mental faculties, Mary's paranoia about malicious animal magnetism being used against her by her enemies increased. She moved to a new house in Chestnut Hill, Massachusetts, in January of 1908 because she was convinced that such magnetism had totally permeated her house in Concord. She had spent 20 years in this house, but the death (probably from diabetes) of a close confidante and attendant and the suicide of the sister of the former First Reader of the Concord church, as well as her own failing health, strengthened her conviction of magnetism's lethality. There was also in 1906 an investigation by reporters of the *New York World* into rumors that Mary was either deceased or *non compos mentis*. The newspaper published an initial exposé claiming that she was a helpless dupe of the members of her household. This prompted her to consent to an interview with reporters to determine the state of her health and whether or not she had any other physician than God. She marshaled her courage and answered the reporters' questions in a satisfactory enough fashion to convince them of her sanity, although she did appear old and somewhat feeble.

Perhaps the cruelest blow of all occurred in 1907 when a suit was filed by her son, granddaughter, and nephew claiming that Mrs. Eddy (then 86 years old) was incapable of managing her business affairs and fortune, and that she was helpless in the hands of designing persons. William Chandler, a U.S. senator from New Hampshire, represented her heirs in this case. In Senator Chandler's opening argument to the court (Daken, 1968) he said

Mrs. Eddy's book [*Science and Health*] alone is proof that she is suffering from the following systematized delusions and dementia: the first one is the delusion—fundamental, widespread, and deep-rooted—of the non-existence and non-reality of the physical universe, organic and inorganic. All her delusions are built upon this fundamental delusion, and they are systematized so that they are part of her whole being. . .Mrs. Eddy, controlled by her delusion, believes that the world is neither real nor existent. . .

Senator Chandler went on to describe other delusions Mrs. Eddy supposedly possessed, including the belief that she was miraculously and supernaturally selected by God to receive divine revelations directly from God, to herself alone, of a new and supernatural mode of preventing and curing disease. In court the senator said that Mrs. Eddy also believed the thought and progress of the universe could be developed only through the science she called hers, and there existed "malicious animal magnetism," a concept implying persecution and diabolism. She termed this "Electricity of Mortal Mind," "The Red Dragon," "The Trail of the Fiend," "The Sting of the Serpent." Animal magnetism apparently was capable of producing all manner of evil, of poisoning mankind, of producing death.

Senator Chandler concluded that Mrs. Eddy had "reached the stage of senile dementia." He further stated that "these delusions of hers include two well-known systematized delusions—the delusion of grandeur and the delusion of persecution."

The court ruled that Mrs. Eddy's alleged delusions should not be presented from the years previous to 1890 as they were not pertinent to the legal proceedings. Because the deed of her trust was signed in March 1907, the court was mainly interested in Mrs. Eddy's state of mind on that date. Therefore, the court ruled that Christian Science and all its literature were not on trial, for most of it antedated 1890. Then the court appointed three masters to interview Mrs. Eddy and determine her competency. Again she mustered her courage for an interview, but the conclusion about her competency was never revealed, as Senator Chandler withdrew his suit and a compromise was worked out by the opposing attorneys. Apparently Senator Chandler was concerned that the court might decide against him, especially since much of his evidence pointing to her "delusional state" was not acceptable as evidence. Mrs. Eddy's attorney may have feared the filing of a new, larger suit over her sanity over a long period of years, not just at the time of her signing the deed of trust. In any case, he offered to create generous trust funds out of Mrs. Eddy's estate to be given the three plaintiffs.

All of these painful events led to Mrs. Eddy's decision to move to Chestnut Hill. When she moved into her new home the doors were closed and barred, and six armed men took their posts on guard outside the house while, within, trusted "watchers" were posted on duty at two-hour intervals to concentrate on guarding her against the evil currents of malicious animal magnetism. When Mrs. Eddy felt ill she would blame her watchers for either shirking their duty or falling asleep on duty. (Incidentally, it is not extremely unusual for financially successful tycoons in their old age, and if living alone, to develop fears of being attacked and therefore hire bodyguards for their homes.)

On the first of December 1910, she was weak and exhausted with a severe cough and, asking for her pencil and paper, she wrote her final words: "God is my Life." Two days later on a Saturday night she was dead, leaving no instructions for an announcement or a funeral. The directors of the Christian Science church ordered that her death be announced in the Boston church after the Sunday morning services. A physician wrote on her death certificate, "Natural causes—probably pneumonia." No funeral was held, but some 50 church officials and servants gathered in her drawing room at Chestnut Hill to witness her body lying in a bronze casket, wearing a white silk gown with a lace shawl. The casket was sealed and buried in a tomb of cement and steel at Boston's Mt. Auburn Cemetery.

A word about Mary Baker Eddy's relationships with other people: as a child she was sickly but friendly, bright, and always "special." She seems to have been given a special status by others throughout her life. She never regularly went to school, so her initial circle of friends was restricted to family members, who must have enjoyed her precociousness, brightness, and spirit. She showed an interest in writing and always was willing to write letters to any family member who was away from home.

During her early adult years, Mary developed a few outside friends (including her first two husbands), but each friendship was invariably transient, usually built on mutual intellectual interests. As she grew older, she was increasingly committed to founding Christian Science and its healing; her friends then were her students, patients, and disciples, and her relationship with each one depended on how wholeheartedly he or she believed in Mary. In several cases when an individual questioned her, incurring her wrath, that individual subsequently defected from her. In time, Mary Baker Eddy came to believe that her friends were those totally on her side and that individuals who did not believe in her were her enemies. By then she experienced herself as God's agent who was on a higher level than her peers; she graciously accepted their worship but could be hateful and scornful toward her enemies. Nobody, not even her third husband during the few years of their marriage, felt really close to her—everyone looked up to her as a demigod. She appears to have preferred this impersonal way of relating to others, and no trace can be found of a solid friendship lasting over a prolonged period in her life, although she had many acquaintances, admirers, students, and devotees. Those in closest daily contact with her worshipped her but were always on guard lest she fall into one of her moods; at times she wanted to be alone and at other times she needed a patient listener when she complained about her enemies; at still other times she needed support and reassurance that she would survive. Significantly, she could not trust any of her fellow Christian Scientists to the point of choosing her successor, but picked a committee of her followers to take over her reins.

\* \* \* \*

If we think of reality in ordinary secular terms, and do not take as ordinary reality the faith in which Mary Baker Eddy was raised, then we can compare the evil genius of Hitler with the angelic genius of Mary Baker Eddy, using regular clinical observations through which we understand every human being, from the most unusual to the most usual. The observations sketched above are far fewer than can be obtained in a first interview with a patient (Saul, 1980, p. 114) in which the data yield at least an initial insight into that individual's main psychodynamics. However, we can compare the status in the devil (Hitler) and the angel (Mary Baker Eddy) of a few dynamic features which we have noted. Most obvious are the narcissism, the hostility, and the grasp of reality.

Hitler seems to have held himself far superior in military knowledge, judgment, and ability to the German General Staff to whom he believed he was God's gift. Also, he felt superior to Jews, gypsies, and all the minority nationals of eastern Europe. This colossal vanity becomes intelligible dynamically as mostly reactive to profound feelings of inferiority, socioeconomically, educationally, esthetically, and emotionally; in lack of maturity and morality, by hating in others what he found intolerable in himself. Yet reactive or not, there is no doubt of Hitler's extreme, pathologically intensified narcissism as vanity and egocentricity, with consequent intensified envy.

Mrs. Eddy certainly believed herself superior to all persons whom she felt to be against her and believed that she understood God and his plans and laws better than anyone else. This in ordinary secular terms might well be the result, at least in part, of her standing up for her views against her father during childhood. However, in diametrical contrast with Hitler and his destructiveness, Mrs. Eddy largely repressed her narcissism and saw her beliefs as "discoveries" of the divine system, as a Christian Scientist. In both Hitler and Mrs. Eddy, their enormous successes after relatively unpromising, even humble beginnings must have reinforced their self-confidence and self-esteem to the point of believing that they must be superior to everyone else, persons of destiny, selected by God or at least favored by God. The intense competitive drive to be superior is seen in a childhood incident when Mary, after learning from the Book of Daniel that Daniel prayed three times a day, made a special point of praying seven times a day. By then she was in serious emotional conflict with her father over God as a loving Father, rather than accepting her father's Calvinistic view of God as punitive. Possibly she was struggling with her mother and siblings to be the favorite in her father's love, to believe in her father as loving, and not strict and punitive, threatening her with hell fire and eternal damnation. This threat probably created severe anxiety and a powerful drive to escape by making her God a loving one. It is inconceivable that a child could grow up under such a strict, harsh, rigidly moralistic, punitive father without much resentment and guilt. Mary must have had her hostilities, as all children do, heightened by her father's attitudes toward her, and she experienced seizure-like states which the family physician judged to be of a hysterical nature—often precipitated by anger or "bad temper." However, if she behaved and thought properly, i.e., in agreement with her father, then she might escape the eternal damnation. She always did fear that perhaps her father's view of religion might turn out to be correct. Therefore, it is safe to conclude that intense, unremitting anxiety was a powerful motivation for her compulsive drive to found her religion of love, in which all evil came from faulty thinking (disagreement with her father), and from hostile and sexual thoughts. How could she manage to stand up to her father in their arguments over religion? Probably because she felt loved and supported by her mother and siblings, and perhaps in part because her father enjoyed these verbal battles over theological dogma with his highly intelligent, deeply interested and motivated daughter.

Mrs. Eddy's childhood with her father suggests a close similarity to that of Emily Brontë with her father. Under the strict, dogmatic paternal pressure, Emily found release, as did her sister Charlotte, in writing —producing her wild masterpiece *Wuthering Heights* (while Charlotte created *Jane Eyre*). Mrs. Eddy, raised in Boston and New Hampshire, not on the bleak and often icy moors, produced a religion based upon love by right thinking, presented not as her own position of closeness to God but as a revealed scientific discovery of God's plans and laws.

Great is the contrast, then, between Hitler and Mary Baker Eddy in the status of their narcissism and their hostility. Hitler was successful as a criminal, venting his hostilities so as to be a leader in killing 50 million people. (Criminality is a psychiatric condition, like neurosis and psychosis.) Mrs. Eddy repressed her hostilities and fled from them psychologically to the opposite pole, trying to help others achieve love and health, but she too sacrificed some elements of her sense of reality. To her credit, she tried to prove her views scientifically, but this could not be done, and even today "psychosomatic medicine" is still a young science. She got around this difficulty by rationalizing that her science was different from all the rest of the body of science, and deciding that those who do not "believe" have some impurities in their minds. Her idea of malicious animal magnetism is a paranoid idea familiar to all psychiatrists. It provided an easy excuse from every illness or failure, and was probably an expression of her own guilt and a projection of her own hostility.

Mary Baker Eddy could not have achieved all she did and suffered through what she did, without some fight-flight reaction generating some anger and resentments, especially with her childhood history of seizure-like states that were precipitated by anger and bad temper. There is a kernel of truth in every paranoid delusion, and perhaps there was some real danger when she surrounded herself with guards to prevent harm from the malicious animal magnetism. Her sense of everyday, practical reality continued intact. Her childhood disagreements with her father were enduring but she could not make this projection fit as a devil or hell's fire into the religion she founded.

The information on both Hitler and Mary Baker Eddy is not adequate to establish their psychodynamics with full scientific, clinical confidence, but a comparison of these two contrasting personalities does provide a simple illustration of how even meager data can yield some features of the psychodynamics. These individuals fit the extreme opposite ends of the *hostilodynamic* scale (Saul, 1980, p. 81)— on the one hand, criminally destructive, and on the other end of the scale, socially constructive.

It would not be surprising if Mrs. Eddy's creation of Christian Science meant psychodynamically a continuation of maintaining her religious arguments against her father. Certainly, though, she must have had enormous drive from her dynamics and also outstanding intelligence and talents to accomplish what she did. And what worked for her emotionally must have fitted the dynamics of the millions who resonated emotionally to the intensity of her feelings. We cannot go into the psychosocial dynamics of her followers beyond remarking that, like all legitimate laws and religions, she provided a way of repressing those animal instincts (dependence and need for authority and love, the fight-flight reaction and hostility, sex, anxiety, and fear, etc.) which must be controlled if people are to live in social organizations. A patient in the earlier days of commercial passenger air travel once said, "My friends and colleagues are afraid to fly, but I am a Christian Scientist and I *know* positively that I will arrive safely."

### REFERENCE

Saul, L.J. (1980): *The Childhood Emotional Pattern and Psychodynamic Therapy*. New York: Van Nostrand Reinhold.

### RESOURCE MATERIAL

Daken, E. (1968): *Mrs. Eddy*. Gloucester, MA.: Peter Smith.

Eddy, M.B. (1891): *Retrospection and Introspection*. Boston: The Trustees under the Will of Mary Baker G. Eddy.

_____ (1875): *Science and Health*. Boston: The Trustees under the Will of Mary Baker G. Eddy (1910).

Glover, M.B. (1876): *The Science of Man, by Which the Sick Are Healed. Embracing Questions and Answers in Moral Science Arranged for the Learner*. Lynn, MA.: T.P. Nichols, printer.

Kappeler, M. (1975): *Aminal Magnetism–Unmasked*. London: The Foundation Book Co. Ltd.

# 21
# PSYCHODYNAMICS
# AND SOCIETY

*Beauty is truth, truth beauty—that is all ye know on earth and all ye need to know.*

John Keats, *Ode to a Grecian Urn*

*The world is my country, science is my religion.*

Christiaan Huygens

*The most incomprehensible thing about the universe is that it is comprehensible.*

Albert Einstein

"Man that is born of a woman is of few days and full of trouble" (Job 14:1). How true, and how ironic. And how miserable people do make others and themselves in their short life span—through wars, futile revolutions, crime, and criminoid behavior. In truth, is this not irrational, a little insane? And is not what makes people cause others as well as themselves so much suffering mostly an excess of hostility (anger, rage, hate, destructiveness)—both emotional and physical?

This craziness of humans is seen in every amount and degree, from mere personal foibles (like "Archie Bunker's") to world wars. Most people fear the insane, but exactly what about them causes fear? Mostly it seems we fear the psychotic's extreme self-centeredness (narcissism), infantilism, lack of reality sense and control, and irrational hostile impulses.

The seeds of such more or less hidden psychoses are in us all, from simple eccentricity to dangerous sadism and murder. Sociologically, the examples are endless: Is there not a psychotic element in the superpowers rushing to build weapons of "defense" against one another, weapons that could destroy all life on our planet? Among the wars simmering worldwide at present are South Africa, Angola, Israel and

Lebanon, Afghanistan and the USSR, Western Sahara and Ethiopia-Somalia, El Salvador, the Philippines, Iran and Iraq, Northern Ireland. Western civilization could try to attribute hostility to less "advanced" nations, were it not for the example of Northern Ireland. Within a gentle and most mature religion, a religion of love, two of the greatest Western races and cultures confront and kill each other. This is the ultimate irony, even more poignant perhaps than the irony of Germany— the fatherland of Goethe, Bach, Beethoven, and Einstein—showing its savagery in World War II. Jim Jones in Guyana should have taught us all a lesson. We call his Temple a "cult" because of the unrealistic worship of one man as a god in a setting of unrealistic delusional beliefs; and there are hundreds of such cults, many very large and incredibly wealthy and powerful, some operating mainly by television. Are the human needs for authority and support in this unhappy life so deep and strong that they will create delusions out of the persisting childhood needs for dependence, love, authority, and relief from guilt—in short, out of the needs for parenting that every child has and the lingering on of these needs into adulthood? There is no doubting the enormous comfort and guidance that even pseudoreligion can give in the sufferings and crises of living. Are people's hostilities too strong and widespread to be controlled by secular laws alone, without threats of hell and hopes of heaven?

Is the enormous proliferation of cults in our country and around the world motivated by these needs in their followers, who bring in the hundreds of millions of dollars which the cults receive?* The labor for these millions is obtained not by physical force but by modern psychological methods. What these methods do is weaken or warp the sense of reality of the adherents by tempting or forcing them into regression back to childish dependence and submissiveness.

Science suggests that the best hope for mankind lies eventually in people's mature sense of reality and instincts for survival. The essence of science is the understanding of reality, psychological as well as physical. The Bible admonishes us: "You will know the truth and it will make you free" (John 8:32). Following Jesus' exhortation to build one's house on the rock of his teaching (Matt. 7:24), we can view the

---

*There are 1,000-3,000 such cults in the United States alone, with more than 300,000 adherents; See Rudin, James, A. and Rudin, M. (1980): *Prison or Paradise*. Philadelphia: Fortress Press.

rock as a dual symbol of reality and of mature morality and ethics, and these boil down to not harming other persons or oneself.

The rational, realistic aspect of religion is the moral and ethical. Moses was a great prophet from the viewpoint of psychological science, because he recognized and expressed clearly and succinctly the basic rules which are necessary for a society of humans to survive. This Decalogue was not improved upon until the Sermon on the Mount: "All things whatsoever ye would that men should do to you, do ye even so to them, for this is the law and the prophets" (Matt. 7:12). "You shall not commit adultery, you shall not kill, you shall not steal, you shall not covet. . .you shall love your neighbor as yourself" (Rom. 13:9). These principles specify the animal motivations and reactions we must control if we are to preserve society and benefit from all it can give us. They are expressed in some form in all of the world's great, ancient, established religions.

It is hard to imagine that the ultimate answer for the survival of human beings can be anything but the basic principles of the Judeo-Christian ethic (shared with all great religions), namely, love or friendship for fellow man. Without love, all the discoveries of science are apt to be used for the destruction of humans. Even the knowledge which is now used to prevent disease can be perverted to bacterial and chemical warfare, and if atomic power is used as weaponry rather than to serve life, that is the way to extinction for all life on our planet. As science advances, there will be many such dangers. Ultimately, it becomes a question of insuring that the enormous powers given to humans by science are used constructively in love, with all the moral and ethical dictates of true religion, and not for domination and destruction. It is indispensable for survival that religion and science join together in cooperation.

\* \* \* \*

The human sense of reality is as delicate and sensitive as it is vitally essential for survival. It is all too easily influenced by feelings and emotions. In fact, one of the great themes throughout all recorded history is the slow progress of the rational, realistic understanding of nature in the thrilling form of the collective, self-correcting comprehension of reality which we know as science. Knowledge is indeed power. Science has given humans control of their own lives and destinies, the power to make a good, secure, enjoyable, satisfactory life for all—but also the power to extinguish all human life on earth. It is not yet certain that further advances in knowledge and understanding will prevent man's extinction. We live in an uncertain period of survival or self-destruction (by overpopulation, because every species breeds beyond its food supply, which results inevitably in pollution, inflation, and nuclear war). We must hope for preservation through religion as it formulates and voices our basic morality and ethics, as it works for human welfare, relief of suffering, and the prevention of disaster. Perhaps psychodynamics, the science of human thinking, feeling, and behavior, will help contribute to solutions of the fundamental problem of human hostility—although psychodynamics, like all science, can be misused for antihuman purposes.

Prior to scientific knowledge, the position of an adult in the world corresponded closely to the position of the child in its family, namely, being little and weak, in constant physical danger, and ignorant of the forces within itself and in the world around it. The inner emotional needs, urges, and desires filled its mind, as both child and primitive adult, with yearnings for protecting parents and siblings who would also grant every form of satisfaction. These needs and desires inevitably created dreams and fantasies, for such is the nature of the human mind.

These desires include all the motivations, all the instincts, all the results of training, and the fight-flight reaction, with impulses to sadism, violence, and even murder directed toward others and, perhaps because of guilt, also directed toward oneself. The less developed a person's sense of reality and the more powerful the force of his feelings, the greater is his confusion in perceiving whether these sensations come from within or without, i.e., the stronger is the tendency to "project" these inner feelings upon the outside world from which they then seem to originate. Thus, imagined spirits once dwelt in every bush and stream, and many of them required appeasement like parents whose goodwill must be preserved if the young child is to survive. The human emotions, projected onto the world, populated it with spirits, gods, and devils, all of which in time and as they were fantasied in common with other people were organized into primitive beliefs. The emotional forces which created these fantasies were mostly the unconscious ones of early childhood toward family members. Thus in the environment of primitive man, still dangerous because of his almost total ignorance of nature, the grown-up recreated his early family in fantasy: an omnipotent father figure who could be giving, protecting, understanding, and loving but also harsh and punishing (Jupiter), a mother figure the same (Juno), siblings, uncles, aunts, and cousins (i.e., all the lesser gods and goddesses who represented the inner emotional forces and also the powers of nature—beauty, sex, the sun, sea, streams, mountains, woods, even wine), all of which developed into the Greek and then the Roman pantheons. In some such fashion nature became populated with projected human fantasies, born of human instinctual needs and emotional forces which teemed in the mind and were perceived as existing in the outer world, just as we experience images in dreams and waking fantasies as apart from ourselves.

Primitive man's reaction to unknown danger by fantasy instead of reality—the knowledge of which was not available in those dark ignorant days—is confirmed by actual history as recently as the Middle Ages. Then, in an England helpless before the Black Death, "weird sects sprang into existence, and plague-haunted cities saw gruesome processions of flagellants, each lashing his forerunner to a dismal dirge, and ghoulish practices glare at us. . . ."*

Perhaps it was the increased stability and security of Periclean society which permitted its great men sufficient tranquility for the mature activities of their personalities to function freely, particularly their curiosity and sense of reality. Archimedes was not so fear-ridden that for him stones and water were spirits or gods to be appeased. He could see them with his sense of reality undistorted by the internal clamor of his conflicting emotions. He studied them and discovered what every schoolboy learns—that "an immersed body displaces its own volume of water and the water displaced weighs the difference between the body when weighed in air and when weighed in water." Thus the mature part of the human mind, when sufficiently freed from the frenzy of the unconscious, conflicting instincts left over from childhood, could understand nature and through this scientific understanding achieve a degree of safety and satisfaction on this planet far

---

*Churchill, W. (1956): *History of the English Speaking People: The Birth of Britain.* N.Y.: Dodd Mead & Co.

greater and more real than that provided by the propitiation of imagined spirits.

Of course the great religions of the world, while ministering to the tensions, anxieties, and dangers of human existence, also represent the insights and principles of maturity for the lives of individuals and of societies. The essence of these insights and principles is basic morality and ethics, namely, a definition of what controls humans must exercise over their instincts in order to survive together in societies. The more a religion promotes morality, ethics, and maturity, the more personally and socially valuable it is, and the more closely do its goals and those of science harmonize. However, the more the sense of reality is warped and the thinking and feelings regress to those of childhood, the more likely is a cult or pseudoreligion to develop, rather than a true religion. Will we see betterment of "man's abominable lot" on earth only as true science and true religion join forces in maturing man's thinking, feeling, and behavior?

As a person goes through life today, the greatest danger to him comes not from earthquakes, volcanic eruptions, astronomical accidents, great storms, other animals, or even from disease, but from other *humans*—in the form of war, accidents, everyday cruelty, and crime (which is a disorder of personality just as are the neuroses, addictions, perversions, and psychoses). Yet paradoxically, an individual's greatest protection and satisfactions also come from other humans. Why this is so is readily understood: however it evolved, human beings come together in societies. These provide the greatest protection from the forces of nature, wild animals, and other humans, and also provide more assured supplies of food, clothing, and shelter. Also, with developed societies comes sufficient leisure for culture and its products, the arts and the sciences, which satisfy more sophisticated needs and even give protection against many diseases. However, humans do not live in societies and adapt to them by nature (at least not yet, in terms of evolution). They must *learn* to adapt to societies. Human young are born completely self-centered and selfish with strong fight-flight reactions, quick to rage and destructiveness. They must be *guided* to adapt to other humans and to society; i.e., they must be *socialized.* There's the rub. For socialization of the human young is a long, slow, gradual process and must be done with much love, understanding, patience, and respect for the child, especially during the first hours, days, weeks, months, and first six or seven years of the child's life. If the child is not slowly "won over" to this social adaptation but is antagonized, it grows up with permanently aroused anxiety and consequent fight-flight reaction against its parents or substitutes which cause urges to withdraw (with or without drugs) as well as rebellious hostility displaced against other human beings and against social behavior. Such a child then becomes a danger to others (as a criminal) or to himself (as a masochist, neurotic, addict, or psychotic).

This is why the quintessence of humanity's problems lies in the proper education and winning over of the young to adaptation to social behavior. Only in this way can other humans be the best protection for an individual, and not the worst danger. Perhaps over the ages, if we survive overpopulation, pollution, and nuclear war, processes of evolution will help humans to adapt better to living harmoniously in their societies. Meanwhile, scientific knowledge of the human mind, emotional life, "spirit," will show us how better to raise children to be good, mature adults, just as science has taught man to raise better corn and cattle.

Psychosomatic disorders, neuroses, addictions, perversions, psychoses, and criminality are the measure of how far man, the mammal, has failed to adjust to living in societies. This failure can be traced to the generally clumsy, atrocious ways in which most parents or their substitutes treat their children, especially during the most formative period from conception until about age six or seven. If all or most children were won over to social behavior by patient, loving understanding and respect for their personalities, then they would develop into relatively mature adults whose instincts are adapted to all that social living requires and also to all it has to offer in terms of security, satisfaction, and enjoyment.

This book expresses the faith that the human mind can be understood objectively, scientifically, realistically, clearly, free from the distorting mists of superstition and mysticism—and the further faith that this scientific knowledge of the realities of the mind will indeed make us free, save humanity from destroying itself, and eventually achieve a good life for all.

# 22
# THE PERENNIAL REVOLUTION

For many people the world from 1900 to 1914 was a beautiful place, as raw nature with the great mountains, lovely lakes, rolling hills and endless fields of grain. Also beautiful were the creations of man in architecture and the worlds of art, music and literature. Sarajevo signaled a sudden, shocking eruption of the blood and gold. Hitler gave the world ample warning of the second greater eruption, World War II. But most people could not believe this either, until the world actually exploded in the Blitzkreig in Poland. Why do people so naively accept the eras of peace, and why do wars and revolutions so regularly burst forth despite mankind's best efforts to prevent them?

The answer is as simple and fateful as the brief formula for the relationship of matter and energy: $e = mc^2$. The answer (or an important part of it) is 0 to 6: violence, war and revolution are *always* beneath the surface, the hostile, violent, cruel, rebellious impulses lie in the hearts of men, i.e., in their unconscious feelings. And why is this? It is because the child we once were lives on in us all, however unconsciously. And most children are full of rebelliousness and violence which are part of a pattern of hostility, hate and defiance against members of their own families (or substitutes) responsible for them and close to them during their rearing, especially during their most vulnerable, most formative years from conception until age about six or seven (0 to 6). Some of these violent impulses are against any person who gets in the way of the small child's attachment to its mother, either the father (Oedipus complex) or brother or sister (sibling rivalry). But basically the hostility is because these natural, inevitable oedipal and sibling reactions were poorly handled by those responsible for the child. And besides these situations, most or all inner urges to cruelty and violence originated from faults of commission or of omission in the treatment of the child by those responsible for him and close to him. The most common of these are deprivation, domination and depreciation of the child. Such abuses leave patterns of rebellion, defiance and implacable hostility in the mind of the child against those in power over him. He grows up with these patterns of feeling repressed by fear and by love, but they live on nonetheless within him, even if detectible only in his taste for violence in literature, art or the media. Secretly, unconsciously his fight-flight reaction, his readiness to escape, (psychologically if need be) and to violence is on a hair-trigger. Most children are so reared as to generate a constant pressure of hostility in them, a pressure and pattern that endure for life. Thus a large part, or probably most of the population, is filled with urges, unconscious if not conscious, to rebel, revolt, vent hostility and even violence—and it acts this out when possible.

Social conditions alone do not cause crime or that form of crime called war. Conditions only release the emotional forces within. As the U.N. Charter says, "Wars begin in the minds of men." The pressures of the residues of childhood patterns of frustration, hostility, rebellion and revenge seek an outlet in action. War satisfies the urge to flight and also to fight. The causes of the urges to cruelty and violence lie in the faults of commission and omission that abused the child mostly before age six. No blueprint is needed for how to rear children nor any special techniques. All humans need do is treat their young as well as other animals do theirs: identify with them, love them, respect their budding personalities, try to understand them—mostly just love them and leave them alone. Give the pine tree favorable soil, sun and moisture and it will grow straight of its own nature. That is the basic—but of course the human animal is not born socialized; the baby must learn eating habits and control of his bladder and bowels, and also of his fight-flight reactions, especially his hostilities to others, but this socialization is a learning process which can be accomplished by the inevitability of gradualness, not by harsh impositions which generate that rebellious hostility which will persist for life as a character trait. Yes, we can prevent mental and emotional disorders and illnesses as well as crime, war and other violence—but only by enabling people to mature emotionally through the rearing of our children naturally and properly, especially during their 0 to 6.

# INDEX

Aggression, 5
Alexander, F., corrective emotional experi-
    ence, 127
    neurotic character, 29, 38
Alloplastic, 114-115
"Animal Magnetism," *See* Eddy, Mary Baker
Animals, and psychosomatic research,
    211-214
Authority, needs for, 217, 294, 296, 297
    and cults, 226-227, 237
Auto-analysis, example of, 93-98

Borderline personality, 9-10, 83-101, 106
    Frosch, 84-87
    Giovacchini, 115
    Grinker, 98-99
    Kernberg, 89
Brainwashing, 224, 226, 231, 256, 294
Buddhism, 239
Built-in conflict, 22

Catatonia, 215
Childhood emotional pattern, 25, 35, 39, 50,
    129-130
    Adolf Hitler, 34
    discerning psychotic elements, 31
    distortion of, 39, 46, 300-301
Childrearing, 11, 15, 17-18, 33, 298-299,
    300
Christian Science, development of, 275-292
Christianity, 238
Civilization, characteristics of, 3, 15,
    216-217
    paralleling individual development, 223
    social cooperation, 6, 298
    sublimation of animal instincts, 4, 6
Compulsion Neurosis, example of, 173-178

Conditioning, 6-7
Criminality, 33-35, 38, 129, 290, 299, 301
Criminoid Personality, 156-162
Cults, 11, 221-261
    Baba cult, 253-254
    brainwashing, 224, 226
    Buddhism, 239
    Christian Science, 275-292
    Christianity, 238-239
    and diffusion, 260
    evolving into religion, 224-225, 240, 244
    Hare Krishna, 236
    Mohammedanism, 239-240
    Mormon, 224-225
    motivation toward, 226-228, 294
    and narcissism, 259
    and paranoia, 225
    People's Temple, 255-257, 294
    and pre-reality thinking, 223, 259, 298
    statistics, 237, 294 (footnote)
    Unification Church, 228-231
    and withdrawal, 258-259
Curiosity, as instinct, 6-7, 12

Darwin, C., instincts, 13 (footnote), 52
Dependence, 5, 33
Depression, 9, 10, 24, 129, 215
Deprivation, 33, 300
    examples of, 61-67, 70, 205
Deutsch, H., "as if" quality, 83
Diffusion, xii, 25, 26, 27, 29, 30, 39, 40,
    258
    as defense, 207-208
Domination, 33, 300
    example of, 61-67
    and sex, 213
Dreams, as road to unconscious, 10, 296

Eddy, Mary Baker, 275-292
  "animal magnetism," 281, 282-283, 285,
    286, 287, 290-291
  case history, 275-283
  Christian Science, founding of, 281-282
    spiritual laws, 283
  externalizations, 289-290
  paranoid delusions, 284-285, 286
  personality, 287-288, 290
Ego, 24
  and borderline personality, 99
  and emotional forces, 121
  functions scale, 116
  Menninger theory of ego under stress,
    115-116
  and neurotic character, 29
  and psychotic personality, 43, 85-86,
    125-126, 130
  and therapy, 26-27, 31
Emotional forces, 4, 8, 9, 17, 24, 25, 35,
    129, 218, 296-297, 301
Envy, 5
Ethics, See Religion

Fantasies, 7, 8, 11, 12, 14, 219, 221-223, 296
  and cults, 226
Fight-flight reaction, 11, 12, 15, 27, 53, 301
  as instinct, 5-6
Fixation, 19, 24, 27, 28, 82, 128
  of narcissism, 68
  in treatment, 78
Freud, S., "after-education," 127
  ego and emotional forces, 121
  Eros-Thanatos theory, 4
  judging character, 263 (footnote)
  narcissism, 51-52
  neurosis, 115
  and psychoanalysis, 16
  regression, 21
  superego, 7, 8, 11-12
  theories challenged by Kohut, 92-93
  "transference love," 124
  Wolf Man, 83
Frosch, J., psychotic character, 84-87

Glover, E., psychotic character, 113-114
Grinker, R., Criteria for borderline syn-
    drome, 98-99
Guilt, 69, 77

Hallucination, 7, 9, 81, 221
Hare Krishna, 236
Hitler, 34, 260 (footnote), 262-274, 288-
    289, 290, 291
  as case history, 263-268
  personality, 268-270
  physical characteristics, 268
  projections or externalizations, 270
Homosexuality, 213
Hostility, 34, 215, 300-301
  analyzing of, 182-183
  and civilization, 6, 293, 299
  controlled by religion, 294
  as criteria for PPD, xii, 25, 30
  and fight-flight reaction, 5, 27
  as force in Adolf Hitler, 273
  in the transference, 206
Hypochondria, 35
Hysteria, group, 257

Identification, 13-14, 27, 217, 222, 260
    (footnote)
  absence of, 32
  in cults, 258
  example of, 58
Insight, 39
Instincts, Freud's Eros-Thanatos theory, 4,
    11-12
  interaction, 14
  list of, 5-8, 12
  meaning of, 4
Integration, 22, 24
  of sex and love, 22

Jung, G., 218-220

Kernberg, O., borderline personalities,
    88-91
Kohut, H., cathexis of self, 91-92

Law, as ethical base, 295
  and psychiatry, 34-35
Lorenz, K., 213, 214
Love, in childrearing, 11, 15, 17-18, 33,
    298-299, 300
  as instinct, 5, 12, 33
  self-love, 5
  "transference love," 124

Masochism, 24, 69, 129, 299
  examples of, 67, 70, 73–77
  and narcissism, 73–77
Maturity, 15–16, 126, 128, 223, 297–298,
    301
  denial of, 261
  failure of, 23
McLean, P., brain and behavior theory, 27–28
Menninger, K., theory of ego under stress,
    115–116
Mental health, definition, 83
Mohammedanism, 239–240
"Moonies," See Unification Church
Mormon religion, 224–225, 240–244

Narcissism, xii, 5, 12, 25, 27, 31, 36, 39,
    51–79, 132–135, 257
  components of, 52
  connection with masochism, 73
  and cults, 245–246, 259
  exhibitionistic type, 67
  as force in Adolf Hitler, 271–272, 289
  in healthy personality, 57–58, 69
  and libido theory, 51
  as link in therapy, 69
  pathological, 87–88
  vanity type, 67
Neurosis, 6, 9, 14, 24, 30, 34, 128, 129, 299
  defined by Freud, 115
  and psychotic personality, 23
Neurotic character, 23, 29, 38, 85, 128
  example of, 49
  treatment of, 26, 196

Oedipus complex, 52, 54, 92, 300

Paranoia, 9, 10, 35
  in cults, 225, 226
  examples, 42–44, 45–46, 130
  in the transference, 122
People's Temple, 255–257, 294
Personality, 16–17
  definition of, 81
  warping of, 17–18
Perversions, 24, 129
Phobias, 9, 10, 92
Prevention, of psychopathology, 14–15,
    215–218, 299, 300–301
Projection, xii, 11, 54–57, 222
  examples of, 42, 46, 59, 130
Psychoanalysis, 16, 211, 219
Psychodynamics, and human hostility, 296
  and motivations, 58
  as science, 4, 8, 12, 14, 16, 27–28, 296
  and society, 293–299

Psychohistory, role in prevention, 216
Psychopathology, 20, 35, 215
  as defense, 178
  determining factors, 24
  Heinz Kohut theories, 92
  and splitting off, 22–23
  variables in severity, 129
Psychosis, 6, 9, 14, 21 (Fig. 3), 25, 30, 34,
    38, 45, 129, 299
  in borderline personality, 99–100
  definition of, 80–81
  group psychosis, 224, 254, 257
  latent, 84
  in psychotic personality, 100
  universality of, 293–294
Psychosocial medicine, 211–220
  psychohistory, 216
Psychosomatic illness, 24, 129, 290
  prevention of, 215
  study of, 211–216
Psychotherapy, 8, 31
  of borderline personality, 90
  length of therapy, 78, 79
  and narcissism, 69
  of psychotic personality, 26, 77–79, 82,
    90, 91, 99, 196, 225
  and resistance, 77, 206
  scale of, 215
  of suicidally depressed, 179–183
  therapeutic alliance, 155
Psychotic personality disorder (PPD), criteria
    for, xii, 40, 49–50, 51, 80–83, 257–258
  diagnosis of, 23, 26, 29, 30, 100–101,
    105–107, 126, 127–128, 139, 208
  and integration, 23
  prognosis, 26, 78–79, 82, 196
  theoretical formulation, 19–28, 127–128
  treatment of, 77–79
  varieties, 38–50
    acting out, 47, 49
    compulsive, 173–178
    criminally destructive, Adolf Hitler,
      262–274
    criminoid, 48
    depressive, 47
    emotional isolation, 184–187
    in marital setting, 188–196
    masochistic regressive withdrawal, 134–149
    paranoid, 42, 46, 47–48, 122
    paranoid-hostile, 150–165
    reactive with psychosis and suicide, 166–172
    simple, 41–42
    socially constructive, Mary Baker Eddy,
      275–292
    suicidally depressed, 179–183

Punishment, fits the source, 69, 70, 77
and law, 34–35

Rationalization, 31, 39, 49
Reality, sense of, and cults, 259
defining human nature, 261, 294, 295
defining psychotic personality, 25, 30, 40, 81, 87, 130, 221, 258
and fantasy, 8, 11, 296–297
as instinct, 7–8, 12
pre-reality thinking, 223
rationalization, 31
warping, xii, 14, 27, 29, 31, 33, 40, 258
Regression, 6, 19–20, 21, 28, 78
example of, 44–45
and narcissism, 67
prenatal, 140
Rehabilitation, of criminal delinquent, 162–165
Religion, 223, 224, 294–296, 298. Also See
Cults, 221–261
Repression, xii
Review of literature, 80–118

Science, definition of, 4
and psychosocial medicine, 211, 294, 295–296, 299
scientific process, 8
vs. superstition, 222
Self-preservation, as instinct, 5, 12, 52–53

Sex, and domination, 213
homosexuality, 213
as instinct, 5, 12
and love, 22
as release, 126
Social cooperation, 6–7, 12, 291, 295, 298–299
Stress, 115–116
Suicide, 166, 171–172, 179–183, 195–196
Superego, 7, 11
Superstition, 7 (footnote), 11, 12, 219, 222, 299

Therapeutic alliance, 155, 206
Transference, 10, 121–131, 208
"analyzing out," 154–155
in borderline personality, 90
paranoid, example of, 122
psychotic, 82, 90, 96, 122
resistance to, 205–206
"transference love," 124, 127

Unification Church ("Moonies"), 228–231, 246–253

Withdrawal, xii, 25, 27, 40, 257, 258–259
masochistic regressive, examples, 136–149

Zilboorg, G., "ambulatory schizophrenic," 83